Pola Negri

Pola Negri
Temptress of Silent Hollywood

Sergio Delgado

McFarland & Company, Inc., Publishers
Jefferson, North Carolina

LIBRARY OF CONGRESS CATALOGUING-IN-PUBLICATION DATA

Names: Delgado, Sergio, 1961– author.
Title: Pola Negri : temptress of silent Hollywood / Sergio Delgado.
Description: Jefferson, North Carolina : McFarland & Company, Inc., Publishers, 2016. | Includes bibliographical references and index.
Identifiers: LCCN 2016029884 | ISBN 9781476664309 (softcover : acid free paper) ∞
Subjects: LCSH: Negri, Pola, 1899–1987. | Actors—United States—Biography. | Actors—Poland—Biography. | Silent films—History and criticism.
Classification: LCC PN2287.N35 D45 2016 | DDC 791.4302/8092 [B]—dc23
LC record available at https://lccn.loc.gov/2016029884

ISBN (print) 978-1-4766-6430-9
ISBN (ebook) 978-1-4766-2435-8

BRITISH LIBRARY CATALOGUING DATA ARE AVAILABLE

© 2016 Sergio Delgado. All rights reserved

No part of this book may be reproduced or transmitted in any form or by any means, electronic or mechanical, including photocopying or recording, or by any information storage and retrieval system, without permission in writing from the publisher.

Cover images: Pola Negri publicity portraits for *The Cheat* (Paramount Pictures, 1923)

Printed in the United States of America

McFarland & Company, Inc., Publishers
Box 611, Jefferson, North Carolina 28640
www.mcfarlandpub.com

Acknowledgments

I would like to thank Pola Negri fans around the world, blog-writers, historians and anyone with something to say about Miss Negri, good or bad. Thanks to collectors who provided photographs for this book. To those who run the Internet Archive, a very big thank you for the treasure trove of old movie magazines from the 1920s and '30s. To the New Zealand newspapers website for invaluable articles about Pola from the other side of the world. To friends and acquaintances who encouraged me to write and finish this book, to my family, mother and father—thank you for your words of encouragement. The author would also like to particularly thank his wife and personal librarian, Marina Vildoso, for all of the love, support and tolerance regarding the author's interest in "another woman."

And at last, Pola, this is for you.

Table of Contents

Acknowledgments v
Preface 1

1 • A Peculiar Public Perception   5
2 • Variations on Apolonia Chalupec   8
3 • The Rise of Pola Negri   16
4 • America Goes Ga-Ga for Pola   31
5 • The Paradox of Publicity   43
6 • Pola Negri in Paramount Pictures   56
7 • The Anatomy of Failure   130
8 • Pola in Purgatory   133
9 • The Wandering Star   141
10 • Der Führer's Favorite   152
11 • All Too Soon Forgotten   161

Chapter Notes   171
Bibliography   181
Index   185

Preface

Pola Negri—that couldn't be the name of anyone *but* a silent movie queen—was the most exotic star of the 1920s cinema. A woman of "otherworldly" and "untranslatable" beauty, she had hair "the color of night" or "black as a raven's wing," skin "white as fine porcelain," and sported "a sensuous mouth painted blood red." Her large blue eyes (or green, or gray—no two descriptions agreed) could flash the blackest of angry thunderclouds or suggest a thousand desires and send shivers up the spines of the strongest men. She was the silent cinema's unquestioned queen of flame and desire. The celebrated British novelist Michael Arlen reverently called her "the kind of woman who in ancient times could wreck empires and bring them to their knees."

You might say she was made for the movies. Her early life story reads like the plot of a Hollywood film. She endured a childhood of stark poverty and persecution in her native Poland, survived a world war, and married and divorced a count, all before her twenty-second birthday. She became a stage star in post–World War I Berlin and rose to fame as the first international star of moving pictures. Audiences that saw her groundbreaking performances in *Passion* and *Gypsy Blood* felt like "they had been hit by an electrical storm." By the time she arrived in America in 1922 to make pictures for the Famous Players–Lasky Picture Company (later "Paramount Pictures"), she was regarded as the greatest actress in the world.

Admiring critics called her acting "colorful," "vital" and "volcanic." She was praised for her "emotional depth" and "real characterizations." She threw herself into her movie roles with total abandon, immersing herself completely, and letting the full range of emotion wreak havoc with her body. In doing so, she demonstrated a frankness and fearlessness seldom seen in other actresses of the era. Even in her most forgettable pictures, Negri burned with passion and emotional intensity. She always made the film worthwhile.

After seeing what she had done in movies overseas, America welcomed her arrival with all of the ardor of a schoolboy's first crush. The press dubbed her "The Negri" or "La Negri." To the legion of gossip columnists, she was "The Queen of Tragedy," to Paramount she was "The Empress of Emotionalism," and to the movie fan magazines she was "a hot-house orchid," or, most spectacularly, "that indomitable tiger-woman." Love her or hate her, she made for good copy. Throughout her career she was the subject of countless rumors and insinuations; all, some or none were true. She was, all at once, an object of fascination, derision and controversy.

During the silent era she was one of Famous Players–Lasky's biggest stars, a top-level talent earning a lavish $8500 a week. She lived the life of a rich-and-famous movie queen draped in tens of thousands of dollars of glittering diamond jewelry; resided in a luxurious Beverly Hills mansion; and rode around town, it is said, in one of her extravagant Piece Arrow limousines with a liveried chauffeur and her pet Russian wolfhounds. Yet this fabled figure, a movie star who was one of the most famous and wealthiest in the world, is virtually unknown today, undone in the end by everything that made her a star in the first place.

If you haven't heard of her, it's understandable. She pales in memory compared to silent picture luminaries Mary Pickford, Gloria Swanson, Greta Garbo and others. Most contemporary film history books only mention her in passing. Today, only a handful of her silent films survive. From 1923 to 1928, Negri starred in 20 full-length features for the Famous Players–Lasky/Paramount studio. Thirteen are lost and two more exist in incomplete versions. Her most critically acclaimed work is now inaccessible. Without movies to judge, most of what is written about her today dwells on her celebrated romantic exploits and her notorious "temperament," relying on old publicity tales that weren't true in the first place.

Until now her narrative has been incomplete. Most of Negri's biographers skim over details they don't care to write about, settling instead for a one-dimensional "highlight reel" of her life and accomplishments. One recent publication of her story reads more like a heartfelt homage and primer than a true biography. She was a far more complex woman than most film historians allow—a paradox of bewildering inconsistencies. Harry Carr, writing in *Motion Picture Magazine,* called her "cruel, condescending, humble, contrite, generous, sweetly reasonable, gracious with a charm that would disarm an ogre, disagreeable, ungracious, winning, forbidding."[1] Even the camera lens couldn't capture her mercurial nature. In the thousands of photographs taken of her during her movie career, she never quite looks like the same woman twice.

Her legend is delicately suspended between subtle contradictions and outright lies. Was she an intimate member of Tsar Nicholas I's inner circle before the revolution? Did she really tour Europe as a celebrated concert violinist? She told countless variations of her own life story, lying if it made her more interesting or if confronted with something she didn't want to discuss. She was both aided and injured by her studio's publicity—loud, brash and exaggerated—that created an exotic personality named Pola Negri that, ultimately, *became* her. As such, her "real" story is a witches' brew of impossible-to-corroborate gossip and ballyhoo, poison-pen distortions and fabrications, and enduring speculation about everything from her true name and date of birth to her sexuality.

Myths about her fill Hollywood lore. Did she really once parade down Hollywood Boulevard with a pet tiger on a leash? (No.) Was she Adolf Hitler's mistress? (No.) Was she a spy? (No, but J. Edgar Hoover suspected so.) Was she the first to inspire a fashion vogue for painted fingernails and toenails and popularize the turban? (Yes.) Did she and Gloria Swanson have a catfight involving real cats? (Well, sort of.) Did she throw herself on Rudolph Valentino's coffin and faint repeatedly at his funeral solely for the benefit of photographers? (No.) Did her "heavy" Polish accent end her movie career when talkies came along? (No, no, no.) Was she bisexual or lesbian or straight? (Well … more on that later.)

All of these misconceptions and exaggerations have obscured the real Pola Negri, reducing her from a talented flesh-and-blood woman to a caricature of an eccentric silent movie queen—think Norma Desmond in *Sunset Blvd*. She deserves a full portrait of her life and films and that's what this book aims to do.

Pola Negri is not an easy figure to write about. In some matters she resists our sympathy. She was never "a regular person" and would never be confused for the girl next door. She was unhappy, temperamental, difficult, pretentious and haughty—sometimes all at once. She was unadulterated in her opinions, far more than what a woman of her time was allowed to or supposed to be. She made terrible and foolish decisions regarding her film career and the men in her life and it cost her dearly. Much to her own detriment, she cared little about the shifting tides of public opinion and, despite studio efforts to temper her ferocious individuality for American consumption, saw no reason to be loved by the public on anything other than her own terms. If you didn't like her, well, that was just too bad for you.

Signed fan photograph, ca. 1923.

Her attitudes on everything from movie stardom to matters of the heart marked her as a woman far ahead of her time. Self-assured and independent, she wasn't what the very conservative public of the era thought she should be: sweet, pretty and demure. They never *got* that she could only be what *she* could be. So they were shocked and dismayed when she lived out her romantic relationships with Charlie Chaplin and Rudolph Valentino in the public eye without caring what anybody else thought of it. When she loved, she did so openly with all of the thunder and lightning of stormy passion. When she grieved over love's loss, it was like an open wound on display for the world to see.

She was a modern and sophisticated woman with a European sensibility free of the puritan mores of small-town America; an intellectual at a time when intelligent women were frowned upon; and a serious *artiste* who believed passionately in her own "art." Her realistic style of acting raised the bar for every other Hollywood movie star and she was one of the first actresses to unabashedly depict sexuality on the screen without any self-consciousness or remorse. She was also the first important foreign star to arrive on these shores in a time of extreme xenophobia. She took the abuse heaped on her and opened the doors for others. Without her to lead, there never would have been a Garbo or Dietrich in Hollywood and she was, ironically, a better actress than both of those well-remembered stars.

Today, any critical history of the silent film, any listing of the most memorable performers of that era, necessarily includes the name of Pola Negri. Therefore, a detailed telling of her life and movie career is needed, if for no other reason than to strip away, like old varnish, the many myths and inaccuracies about her, and return her to her rightful place as one of the greatest stars in motion picture history.

1

A Peculiar Public Perception

In his book *An Evening's Entertainment: The Age of the Silent Feature Picture, 1915–1928*, Richard Kozarski opines, "Negri's place in American film history has never been adequately evaluated."[1] It's true. With so few of her films available for viewing, there is insufficient evidence to adequately judge the acting that won the acclaim of critics in her time. Or perhaps she was less the great dramatic actress and more the "exotic" personality that her publicity always made her out to be. Kozarski asks, "[H]ow much of the Negri phenomenon was real and how much was purely manufactured?"[2]

It's a question worth exploring. Although Negri earned a reputation as a great dramatic artist in European films, her American identity was entirely invented by the Paramount press machine. Publicity, never the most honest of literary forms, made her a star and what was written about her became, over time, honest-to-goodness "truths" taken as celluloid gospel in Kenneth Anger's *Hollywood Babylon* and other scandal-filled tomes on film culture. Today, a false "historic record" perpetuates a peculiar perception of Negri as an over-the-top, headline-seeking opportunist, a self-aggrandizing scene-stealer whose main (and perhaps only) talent was self-promotion.

So instead of objective critical appraisals of her films and acting, authors and bloggers offer opinions that she was "more famous for being famous then she is for her films."[3] We read, as a stated fact, that she "flaunted" her marriages to a count and a prince "at every opportunity" and deliberately alienated herself from the rest of Hollywood.[4] We are told she was a "foreigner" and "stuck up" and that Americans audiences "found her silly."[5] We hear of her "annoying publicity," her feud with Gloria Swanson and her "hysterical scene-stealing" at Valentino's funeral.[6] It is concluded that by the late 1920s she had become "somewhat of a joke—and the wacky PR put out by her American studio, Paramount, had turned her into a parody of the heavy-breathing silent screen vamp."[7] Even her *Los Angeles Times* obituary from 1987 relates how she endlessly expressed a Garbo-like wish to be left alone, which was certainly *not* the case, and then offers the "truth" that she seized upon any opportunity that came her way to obtain publicity for herself.[8]

She is depicted as a demanding diva, imperious and insufferable. In her book *Silent Film Stars*, Jeanne Basinger writes that Negri demanded that her dressing room floor be strewn daily with fresh orchid petals. Stories have her yelling at wardrobe mistresses, slapping men who displeased her, hurling flower vases at her maid, and asking hotels to evict paying guests from adjoining rooms so that she would have more space for herself.

One writer referred to her as an "egomaniac to upstage every other egomaniac" and described how, in the era of Prohibition, she insisted on her dressing room being fully stocked with bottles of champagne and cognac, fresh flowers and tins of caviar.[9] He also noted that Negri was proficient in cursing in seven languages and used them quite liberally when she lost her temper.[10]

None of this is actually true (though she was proficient in cursing in *six* languages).

Despite what is written about her now, Negri was one of the brightest stars in the Hollywood firmament during the silent era. Newspaper writers of the time called her a "dynamic and bewitching" actress.[11] She had "the fire and temperament of the Slav" and threw herself "into whatever part she is playing with all of her soul."[12] She was described as a woman of "elemental naturalness."[13] A review of one of her early pictures stated, "Pola Negri, as always, dominates each scene. Her manner is statuesque, silent suffering, and then impulsively dramatic." In a magazine article from 1923, author Russell P. Mallinson wrote:

> Pola Negri brings to the screen devastating love on the heels of which tragedy barks. She inspires passion in the hearts of her lovers, which burns with a fierce flame until it consumes them. Hers is the type of love which has created the tragedies of history, overthrown monarchies and ravaged kingdoms ... which brings men in the pride of manhood and those in the autumn of their lives, pleading at her feet.[14]

A letter-writer in a 1923 issue of *Picture-Play Magazine* simply asked, "Why can't they all act as well as Pola Negri?"[15]

She wasn't what America expected in a movie star. Upon arriving here in 1922, Negri knew little of the ways of the American press and deeply resented their asking what she thought were very personal questions, particularly regarding her private life. For such reticence, she was portrayed as cold, aloof and *difficult*. Journalists complained in print that she was too *serious* and that all she wanted to talk about in interviews was her "art."[16] The usual celebrity gossip—fashion, who else she considered to be a good actress, what she thought of American pictures—bored her to impatience and she was sharply criticized in the tabloids for her refusal to be "public property." Never one for false humility, she considered herself a great actress, and for saying so was branded "self-important" with all of the malice the term could muster.

She certainly wasn't shy—"demure" wasn't in her vocabulary and definitely not in her makeup. She was—and still is—famous for her "fits of temperament." One "true" story has her holding up filming on one picture because the color of her slippers did not match the ruffle on her dress and she would not go on until they were dyed to the proper shade of purple. Another "story" has her throwing canisters of face powder at a makeup man who suggested her own makeup was wrong for her face. She could be difficult, yes, but it was never the case of a spoiled "diva" making waves for the headlines. For Pola Negri, being temperamental was a manifestation of her determination to succeed despite all difficulties. As an artist intensely dedicated to her craft, she needed to be the best actress that she could be, even if it meant cursing wildly in a fit of pique and in six languages at ineffectual directors, bumbling stage hands and rude makeup artists; demanding script revisions; or angrily storming off sets and refusing to return until she got what she needed to play her role to the best of her ability. Even her highly public love affairs were stormy and if they ended dramatically, well, how could she have handled them in any other way? Negri lived her emotional life on the outside and the buttoned-down Babbitts of the moviegoing public of the 1920s never understood that about her. She was uninhibited *and* foreign—two qualities that made small-town America uncomfortable. As one might expect, her pictures never drew well away from the big cities, yet for the most part she still had the adulation of the critics and the fans who flocked to ornate movie palaces, eager to witness her dramatic fireworks.

She was the perfect embodiment of the fiery and exotic Continental actress that most Americans had heard about, but never seen in person. Talent-wise, there was nothing "synthetic" about her. She was the "real thing."[17] There were other celebrated dramatic actresses in the silent film era such as Lillian Gish and Norma Talmadge, yet no one equaled Miss Negri for intensity on the screen. Critic Lotte Eisner called her "the Magnani of the silent era, full of exuberant vitality" and wrote that she "does not act; she is scarcely an actress. Quite simply, she exists. She has that intangible quality called 'presence'; she is her role."[18]

She was light years ahead of her competition in dramatic potential. Most silent picture actresses of the time primped and posed coyly in front of a gauze-covered camera lens and called it "acting," Negri, however, was a spontaneous talent who created "fully formed natural characterizations" bereft of artificial mannerisms, and she was willing to emotionally bare all. She was something new and different, a natural actress of wide range who played strong, independent and sexually aware women, a historic departure from female roles up to then. Wrote one author: "At a time when ladies blushed if sex was mentioned, Pola talked about it openly as if it were another everyday function, like brushing one's teeth."[19] According to film lore, she had to be "taught" to kiss "chastely" in the American manner. Film historian Robert Griffith called her "sexually irresistible" and said she "seemed concerned about nothing but her own pleasure, and the pleasure of the moment.... What she stood for is illustrated by the fact that American fathers took their sons to see Miss Negri as sort of an initiation into the facts of life and womanhood."[20]

Prim-and-proper "America's Sweetheart" Mary Pickford may have been the highest paid woman in silent pictures, but Pola Negri was essential in championing the image of women as sexually liberated beings both on and off the screen. For her time, she was revolutionary, and the first modern actress in American movies.

2

Variations on Apolonia Chalupec

Detailing Pola Negri's early life is a Sisyphean task. Facts and lies about her beginnings are so entwined that no one can ever hope to completely discern the truth. Negri didn't help matters either. "She could out-hawk her own press agents with whoppers about her past," according to one source.[1] Her favorite director, Ernst Lubitsch, once said, "Pola is a greater character than in any fiction. She act, she act so much she don't know who she is herself [sic]. She is fiction."[2] Herbert Howe, a Los Angeles newspaper columnist, wrote in 1930, "Pola once told me her story. How much of it is fiction neither she nor I will ever know."[3] It's a bad start for any would-be biographer.

What about historical sources? Her beginnings were chronicled in movie magazines like *Photoplay, Movie Weekly* and *Picture-Play*. Her ghost-written "autobiography," *Memoirs of a Star*, was issued in 1970.[4] Nothing ever written about her can be considered authoritative. Much of her life story was the product of press agents and ghost-writers. Many of the magazine articles about her offer strikingly different variations on her tale. To piece her complete story together, you have to read everything and even then the answers come with question marks. Who exactly was Pola Negri?

By most accounts, Pola Negri was born Barbara Apolonia Chalupec on January 3, 1897, in Lipino, Poland—though sources differ on most everything. For her serialized 1924 "autobiography" for *Photoplay*, she declared she was born in Yanowa, near Lipnau.[5] In other sources, the name of the town is spelled "Janowo" and "Janowa." The *Blue Book of the Screen* from 1923 lists her birthplace as "Bromberg near Lipino." She was Polish by nationality, but articles written during the 1920s also describe her, in no particular order, as German, Russian, Austrian and Hungarian.[6] Variations on the spelling of her surname include "Chalupez," "Chalupek" and "Chalupiec."

Negri's *Los Angeles Times* obituary called her the "last child born in the 19th century—born a few minutes before midnight in the final hours of 1899."[7] Other sources cite the year of her birth as 1894, 1897, 1899 or 1901. Take your pick. Pola herself once coyly admitted that the year of her birth became later every time that she was asked about it. She called such subterfuge "a ladies prerogative, I believe."[8]

The original source of her reputed first name, "Barbara," is a mystery. She isn't referred to by that name in any magazine article or biographical sketch from the 1920s or afterward. In his Negri biography, Mariusz Kotowski offers a still photograph of an official birth certificate recorded in Lipino, Poland, in 1978 (her original had been lost) that lists her full birth name as Apolonia Chalupec—no "Barbara" to be found—yet, for whatever reason, most profiles of her still assert that "Barbara" was her first name.[9] For this author, the argument is settled by the fact that Apolonia Chalupec nee Pola Negri identifies her final resting place at the Calvary Church in East Los Angeles. "Apolonia" was her paternal grandmother's first name—"Pola" being the diminutive form of that—and she was affectionately called "Polita" by her family and childhood friends.[10]

She was the third child of Jerzy Mathias Chalupec and Eleonora de Kielczeska/Kelczewska. In *Memoirs* she passingly refers to two sisters, both of whom died in childhood before she was born, but one of the first *Photoplay* pieces about her describes her as "devoted to her sisters."[11] Another story mentions an older brother killed in an outbreak of plague.[12] There is no mention of a brother in *Memoirs of a Star*. Yet in the June 2, 1923, *Film Daily*, Rockford, Illinois, film exhibitor Bill Danzinger told of a telegram received from Negri expressing her interest in locating her brother, "Ian Chalupez," who left Poland in 1909 and allegedly settled in Rockford and worked as a translator in an "exchange house." He was said to be 34 years old and strongly resemble his famous sister. The exhibitor's claim was actually a publicity stunt to promote one of her pictures opening in town. *The Blue Book of the Screen* for 1923 says "Ian Chalupez" was the name of her father. Was any of this true? The answer is unknown.

Pola's mother, Eleonora, "a refined young woman," was born in the town of Brdow, Poland, into a family of "impoverished nobility."[13] Once-wealthy Polish gentry, her family had lost most of its fortune and land after its support of Napoleon and the French Army against the occupying Russian forces in 1812. Another source refers to Eleonora's family as Russian impoverished nobility, "as Pola has always insisted," although she never actually said that.[14] In her *Memoirs,* Negri describes her mother as strict and stern, a very devout Catholic, an able cook and her "greatest friend."[15] Eleonora was the one person—really the *only* person—Pola was ever truly close to during the course of her life.

Her father Jerzy was "a Slovakian immigrant with probably more than a touch of the Bohemian gypsy in his blood—you only need to look at that dark hair, that olive skin, those deep brown eyes."[16] For *Photoplay*, however, her father became "George"—the Anglicized version of Jerzy—and instead of a Slovak he was a Hungarian gypsy.[17] The same article calls him a manufacturer of paper, although in *Memoirs* he is described as a tin master. Other sources say he was a furrier or a fabric-maker.[18] One source confuses its facts to such an extent that it describes Pola's *father* as Polish and calls her *mother* a gypsy.

Eleonora was 31, ten years older than Jerzy, when they wed in the Catholic faith on July 10, 1892. Their union did not meet with the approval of her family, who did not believe that she should mix with what they called "swarthy people."[19]

After their wedding, Eleonora and Jerzy settled in Lipino, in the Russian-controlled section of Poland. Eleonora used most of her meager inheritance to help her husband buy a tin factory there. According to *Memoirs*, the family was prosperous, living in a large country house surrounded by trees and gardens. Although skinny and prone to illness, Pola enjoyed a carefree childhood: playing games, hunting for mushrooms, and climbing trees in the nearby forest. One tumble out of a tree resulted in a head injury that required her to undergo surgery to restore her sight. Her family was close-knit. Her namesake grandmother lived in the same house and her uncle and aunt lived nearby. Yet despite happy times, she was a melancholy child and quite often alone with her books, an early foreshadowing of the lonely adult she would eventually become. Her father could always snap her out of one of her dark, pensive moods with a smile and calling her by his pet name for her, "Zamyslona," the Meditator, referring to her need for solitude. In a 1924 magazine article, Negri described a childhood full of pain and suffering. Death seemed to be everywhere: war, revolution, starvation, plague, torture, imprisonment and killing. She told of a Warsaw terrorized by marauding bands of Russian Cossacks who tossed vicious feral cats into the crowds. The cats clawed out eyes and scratched at faces as the victims screamed in pain.[20] Negri told how she saw mothers and friends mercilessly shot down in front of her eyes.[21]

If that all sounds like hokum, that's because it is. Let's just called it "flavored" for dramatic effect.

What is absolutely true is that the most traumatic event of her childhood, perhaps of her entire life, was the loss of her father. According to Negri, her father, although a Slovak, was filled with nationalist zeal and joined the campaign for independence from Russia during the Polish Revolution of 1905. Hopes for Polish freedom were swiftly crushed by the Russian army and Jerzy was arrested by the authorities and sent to the Citadel Pavilion in Warsaw to await trial on charges of revolutionary activities.

Negri's *Memoirs* offers up an alternative version of her father's story. Jerzy, she claimed, used his frequent business trips into Warsaw as cover for clandestine meetings with underground cells of Polish freedom fighters. In a variation on the story, Jerzy was twice arrested on charges of forging identity papers for suspected revolutionaries. After a high-ranking Russian general was killed by a bomb thrown during a Warsaw riot in 1905, military authorities rounded up all known political activists. Jerzy was arrested at home, jailed, tried by a military tribunal and, as expected, found guilty of treason. He was sent to Pawiak Prison in Warsaw to wait while his appeal ran through the courts. Negri claims in her autobiography that she saw him only one more time during her lone visit to the prison, describing a sad and dramatic scene where the authorities prevented her from giving her distraught father one final embrace.

There is, not surprisingly, a third variation of the story stating that her father died in 1905, about the time that she was six years old.[22] This version omits any mention of patriotic heroism on Jerzy's part. Negri suggests in her autobiography that Eleonora long suspected her husband of philandering during his trips away on business. With so many variations of the story to choose from, it may not be much of a stretch to offer the theory that Jerzy became a necessary "martyr" to the Polish cause in Negri's narrative in order to absolve him of the sin of infidelity in his daughter's eyes.

According to *Memoirs*, within days of her father's arrest the government confiscated everything from the family that had been in his name. "There was no question of waiting for the outcome of a trial, of his guilt or innocence, of what was to become of his family."[23] Her uncle took her grandmother back to Slovakia to protect her from further Russian reprisals. Pola never saw her again. *Photoplay*'s version of the story has Eleonora secretly working for the Polish cause in spite of Jerzy's imprisonment until one cold winter's night when mother and daughter were driven from their home by the dreaded Cossacks. Their house was set aflame as they huddled shivering in the snow and, Negri wrote, "in response to my mother's cries of 'Why?' they only said, 'You are the wife of the revolutionist Chalupec.'"[24] Pola and her mother fled to Warsaw, nearly starving and freezing to death on that perilous journey.

The same *Photoplay* article adds an extra layer of tragedy: Jerzy's arrest and the death of Negri's (imaginary?) brother from bubonic plague drove Eleonora insane, and she was placed in a mental hospital. Without a mother or father to care for her, seven-year-old Pola was sent to live with her aunt and uncle in Warsaw.

Memoirs omits any mention of rampaging Cossacks or of her being sent to live with relatives, so we will assume they are tales of fiction. Instead, Eleonora sold their home in Lipino after Jerzy's arrest to move to Warsaw to be nearer to her incarcerated husband. The money from the sale enabled her to purchase a small grocery at 11 Browarna Street in Warsaw, although she had no experience at running a business. The area they relocated to, Powisel, is described as "squalid," more slum than neighborhood and adjacent to a "filthy" river. Among their lower-class neighbors were two "ladies of pleasure"; Negri became very curious about the steady stream of male callers who visited the ladies' apartment at all hours.

Pola was enrolled in a general admission parochial school in Warsaw for her primary education, although *The Blue Book of the Screen for 1923* describes the establishment as a very exclusive finishing school run by a "Countess Platen." Either way, she hated it. Even at a young age she sensed she was different from the other students. The other girls' main goal was to grow up and get married like young girls were *supposed* to do. Pola's main desire was to get noticed. For such iconoclasm, she was bullied by classmates. According to Kotowski, they pulled on her long dark braids or cruelly tied them to the fence outside or spilled ink on her clothes, reducing her to tears.[25] She was also subjected to physical abuse from her teachers. With no interest in becoming what she was supposed to be, she was a very bad pupil and did her best to get expelled. "How I worked at it! I neglected my lessons, talked out of turn, pulled pranks on the other girls in front of the Sisters … but it was all to no avail."[26] She told nothing of her problems to Eleonora, who was consumed by the slow progress of her husband's legal appeal and the failing finances of the market. After the store was lost, Eleonora took a job as a cook for a wealthy Jewish woman.

Outside of school, Pola spent her free time in the street playing with other neighborhood children. Although a mere slip of a girl, she could outrun the boys who chased her during games and eluded their clumsy grasps like a graceful dancer. Passersby, seeing her at play, suggested to Eleonora that her daughter might be a good candidate for the Warsaw Imperial Ballet School.[27] Delighted by the idea, Negri pleaded with her mother for the chance to apply as a way to escape from schooling. It took a great deal of convincing. Eleonora, a very practical woman, considered most entertainments frivolous and unnecessary, but she loved opera, and ballet was a close enough kin. When Pola broke down and tearfully told her about her mistreatment at school, Eleonora decided to let her apply to the ballet school as long as she agreed to being tutored in regular school subjects by a neighbor.[28]

According to dozens of accounts, even present-day ones, Negri was admitted to the Russian Imperial Ballet School in St. Petersburg, Russia. It isn't true, although her early publicity played it up as though it was the case. In one article, she is quoted as saying that during her training in Russia, "we were made to dance in three feet of snow for an hour every day during the winter months. This was considered to give our limbs grace and strength. When we danced on a polished floor after the snow we felt as light as birds!"[29] In *Photoplay* she claimed that Imperial Ballet School students were treated like animals, subject to beatings with a whip by the masters.[30] She also told of dancing for the Tsarist court and meeting the Tsarina Alexandra, who presented each of the students with gifts at Christmas.

According to another article, her dancing was so admired by the tsar and tsarina that she was welcomed into the Russian royal family's inner circle. In another piece, Pola denied that the tsar had been a heartless autocrat, that he had perhaps been autocratic in his ruling but that he had "deplored unnecessary rigors" in the conduct of affairs of state.[31]

All of this is Grade A baloney.

Miss Negri was actually accepted to the less-important Warsaw Imperial Ballet in 1911 and spent the next two years studying ballet technique and awaiting her professional dance debut. From the beginning, she said, the school's ballet mistress saw something special in her that compelled people to watch her. With her black hair, pale white skin and large, haunted-looking grey eyes, she readily attracted attention and left an impression on whomever she met.

During this time, Jerzy's appeal was denied and the Russian authorities transferred him to a prison in Siberia. Much of Pola's early publicity claimed he died in confinement there. *Memoirs* stated that he was released after serving ten years, yet never returned home to his family. After his release, Jerzy allegedly became involved with a woman in Warsaw and later served as an officer in the Polish Army. According to Negri, he was killed in action against Russian Bolshevik forces in 1920, giving his life for the cause of Polish independence. Whether the story of his fate is true or not is unknown.

Upon graduation from the ballet academy in 1913, Pola joined the Warsaw Ballet Company with hopes of someday becoming a lead dancer. Her first solo turn was in the role of the "Dancing Doll" in the ballet *Coppelia*, choreographed by Michael Folkine, considered at the time the greatest living choreographer after Nijinsky.[32] Her promotion to the ballet company came with an increase in salary, allowing her and Eleonora to finally move away from 11 Browarna Street and into a more respectable neighborhood.

Her dancing in *Coppelia* got her good notices and, more importantly, the attention of a wealthy and refined Ukrainian patron, Casimir de Hulewicz, Director of the Imperial Ballet. He took an interest in the family's well-being and served as something of a surrogate father figure for Negri. When she contracted a mild case of tuberculosis,. he generously paid for her three-month stay in a sanitarium at Zakopane in the Carpathian Mountains. She gradually recovered, but it was painfully clear that her lungs had been damaged to such an extent that she would never be healthy enough again to endure the grueling training of a star ballerina. Her dreams were shattered. It was a bad break she still lamented years later, declaring, "If I had the chance, I would be willing to trade places with the poorest ballet dancer in the world."[33]

What could she do now? If she couldn't dance, how would she support her mother? According to a 1923 newspaper piece, the idea of becoming an actress came to her during her time in Countess Platen's school in Warsaw. Her entire class was taken to the theater to see a stage production of *Cinderella*. Negri was spellbound by the story and acting. Memories of the production kept her awake most of the night. "[The] next day I told my schoolmates of my wonderful adventure at the theatre and my decision to become an actress. And for the benefit of those who had not seen the play, I re-enacted it, impersonating the heroine and several other characters."[34]

Her ambition to become an actress ran into stern opposition: Eleonora, concerned about her daughter's still-fragile health, adamantly refused to let her to apply to the Imperial Academy of Dramatic Arts. De Hulewicz, offered her no help at all. Ever the willful child, she applied for admission behind their backs; fearing that they would find out, she used a pseudonym on her application. "Pola" for a first name was a natural, but she needed a surname that would not give her true identity away. She recalled a book of poetry from

Italian poetess Ada Negri she had admired as a child and took her last name as a homage. So, Apolonia Chalupec became "Pola Negri."[35]

Conspiring in secret with her tutor, she prepared for her audition by learning scenes from Moliere's play *L'Ecole des Femmes* and one of the songs from Konopicka's *Imagina*.[36] The day came and despite her nervousness, she delivered a dramatic, tear-stained performance before a panel of instructors and was accepted to the academy. At 15, she was five years younger than most of the other students. Negri made no friends during her time there, but she chose not to dwell on loneliness. Acting came first for her.

It must have been daunting, at her young age, to be burdened with her family's support. With her scarred childhood and her lonely nature, one might conclude that acting was her lifeline, her saving grace, her escape from the harshness of her existence. Indeed, acting was the one thing that defined her sense of self. She took to her dramatic training with a vengeance. In her *Photoplay* autobiography, she claimed to have completed the three-year course in one year.[37] "I learned how to gauge an audience accurately and elicit greater laughs or tears by certain little tricks of technique—a cocked eyebrow, a break in the voice, a way of walking across the stage."

For her graduation performance. Negri played the plum role of Hedwig in the fourth act of Ibsen's *The Wild Duck*. On the strength of her performance, she received an offer to join the Rozmaitości, Poland's national theater. De Hulewicz advised her to decline, suggesting she hold out until they came back with an offer of more substantial leading roles.

As a favor to Negri, De Hulewicz persuaded Kazimierz Zalewski, owner of Warsaw's Little Theatre, to give her an opportunity to work with its acclaimed artistic director, Josef Podemski. Negri made her lead debut in Hauptmann's *Hannele* and received some praise. According to *Photoplay*, on the night of her triumph it was not Pola Negri who received flowers and applause, but little Apolonia Chalupec, who wept with happiness in her mother's arms.[38]

Very touching, but, again, it's not true. *Memoirs* says her first lead role was in the play *Śluby Panieńskie*, a drama originally written as a vehicle for the legendary Polish actress Helena Modjeska.[39]

When the play was in rehearsals, Warsaw heard the news that Austria's Archduke Ferdinand had been assassinated by Serbian nationals in Sarajevo. While mobilization for war ensued among the Great European Powers, no one believed that war was actually imminent, nor did the possibility of military conflict prevent Negri from concentrating on her acting. Her dramatic performance garnered enthusiastic praise in several of Warsaw's newspapers. One newspaper critic declared: "Not since I was a very young man and fell in love with Helena Modjeska has any actress so completely captivated me the way that Pola Negri has."[40]

True to De Hulewicz's prediction, the Rozmaitości called back, this time offering her the role of lead actress. She accepted their invitation and joined the Polish national theater for new versions of Ibsen's *The Wild Duck* and Hauptmann's *Hannele*.

Fame in the theatre, however, was not quite what she had expected it to be. It was exciting, yes, but she quickly learned that fame and art came at a price. At the summit there would always be loneliness. There would never be room up there for anyone else in her life.[41] Being an actress required her to go at it alone, and she always would.

Her debut season at the Rozmaitości was interrupted by war. Despite their hatred for the Russian occupiers, courageous Poles took up arms alongside the Russian Imperial

Army to defend their nation against the invading German forces. As battles raged in the countryside outside the capital, the Warsaw Opera House became a makeshift hospital. Negri joined the Red Cross as a volunteer nurse, tending to soldiers recuperating after surgery. The horrors of war were too much for her and after a few months she suffered a nervous breakdown, rendering her incapable of further service to the hospital.

As the war ground on, defeat became inevitable. A pall hung over the city. In the bleak summer of 1916, with the Germans still advancing, the depleted Russian forces abandoned Warsaw. De Hulewicz persuaded Negri and her mother to flee with him to safety in Russia. They packed to leave, but the bridge they were to cross was blown up by artillery and De Hulewicz, cut off by the German forces, was unable to reach them before evacuation. The Russian troops withdrew to the city of Praga and from there launched a heavy bombardment at the German positions that lasted well over a week. Despite the continual shelling, the Germans insisted the Imperial Theatre remain open and the show went on, sometimes in front of an audience of German officers and sometimes to empty seats.[42] It must have been a harrowing experience for the actors, trying to put on a play when an artillery shell might fall on the opera house at any time.

The chaos of war engulfed Warsaw. Terror seized the population and there weren't enough hospitals or surgeons to tend to the growing numbers of the wounded. Negri claimed she had several narrow escapes and saw friends die from stray gunfire. The demands of performing under such stress so exhausted her that she had to be put under a doctor's care.[43] After a week's shelling, the bombing ceased and the Germans had control of Warsaw. The city under the Germans wasn't much of an improvement, but life went on and gradually went back to normal.

Negri made her first foray into moving pictures before the war. According to publicity, she financed, wrote and starred in her own production, *Love and Passion,* in 1914. She completed her maiden picture within a month, but was so disheartened by the primitiveness of the production that she sold the rights to it to an exhibitor for about $50. The purchaser of her crude little effort later made a small fortune exhibiting it in Poland and Russia.[44]

Memoirs omits any mention of *Love and Passion,* instead identifying the two-reeler *Niewolnica zymslów (The Slave of Sin)* as her first feature film; it was released in 1914 by a small Polish production company, Sphinx.[45] The picture was, ironically, the story of a dancer. Negri claimed to have found the script lacking and revised it herself. If her story can be believed, she seems to have quickly grasped the potential of moving picture acting as a career.

Her earliest films were marked by a hearty camaraderie and *esprit de corps* between cast and crew that she would find sadly lacking in her later American productions. As she recounted, "[L]ife at the studio, in those hectic days, was simple and it was fun. There were very few temperamental flare-ups or arguments; we all felt too much a part of every aspect of what was happening for that. It was in every sense—*our* film."[46]

Slave of Sin, now available on DVD, is technically crude, shot on what looks like two flimsy sets with interchangeable furniture, and suffers from staginess due, no doubt, to the almost non-existent budget. Negri plays a girl named Pola who runs away from her parents and steals money from her boyfriend Dimitri. He vows revenge. She becomes a nightclub dancer and attracts the attention of the married Alexei (played by Alexander Hertz, the owner of Sphinx *nee* Sfinx films). Smitten, Alexei deserts his wife Sonia and moves the young dancer into her own apartment.[47] Sonia becomes ill from heartbreak.

Pola discovers that Alexei is married and leaves him. Suitably chastened, Alexei asks his wife for forgiveness—but too late. She dies. The vengeful Dimitri finally catches up with Pola and shoots her. She dies. Roll credits.

It's all very melodramatic and looks more like a filmed play than a movie. The cast, for the most part, are amateurs and it shows. Even Negri's acting is more suited to the stage. She does convey a subtlety of emotion here and outshines her castmates.

The film was a moderate success and Hertz signed her to a long-term contract with Sphinx for the equivalent of 500 American dollars a week. Between stage performances she made a handful of movies for the company, including *Zona* (Wife) and *Czarna Ksiazeczka* (The Black Pass) in 1915, *Studenci* (Students), *Pokój Nr. 13* (Room #13), *Tajemnica Alei Ujazdowskioch* (Mystery of Uyazdowsky Lane), *Arabella* and *Jego ostatni czyn* (His Last Gesture), all in 1917.[48] All of these pictures are lost.

As a result of her performance as "The Dancer" in the Rozmaitości's version of Max Reinhardt's *Sumurun* (1917), she received an invitation from Reinhardt to appear in his re-staging of the play in Berlin. Excited at the prospect of leaving war-shattered Warsaw and working with the celebrated Reinhardt, she accepted the offer although she still had an "iron-clad" contract with Sphinx, and Hertz refused her request to set it aside so she could go. Undaunted, Negri took her plight to a lawyer who obtained her release from Sphinx on the grounds that she had signed her studio contract while still a minor, rendering the agreement unenforceable. With *Sumurun* set to begin rehearsals in Berlin, Negri bid goodbye to her mother and left by train to travel to a nation that was still at war.

3

The Rise of Pola Negri

In 1917 Negri arrived in Berlin, a city just beginning to realize that the war they had come so tantalizingly close to winning was lost. She described the feeling that engulfed the beleaguered city as "the chill of approaching death."[1] Without the *Sumurun* rehearsals to distract her, she might have immediately returned to Warsaw.

Settling into a new city, she rehearsed hard to master her role, cognizant for the first time under Max Reinhardt's direction of the possibilities her part held. Her character did not speak; the role was entirely performed in pantomime. She had to convey every thought through movement. Her training in ballet served her well.

Max Reinhardt graciously took Negri under his wing. He offered her acting tips, set her up in an apartment with a local woman to look after her, and made sure she received German language lessons.

At that time, he was the most famous stage director in Europe—and the most unconventional. He encouraged actors to look within themselves, allowing their personalities to create their stage performance. He preached that acting should be organic—spontaneous—instead of rigidly structured by a script. As a result, every performance was fresh as actors were encouraged to reinterpret their roles as they liked. Negri was inspired by her director's encouragement and faith in her talents. It must have excited her to see placards around Berlin announcing "*Sumurun—with Pola Negri.*"[2]

If she felt any anxiety about her situation, it's understandable. Here she was, an unknown Polish actress "on trial … in one of the most discriminating art centers of Europe."[3] Her pantomimic ability, however, won her applause, and Reinhardt was credited with a new star "discovery." Predictions of future success on the stage brought her name to the forefront as the play's run was extended.

Life in Berlin was difficult during the war. Negri took a small apartment with a maid on the Emerstrasse, one of the city's main streets. Food shortages were common—grocery store shelves were often empty while the black market thrived. There were times she did not have enough to eat. Warsaw, by comparison, was in better condition even under German occupation, and from time to time she received boxes of food from her mother that she happily shared with her castmates. Sometimes, however, the boxes only contained rocks, the contents stolen by thieves.

According to *Memoirs*, while playing in *Sumurun*, she was dismayed to learn that her first film, *Love and Passion*, had been booked into a seedy Berlin theater to capitalize on her new fame under Reinhardt. She became concerned that this cheap little picture would make it impossible for her to be taken seriously as an actress. To her surprise, the picture was a hit and, even more surprising, brought her an offer from Ufa—the Unversum Film Aktien Gesellschaft—to make pictures at a salary 20 times what she was making on stage."[4] In her autobiography, Negri wrote that she accepted the offer in April 1917 and for about a week she filmed at the studio during the day while appearing on stage in *Sumurun* at night. When she realized that doing both meant doing neither well, she abandoned her stage career after the *end of Sumurun*'s run and dedicated herself to being a motion picture actress.[5]

Her timeline, however, omits the six pictures she made for Saturn Films prior to joining Ufa: *Nicht lange täuschte mich das Glück*; *Zügelloses Blut*; *Küsse, die Man stiehlt in Dunkeln* (*Kisses Stolen in the Dark*); *Die toten Augen* (*The Dead Eyes*); *Wenn das Herz in Hab erglüht* (*When the Heart Burns with Hate*); and *Rosen, die der Sturm entblättert*. Out of all of these pictures, only *Wenn das Herz in Hab erglüht* survives today.[6]

Sumurun's Berlin run also introduced her to Ernst Lubitsch, a fellow cast member. Lubitsch had film acting experience portraying an ethnic Jewish character in a series of Ufa comedy shorts. He was eager to direct pictures and he persuaded Negri to sign with the studio after Saturn went bankrupt at the end of the war.

Ufa, Germany's largest film studio and the center of its film industry, was never on solid financial ground. Negri spent three years under contract there, making pictures at a prolific pace, both with and without Lubitsch behind the camera. In 1918 she appeared in *Mania, Die Augen der Mumie Ma* (*The Eyes of the Mummy*), *Der gelbe Schein* (*The Yellow Ticket*) and *Carmen*. All of these films survive today; *Mania* was fully restored in 2011.

In *The Yellow Ticket*, a remake of the lost Polish-made *The Black Passport*, Negri plays Lea Raab, a Jewess who passes herself off as the dead sister of Ossip Storki, her school tutor, to gain entrance to the University of Petrograd to which Jews are not admitted. A brilliant student, she rises to the top of her medical class and becomes her professor's prize pupil. Demetri, a fellow student, falls in love with her but rejects her when he discovers her working

Top: **Postcard of Pola Negri, ca. 1917, Phtochemie Berlin No. 1106 (photograph by A. Binder).** *Bottom:* **Postcard of Pola Negri, ca. 1918, Verlag "Ross," Berlin, No. 1012 (photograph by Ernst Sandau).**

in a seedy nightclub, coerced into prostitution by her abusive landlady. Lea, ashamed, jumps from a window in a suicide attempt, yet survives. She is found in the hospital by Storki, who has learned of her use of his sister's name. He also discovers that her school professor is also her biological father. Moved to help, the professor performs surgery on her and Lea recovers, providing for an unusual happy ending.

Beneath the ragged melodrama of this picture is a serious subtext: anti-Semitism. "The Yellow Ticket," or as it is referred to in the picture, "The Yellow Passport" is a document—official permission—needed by Imperial Russia's Jews to do *anything*, be it travel, be admitted to the university, obtain housing, etc. Lea's desperation to keep her ticket leads to dehumanization, the plight of many Jews in those Tsarist times. Negri was convincing enough in her portrayal here that many believed that she *was* Jewish. She was, however, Catholic in various degrees of practice throughout her life.

The Yellow Ticket displays her growing sense of comfort in front of the camera. Although her acting here still sometimes comes off as a bit stagy, particularly in displays of grief or despair, these occasions are offset by a very natural and effortless style of performance in most scenes. There are a few stock characters in the picture that border on racist caricature, such as Lea's ailing adoptive Jewish father, but Negri's heroine rings true. She is riveting to watch, even in such a creaky old picture, and has an intensity unrivaled by anyone else in the cast.

The picture's flat lighting lets her down. In one scene, she leans into a mirror on the wall and her reflection seems to be of someone in her forties. Her makeup is mostly greasepaint. Her kohl-ringed eyes and very black hair give her a theatrical look that jars violently with her natural acting style, but such was the way of moviemaking in Germany in 1918.

In 1919, she starred in *Madame DuBarry* (*Passion*), *Das Karussell des Lebens* (*The Carousel of Love*), *Kreuzigt Sie!* (*Crucify It!*), *Komtesse Doddy* (*Countess Doddy*, aka *Countess Baby*) and *Vendetta*. *The Carousel of Love*, *Vendetta* and *Crucify It!* are lost films.

The Carousel of Love is the story of Lola, a conscienceless French model with a string of lovers. She marries a man who embezzles money from his own firm to pay for her extravagances. After he is sent to prison for theft, she divorces him and marries a wealthy South American cattle man whom she hates. He is killed and she returns to France on the arm of a young man smitten with her. He proposes marriage, but she cruelly rejects him and marries his father. The jilted young man kills himself out of despair and the father, after learning of their affair, banishes his new bride from his home. A distraught Lola throws herself under the wheels of an express train.

In *Vendetta*, a young Corsican noblewoman's brother is killed in a duel. She swears to take vengeance on his slayer. Her guardian pressures her into a promise to marry him if he discovers the identity of the killer. She subsequently meets a young Englishman in a hospital and nurses him through a fever during an epidemic. They fall in love and marry. After their wedding—and you can probably guess what's coming next—the opportunistic guardian reveals her new husband to be the killer. But it is the guardian who is slain at the conclusion of the picture by the former servant of the Countess' brother.[7]

In 1920 her work included the lead in *Die Marchesa d'Armiani* (*The Marquise of Armiani*), a film version of *Sumurun*, *Das Martyrium* (*The Martyrium*), *Die geschlossene Kette* (*The Closed Chain*), and *Arme Violetta* (*Poor Violetta*). Apart from *Sumurun*, her 1920 output is lost.

Her final German pictures were made in 1921: *Die Bergkatze* (*The Mountain Cat*),

Sappho and *Die Flamme* (*The Flame*). *The Mountain Cat* and *Sappho* are extant and complete. Only one reel of *The Flame*, 20 minutes or so, still exists.

Her pictures weren't all hits. It was the pictures directed by Lubitsch that were the notable standouts. Most of the others are long forgotten and very little English-language material on them exists. Negri doesn't even acknowledge the majority of her early German films in *Memoirs*, preferring to dwell on the ones which made her an international star.

Die Augen der Mumie Ma (*The Eyes of the Mummy Ma*), her first feature with Lubitsch, co-starred Swiss actor Emil Jannings and German actor Harry Lietdke; the latter was her leading man in most of her Lubitsch-directed pictures. Although the title makes the picture sound like a horror film, it is more in the style of an Edwardian penny-dreadful stage melodrama.

An English painter, Albert Wendland (Lietdke), is in Cairo touring the pyramids. After hearing of the tragedy that befell a hotel guest who dared visit the tomb of Queen Ma ("The eyes, the eyes are alive!" the haunted guest cries to Wendland), he decides to investigate. At the tomb he meets its crazed keeper, Radu (Emil Jannings), and discovers he is holding a young woman, Mara (Negri), captive. He frees her from the queen's sarcophagus and, smitten by her beauty, takes her back to Europe. Radu vows vengeance on both and follows them to England.

In London, Wendland weds Mara. Her oriental style of dancing makes her a celebrated variety performer. As the unrelenting Radu closes in, the terrified Mara can feel his presence and suffers fits of hysteria. When Radu finally catches up with her at the Englishman's home, she falls down a flight of steps while trying to escape and dies. Radu, stricken with remorse, stabs himself to death.

It's a primitive-looking production shot under wartime conditions. For most of its running time, a youthful-looking Pola wears no makeup and is practically unrecognizable. The most striking aspect of her performance is her use of physical motion. She moves with a cat-like agility during her dance scenes, imbuing her character with a slinky and sensuous air. Although her acting is still a bit stilted in spots, she has complete command of the viewer's attention.

During the filming of her climactic death scene, Negri told her director it would be more realistic for her to fall down the entire length of stairs instead of staggering down a few steps and then collapsing at the bottom of the staircase as was done in most similar scenes. Lubitsch resisted her suggestion, fearing for her safety. "I might need you for retakes," he jokingly told her. When she did the scene, Negri threw up her hands, and as she went to stagger back on the steps, caught her heel in the hem of her dress and tumbled down the stairs, landing in a heap at the bottom. A startled Lubitsch had harsh words for Emil Jannings, her co-star, for his failure to catch her. "How would I know she was going to do that?" Jannings protested loudly. "Did I ask you to hire this crazy Pole?"[8]

With *Die Augen der Momie Ma* a hit, Ufa asked for another Lubitsch-Negri collaboration. Lubitsch decided on a film version of the opera *Carmen*. Negri was initially dubious about the choice of subject material. How do you film a world-famous opera without obtaining the rights to Bizet's musical score? The studio didn't have the funds to do that. Her director, however, ingeniously circumvented the problem by opting to base the picture on Prosper Mérimée's original story of *Carmen*, the inspiration for the opera. Ufa approved a higher budget, and sets were built on the grounds of their Templehof Studio in Berlin.[9]

Carmen is a daring picture devoid of movie glamour. Pictorially, it is crude and its tone is mean-spirited and tragic. The inhabitants of squalid Triana, the gypsy quarter of old Seville, are depicted as a motley collection of drunks, smugglers, killers and philandering soldiers, all generally treacherous—the lowest of the low. One can argue that the depiction of the townspeople in the film reflect the traditional prejudices against Southern Europeans as lazy, shiftless souls: dirty, ignorant and primitive. The only well-meaning character among the undesirable lot is the "hero" Don Jose, a military man, whose mistake is to fall for a heartless temptress who ruins his life.

Carmen was Negri's favorite film role. She said years later, "Carmen—oh yes, Carmen. I understood her. I loved her. I was her. It was like playing on an organ with innumerable stops. Every emotion could be touched upon."[10]

She is the quintessential female "vampire," a pitiless seductress who destroys lives on a whim and enjoys it. The dirty and unkempt Carmencita has no qualms about compelling her smitten fool of a lover (Harry Liedtke) to abandon his military career, disavow his loving fiancée and commit murder. Pola plays her as an animal, a base and amoral woman. She delights in cruelly dangling her affections and laughing at the poor romantic sap who suffers at her hands. When Don Jose threatens to kill her rather than lose her to another man, she dares him to do so and calls him a coward when his nerve fails him. She later urges him to stand up to his commanding officer, who has also fallen for her. A jealous Don Jose kills him in a duel—making him a murderer and fugitive. In the end, when Carmen shifts her romantic attentions to a famous bullfighter, the spurned lover stabs her to death.

Lubitsch wisely gave his leading lady the freedom to be physically ugly, an opportunity she would never have again. Her clothes are filthy. Her white facial makeup and black kohl-ringed eyes give her a grotesque harlequin-like cast. Tight close-ups of her face, of the cruelty in her eyes, allow us to view the ugliness of her soul. It's a very brave performance. No other silent era actress took the risks that Negri did in *Carmen*, daring to play a character so devoid of sympathy. Her first-rate acting wins the viewer's admiration.

As *Carmen*'s Berlin premiere took place, the sound of gunfire was heard outside the theater. The Western Front had collapsed, and as the German government negotiated a surrender to the Allies, the country teetered on the brink of a civil war. At the conclusion of the screening, Negri left the theater for a subway station a few blocks away. As she walked along the darkened street amidst another round of gunshots, she walked in short steps and kept her back to the wall so as to not offer a target for snipers.[11]

Her next Lubitsch picture was the internationally acclaimed *Madame DuBarry*. This "historical costume drama" traces the rise of humble Paris milliner Jean Vaubernier from courtesan to a titled marriage as Countess DuBarry to the official mistress of King Louis XV (Emil Jannings)—making her, for a brief time, the most powerful woman in France. As her influence with the king grows, her former lover, Armand (Harry Liedtke), and the people turn against her. After Louis' death, she leaves the palace to live in seclusion, but is arrested during the French Revolution and sentenced to be guillotined. A last-minute rescue attempt by a repentant Armand fails and she is beheaded to cheers from the mob. The last shot is of her severed head lying in the street.

The picture was a sensation across Europe. Critics marveled at its sumptuousness and praised Lubitsch's handling of the crowd scenes, which earned him the title "The German Griffith."[12] The director trained his camera on the characters rather than on events, presenting the story from a point of view never before seen by audiences of the day.

Harry Liedtke and Pola Negri in a scene from *Carmen*, Ufa, 1918 (Germany). Directed by Ernst Lubitsch.

Madame DuBarry made Pola Negri a huge star on the Continent. In an era where female characters were either entirely good or bad, her DuBarry is neither. She is cunning and ambitious and has no regard for anyone but herself. She is clearly not ashamed to use her sexuality to her advantage. In fact, the film makes it clear she enjoys sexual pleasure, a genuinely radical notion in 1919. In the end, her willfulness and selfishness doom her. Proto-feminism is crushed by strict conservative paternalism.

Pola Negri and Hans von Winterstein in *Madame DuBarry*, Ufa, 1919 (Germany). Directed by Ernst Lubitsch.

Lubitsch gets most of the credit for *Madame DuBarry*'s success, but it is really Negri's picture. No other silent era actress so dominated a picture. After seeing it in a Berlin theater, *Picture-Play Magazine*'s Herbert Howe hailed her as Europe's greatest actress and called her "incomparable."[13] In *An Index to the Films of Ernst Lubitsch*, Theodore Huff states:

> Miss Negri gave a colorful performance almost never equaled for vitality and emotional depth. Never before had a screen star burst on the public in such full bloom. With grace, verve and vivid radiance, she created a living character who was simple, vivacious, a capricious child one minute and the next a restless and passionate woman, carried away by her love of luxury. In spite of the character of Du Barry, Miss Negri made her a fascinating and disturbingly sympathetic figure who was actually pathetic towards the end—a "toy of erratic destiny" in the grip of events beyond her simple and extremely feminine nature.

Negri shows an outstanding dramatic range in the role. In the first half of the picture there are glimpses of comic ability in her flirtatiousness with Jannings' King Philip.

Instead of bowing to him as dictated by royal protocol, she playfully jumps on his lap as if offering herself to him—which is exactly what she's doing. After taking her on as his mistress, the besotted king tends to her feet, clipping her toenails and making sure her shoes fit properly. You can tell from the look on her face that she's thrilled to hold such a powerful man in her thrall, yet it is a power she uses foolishly. Humiliated by a mob protest against her outside the palace gates, she asks her lover to get rid of them and sees the palace guards open fire on the demonstrators. The look of horror on her face, the realization that she is the cause of dozens of deaths, seems absolutely genuine.

During the course of the picture, in fact, Negri hardly appears to be acting at all. Her reactions to events are natural, logical and honest. At the end, when DuBarry goes to her death, she is not brave or heroic. As she struggles in vain against her captors, you can sense her fear and desperation as she is dragged towards the waiting guillotine. When she begs her executioner for one more day of life, you feel sympathy for her. Playing DuBarry was the finest moment of her career and one she would never top.

Negri later recounted a tense moment during the production of the picture. In 1919, unemployment was rife in Germany and resentment ran high against the ousted Kaiser. When Lubitsch advertised for a thousand extras for a mob scene, over 3,000 turned up at the studio for the chance to earn a few Deutschmarks for a day's work. They refused to be turned away. Ufa, fearing a riot, hired them all.

At German Emperor Frederick the Great's summer palace in Potsdam, Negri was rehearsing a scene in her powdered wig and court costume. Suddenly a peasant woman hired as an extra caught sight of her. "The Kaiserin!" she cried out, convinced that the actress was the hated Kaiser's wife. Pola had to persuade the skeptical woman that she wasn't the former empress, avoiding a potentially ugly scene that could have shut down the production.[14]

After completing *Madame DuBarry,* Negri returned to her native country for the first time in three years. At the end of the war Poland had freed itself from its Russian occupiers and was now an independent nation. Negri was overjoyed to see her mother again and spent time visiting old friends. Soon Ufa was summoning her back to begin her next picture, but her return to Germany was unexpectedly delayed—by marriage.

It is tempting to conclude that the lack of a father colored Pola's adult relationships with men. She was strong and intelligent and yet always chose men who were wrong for her. All her love affairs failed or ended in tragedy, leaving her with loneliness to endure. More than once she described herself as a "fatalist" in matters of the heart, so it would seem that most of her romantic troubles were pre-ordained, beginning with her unexpected marriage in 1920 to Count Eugene Dombski.

According to most accounts, upon leaving Poland to return to Berlin, she was informed at the border by a customs official that she would not be allowed to take her jewelry out of the country.[15] In *Memoirs,* however, it was a copy of *Slaves of Sin* purchased from Alexander Herz that she was not allowed to take with her.[16] Whichever it was, she was furious at the prospect of being delayed by bureaucratic red tape and demanded to see the official's superior. She was directed to the office of the military district commander, Count Eugene Dombski—sometimes spelled "Dombska," "Damski" and "Domski."

She described him as "an extraordinarily handsome young man in his mid-twenties. He had lively blue eyes and carried himself with such awesome bearing that he seemed taller than his medium height."[17] Dombski graciously waived the restriction against whatever she was taking from the country and invited her to dinner. Charmed by the count, she accepted. He must have made quite an impression that night because by the time that Negri returned to Berlin, she was smitten with him.

They corresponded frequently over the next few months, letters she characterized as "filled with friendship, more than friendship, and then finally with love."[18] When Dombski told her he was going to be in Warsaw and asked if she would meet him there, she cajoled Ufa into giving her three weeks of vacation and went to see him. She had convinced herself she was in love with him, yet Dombski did not seem to return her feelings. According to Negri, he was "courtly and filled with extravagant gestures, but he never put his arm around me except to lead me in dance. Perhaps he loved me as a friend but did not find me physically attractive. I did not know what to think."[19] She returned to Berlin at the end of her vacation, but with all motion picture production at Ufa at a halt due to financial problems, there was no work and all she could think of was him. When he unexpectedly sent her a letter containing a marriage proposal, she agreed without hesitation.

She married Dombski and went to live with him at his apartment in Sosnowiec. It was an impossible situation for her. Sexually, she and her new husband were incompatible. "In bed, I was not his wife sharing the pleasures of marriage. I was simply an object at which he hurled his passion."[20] Dombski spent most of his time away from home. They had very different views of the world. He was comfortable living in a small town and unconcerned by anything that occurred outside of his Army job. Any time she tried to discuss art or politics with him, he chided her for cultivating interests outside of her "job," which was to be his wife and nothing else. Negri, on the other hand, was used to far bigger things than what her husband's little town offered. She missed the excitement of Berlin and the attention she received as a famous actress. Her notion of marriage was little more than a romantic fantasy that quickly withered, leaving her frustrated and lonely.

A visit from Lubitsch convinced her to abandon Dombski and return to Germany. Ufa had acquired new financial backing and they were gearing up again. Lubitsch told her that exhibitors were asking for another picture from the Lubitsch-Negri team. Eager to resume work, the countess informed her husband of her intention to return to Germany. To her surprise, he did not object to her leaving. Negri left for Berlin the next morning. For all intents and purposes their union was over. She would never reconcile with the count. The marriage had lasted less than a year. Negri summed up its failure by saying that her husband could not provide her with the intellectual stimulation that film work gave her. "I realized my work was more vital than such love. I went back to it."[21]

After she became a Hollywood star, the end of her marriage to Dombski became a tale of stormy passion and heroic determination. According to one publicity piece, the count was enraged over her desire to continue her movie career and forbade her to have any contact with Ufa or any other film studio. When she was called back to Berlin, he became violent and held her at gunpoint, telling her she would leave over his dead body. Negri waited until he was asleep to make her escape, packing up only as many clothes as she could carry and walking on foot for miles in the black night towards the train station, arriving in the nick of time—imagine that—to catch the next train for Berlin.[22]

Her next Ufa picture was an adaptation of *Sumurun*, directed by Ernest Lubitsch. Over the years, Negri claimed to have invented the depiction of sexual arousal on-screen and *Sumurun* was Exhibit A in her case. The role provided her the opportunity to display her charged sexuality to the fullest. In 1920 there was no other character on the moving picture screen quite like her: feral, carnal, unrestrained. She literally smolders. Her

"Desert Dancer" is sexual abandon incarnate, the object and embodiment of unbridled and deadly lust. Even by today's looser moral standards, her performance is still frank and irresistible.

Clad in a satin halter top and harem pants, she slithers like a snake to the music of a snake charmer. She sidles up to men, smiles, undresses them with her large, expressive eyes and gives off an intense air of ardor. She even dresses the part. Her costume must have caused audiences to gape in wonder, as her bare navel is exposed for most of the picture. One wonders how they ever got those belly shots past the censor at a time when a woman appearing in public in a modest one-piece bathing suit could be arrested.

The Dancer's story in *Sumurun* is by far the most compelling subplot of this Arabian Nights fairy tale. The Dancer is the woman that everyone wants and no one gets. She pits father and son against each other and is loyal to neither. By the end of the picture, most of the male characters are dead by each other's hands and the Dancer has been murdered due to her own wantonness. Negri injects a pathos into her performance that humanizes the Dancer and prevents her from becoming a mere caricature. It's a sensational part for a skilled actress and she pulls it off without a single false note.

Away from the camera, and with her husband still in Poland, Pola fell into a passionate affair with Wolfgang George Schleber, a wealthy German industrialist she nicknamed

Paul Wegener and Pola Negri in *Sumurun*, Ufa, 1920 (Germany). Directed by Ernst Lubitsch.

"Polonius" because his profile reminded her of a Roman sculpture. Until she met Rudolph Valentino years later, he was the great love of her life. As Kotowski points out, he introduced her to museums and bookstores and taught her about fine wine and classical music. They were out almost every evening, enjoying Berlin's nightlife, attending concerts, attending the theater, etc. Polonius cultivated both her cultural and sexual instincts. He was exactly what she had been missing in a lover: someone who challenged her intellectually and would not leave her.[23]

There were fights and arguments, of course. Negri had a jealous streak and never held back when she was displeased. She did everything passionately and demanded the same loyalty from a man that she did from an adoring audience. When she wanted attention, she would not be denied.

Under Polonius' influence, she developed a love for jewelry, both for looks and, never forgetting her earlier poverty, as a financial investment. From the former Kaiser's family she purchased the fabled Hohenzollern collection of jewels. As one of the highest paid women in a Germany where inflation ran rampant—a laborer would be paid for a day's work in millions of worthless Deutschmarks and carry the mountain of bank notes home in a wheelbarrow—she could afford them, and in time they would certainly be worth far more than what she paid for them.[24] It would prove later, during the tough times, to be a very smart move on her part.

Meanwhile, *Madame DuBarry*'s success in Europe caught the attention of an American studio, First National Pictures. Needing a hit picture, they purchased the rights to exhibit the film in the U.S. for $30,000.[25] Due to an unofficial ban on the importation of German pictures into New York City, they didn't dare book the picture into their top house on Broadway, the Strand Theater. But legendary movie showman Samuel L. "Roxy" Rothafel defied the ban and offered to play the picture, now retitled *Passion,* for one evening, December 12, 1920, at the Capitol Theatre.[26] To avoid controversy, the picture was initially billed in newspapers as an *Italian* production starring "Poli Negri." Exhibitors took notice when *Passion* set a one-day record at the Capitol with 21,000 paid admissions and takings of $12,000. The picture then had a then-unheard-of two-week run with 350,000 tickets sold and turn-away business every night, making it the most profitable foreign film released in America to that date.[27] Importantly for Negri, the *de facto* prohibition against German films was lifted due to *Passion*'s success.

On the strength of *Passion*'s New York popularity, an American studio, Famous Players–Lasky, took advantage of another financial reorganization of Ufa and got both Lubitsch and Negri to agree to jump ship after their current contracts expired. They also hired away Paul Davidson, the founder of Ufa, tapping him to run their new German subsidiary EFA.[28] At the time of Negri's signing, there was no plan for her to make films in the U.S. She and Lubitsch would be making German movies *in* Germany for domestic consumption and for foreign export.

Negri was supposed to re-team with Emil Jannings in a version of *Macbeth* with Lubitsch directing,[29] but her next production was the little-known *Die Bergkatze* (*The Mountain Cat* aka *The Wildcat*). It's a treat to see Negri in an out-and-out Lubitsch comedy filmed on location in the snow-capped mountains of Bavaria. In her autobiography, she relates how Polonius sent coats and daily boxes of food to keep the cast and crew from freezing and starving to death.[30] Yet despite the hardships, it looks like everyone had a grand time filming this comic romp. There are plenty of surreal Lubitsch touches on display, from the sack of mice used to disperse a crowd of women to the bandits willingly and gleefully offering up their backsides to the whip. The picture is absurdist in tone and Negri is wonderful in it. She plays "Riska," daughter of the chieftain of a group of inept mountain bandits. Riska is a wild one, and her tousled black mane of hers, free and sexy as all-get-out, summarizes her German film persona perfectly. Riska is the equal of any one of her father's men. She shoots and wields a whip with ease and is unquestionably the brains of the operation. Certainly she is the only competent bandit in the bunch. She leads the group's raids on military caravans and single-handedly routs the inept military garrison sent to stop them. This is not a woman easily tamed.

Enter Lt. Esterhazy (Paul Heidemann), a smug ladies man who is sent to the far-off garrison as punishment for philandering. Riska robs the smarmy lieutenant of all his clothes and sends him on his way, but not without falling in love with him first. Although she dreams of a romantic life with him, she ultimately cedes him to the garrison commandant's daughter after persuading Esterhazy that they aren't really suited to each other. She winds up married to one of her fellow bandits, a shy man she responds to with an almost maternal love.

Variety, which had established a Berlin bureau after *Passion*'s success to cover the newest German productions, felt the picture was undeserving of the drubbing it received in the Berlin press.[31] They described it as a "burlesque on militarism" and called Lubitsch's direction "original and brilliant" but just short of the mark. Negri was described as "charming and very easy," but they criticized her acting as too "straight" for a farce of this nature.[32]

Her last picture under her Ufa contract was *Sappho*, directed by a Russian, Dimitri Buchowetzki. Negri plays the title role of Sappho, "queen of the women of pleasure." As

Miss Negri and John Frederson in a scene from *Sappho*, Ufa, 1921 (Germany). Directed by Dimitri Buchowetzki

the picture opens, she has betrayed Andreas, a young engineer, by having a tryst with his employer, George. Andreas goes insane from grief and is committed to an asylum. His brother Richard learns from the asylum doctor that Sappho was the cause of Andreas' mental collapse, and he vows to get revenge. When he goes to the city to find her, he meets her by chance and, without learning her name, falls in love with her. Sappho, equally affected, leaves George to start a new life with Richard. This does not sit well with George, who tracks the couple down at a seaside resort and reveals her identity to Richard. Furious, Richard casts her away and returns home to his village, where his long-suffering girlfriend is waiting to for him to marry her.

They are wed, but at the wedding breakfast, Richard is overcome by memories of Sappho. He runs out on his new wife and races back to the city to find her. Meanwhile, Andreas kills his guard and escapes from the asylum.

Sappho, mourning Richard's marriage, attends a masked ball with her latest admirer. Richard finds her and the lovers are reunited in one of the private dining rooms. Andreas turns up and shoves Richard out of the room, locking the door. By the time Richard manages to break the door down, Sappho has been strangled by Andreas.[33]

Sappho is a tragic character. Men fall in love with her and desire her. She can't help that, but it makes her "dangerous," according to the insane asylum doctor. Whenever she leaves a man, he goes mad or threatens to ruin or murder the new suitor. A man who romances her is invariably "ruined." It's interesting to note that behind the myth of the female "vamp" is a male too weak or flawed to resist the charms of the "she-devil" seductress. Who is really to blame for the lethal attraction between them? More often than not it is the vamp who pays with her life in the end. Here, Sappho is strangled at the hands of the man she has driven mad with her cheating heart.

Sappho is evidence that the quality of Negri's performance depended heavily on the caliber of her director. Most directors other than Lubitsch did not know how to use her to her best advantage. Buchowetzki gives her very little to do here dramatically and in such a choppy, disjointed and cheap-looking picture her naturalistic performance is lost amidst the rudimentary plot and slapdash acting of her co-stars. It is a very pedestrian production and there is really little to commend it other than Negri's performance.

One note of interest: In the first act, Pola appears without any kind of makeup other than the mask-like white base that she uses in most of her German work. Add that starkness to her magnificent black curly hair and black clothing and she takes on an expressionistic appearance. It's a fascinating look, refreshingly modern and striking.

Despite the weaknesses of this picture, it's still interesting to see how far ahead of her contemporaries Pola Negri was in terms of dramatic ability. No other European actress of the time came close and no other American actress, excepting Lillian Gish, could match her talent as a tragedienne.

Leaving Ufa after the expiration of her contract, Negri started making EFA's *Die Flamme* with Lubitsch in 1922. She plays a former prostitute who finds that new love with a young composer cannot erase her sordid past. Their marriage tragically unravels due to family interference. His sudden success with his music makes her past life all the more painful.

EFA's original plans called for Lubitsch to direct every one of her pictures.[34] In retrospect, that might have been an impossibly tall order. Although their creative partnership was generally successful, Lubitsch's use of Negri has a sadistic bent to it. In her director's scenarios, Negri was always "the other woman" and always came to a violent end in that "fatal association between sexuality and guilt."[35] She is scared to death in *The Eyes of the Mummy,* stabbed in both *Sumurun* and *Carmen,* beheaded in *Madame DuBarry,* and takes her own life in *Die Flamme.*

Negri never had a bad word to say about Lubitsch. He was the perfect "collaborator" for her. Her most memorable performances came under his direction and it's too bad that, except for *Forbidden Paradise,* she did not have Lubitsch to guide her in her American pictures.

In interviews Lubitsch always complimented her, saying that she had "natural color," the ability to get herself talked about, and a "highly developed and sensitive artistic instinct."[36] Yet in 1932 he wrote, "[T]he relation between a director and an actress is like the relation between a man and his mistress. They are bound together by contact, but there is no sentimental attachment."[37] According to Lubitsch biographer Scott Eyman, the director prepared two shooting scripts for *Die Flamme,* one for Negri and one for the rest of the cast. That way he could shoot her scenes first and get those out of the way rather than hear her complain about his direction or wait around for her to show up on the set well after noon or whenever she pleased. Fame had made her too difficult for his taste. He felt she treated him subserviently and didn't give him enough credit for *their* pictures. Perhaps killing her off all those times was his own way of getting back at her.

Die Flamme's original downbeat ending was altered by the studio in favor of a "nice" ending—shades of what was to come—and an unhappy Lubitsch was fired after refusing to shoot more pictures for EFA. After his departure it was first announced that Negri would make four movies, two to be shot in Germany and two in America.[38] Then it was announced that her next picture would be shot in Berlin with a director imported from New York. Realistically, however, with Lubitsch already in America, there was no real reason to keep Negri in Germany. On July 1, 1922, it was announced that she would soon arrive stateside to make *one* picture,[39] but it's likely that Famous Players always intended to make her an American movie star.

In *Photoplay,* Negri later explained the reasons for her departure from Germany. She blamed it on the harsh criticism she received from the German press. They had learned that she was donating money to Polish charities and accused her of supporting Germany's enemy, Poland. Pola insisted that she wasn't giving money to the Polish military. She generously donated to a number of Warsaw orphanages and to several German charities; and regardless, she felt she had the right to dispose of her money as she chose.[40]

Picture-Play Magazine, however, offered an alternative reason for her leaving:

> Pola is in trouble in Germany and is rather glad to get out. It seems that she contributed toward erecting a statue in her home town in Poland. All would have been well if they hadn't learned in Germany that the statue was of a Polish gentlemen who had fought with no small success against the Germans. And to make it tougher, in order to make a place for the statue they tore down one of some German ancient and dumped him into the alley. All in all, Pola had a good deal to explain.[41]

Later there would be gossip suggesting that certain agencies within the German government suspected Negri of being a spy for Polish intelligence and that her 1922 departure from Berlin was a matter of necessity, not choice. As ridiculous as this sounds, this charge against her would be resurrected a decade later by the Nazi regime. Strangely enough, it is said that during her time in Hollywood the U.S. State Department kept a file on Negri as a suspected *German* spy in America.

Departing Germany meant the end of her relationship with Schleber. His business was in Berlin so he could not accompany her to America. Negri suggested they maintain a long-distance relationship and promised to return to Germany when her contract expired. *Memoirs* makes it clear that that if Polonius had simply asked her to stay with him in Berlin, she would have stayed. He promised her instead that he would meet her in Paris before she left for the States.

Pola traveled to St. Moritz for the local premiere of *Madame DuBarry*. The fresh mountain air was good for her ailing lungs. Exhibitors and Swiss royalty wanted her to make personal appearances. The press followed her constantly. She soon tired of Switzerland and left for France without informing her hosts of her departure. She was anxious to reunite with Petronius, yet after her arrival in Paris he did not appear. Her letters and telegrams to him went unanswered.

While in Paris, she sat for a portrait by famous Polish painter Tadeusz Styka. She also received a visit from her mentor Casimir De Hulewicz, who had lost most of his fortune after the war. He was still convinced that she was going to be a great moving picture star. He arranged for her to meet a friend of his: Sarah Bernhardt. The legendary French actress declared her admiration for Negri's screen work and told her she was the future of film acting.

According to her autobiography, Pola was on the eve of her departure for America when she received divorce papers from Eugene Dombski. He had converted to Protestantism to marry his Danish fiancée, so there would be no need for an annulment of their marriage from the Catholic Church. She signed them, willingly relinquishing her title as Countess Dombski. She would later state she had received her divorce decree in 1921. If true, this begs the question why she didn't marry Petronius earlier. In any event, her further letters and telegrams to him again went unanswered and she was soon made aware by mutual friends that he had taken up with another woman.

Once again, a man she loved had abandoned her. Heartbroken, she left for America and her new life.

4

America Goes Ga-Ga for Pola

At the time of her arrival stateside, Salt Lake City's *Deseret News* wrote that Pola Negri "has the paradoxical distinction of being one of those famous and yet at the same time one of the least known of motion picture stars."[1] In 1921 and '22, many of her German-made pictures were distributed in America, mostly by First National and Paramount. Critics were astonished by her talent. Audiences were intrigued by her personal magnetism and beauty, yet no one knew anything about her. She was a complete unknown.

The press was faced with a difficult challenge. How could they write about an actress in Germany they could not interview? Without knowing much about her, they "invented" her. It bothered no one in the press that most of what they wrote about her in those early days were lies. After all, they had pictures to promote. Publicity depicted her as the seductive real-life vamp, a charming stunner and the essence of Continental sophistication. They made her fiery, mysterious, dangerous to desire. The difficulty came later when her studio got a case of cold feet and tried to undo what they had wrought, only to find that they'd made it impossible for the real Pola Negri to succeed.

The first mention of her in the American press came courtesy of Charlie Chaplin, who in 1920 wrote about his trip to Europe for the Hearst newspapers and later published his reminiscences in a 1921 booklet, *My Trip Abroad*. He was introduced to Negri at the Palais Heinroth restaurant in Berlin during a party to celebrate the premiere of *Madame DuBarry*. In a dispatch he described her beauty, highlighting her black hair; white, even teeth; and her coloring—her white, pale skin. He wrote, "What a voice she has! Her mouth so prettily speaks the German language. Her voice has a soft mellow quality with charming inflection. Offered a drink, she clinks my glass and offers her only English words: 'Jazz boy, Charlie.'"[2]

When *Passion* triumphed in New York, Negri was the center of publicity. First National's ads focused not on Lubitsch's directorial accomplishment, but on *her*. "You'll see Pola Negri, the toast of Europe's gay capitals and soon to be famous throughout America…. You'll feel her strange personal magnetism, which in woman opens all doors, levels all class distinctions, makes all men vie for her smile."[3]

The *New York Times* called her DuBarry "as fascinating as she has to be, with as much of the appearance of dignity as she must have on occasion, as and as contemptible and cowardly as she was. She actually wins sympathy for a woman who cannot at any time be admired. This is an accomplishment."[4] It seemed she was the actress that critics had been waiting for. The *Salt Lake Telegram* speculated that Negri's attractiveness "lies in the perfect contour of her face and the remarkably large and expressive eyes—eyes which tell everything and nothing as she wills." Her type was described as "soulful-capricious, simultaneously intense and fancifully fantastic."[5]

Picture-Play Magazine waxed enthusiastic over her:

> We have seen the Negri and we are hers! What a thing these Germans have done to us! They send us a stupendous picture like *Passion* and they put in the leading part a Polish charmer who makes us forget everything except the fact that here is an actress of tremendous appeal.... Only is the great Chaplin to be compared with her in skill of pantomime. Nazimova we thought was an artist; Pauline Frederick, we thought had great moments of emotional appeal, but these two—probably our greatest screen actresses—fade before the Negri.[6]

Motion Picture Magazine called her "fascinating and vivid—a finished actress who brings to the screen the grace of the Russian ballet from which she comes."[7] According to The *Wyoming State Tribune*, her performance in *Passion* was "one of the finest characterizations ever achieved by any actress.... [I]t is recorded that whole audiences have arisen to their feet and cheered her artistic triumphs despite the fact that the character she portrays is a peculiar mixture of virtues and faults with the latter for the most part prevailing."[8] The *Salt Lake City Telegram* said she had an abundance of "dramatic fire" that engaged the audience's admiration.[9]

American actors and directors also offered praise. Norma Talmadge said, "Pola Negri is marvelous, absolutely. She brings a freshness and buoyancy to the screen that no one else I can think of possesses." Betty Compson declared that she had depth, spontaneity, beauty and—well, everything. Director King Vidor lamented that America had no other feminine star that approached "the genius of Pola Negri." His wife, actress Florence Vidor, thought Negri was "divine."[10]

Most exhibitors were thrilled with *Passion*. The manager of the Lehigh Orpheum Theater in Bethlehem, Pennsylvania, said the picture "drew mostly to capacity and appealed to lovers of the historical and literary side of the picture business."[11] In Georgetown, Ohio, an Auditorium Theater exhibitor called *Passion* a "wonderful production with a wonderful star. Drew large crowd with advance prices."[12]

On the other hand, *Screenland Magazine* called *Passion* "pretentious"—which meant it was too highbrow for regular audiences. Ida Wallace's letter to *Motion Picture Magazine* called Negri "completely charmless" and "decidedly ugly." In her opinion, Negri was about the worst actress she had ever seen: "[I]f she has expression I fail to see it. She acts just about as well as a three months old babe. If one really can act, the looks do not matter, but if one is not attractive, and can't act—!!"[13]

Postcard view of Miss Negri and her wild, wonderful head of hair, Verlag "Ross," Berlin 407/5 (photograph by Rembrandt, 1921).

E.A. Baughan, film critic for *The Daily News* in London, took issue with the notion of Negri as the next coming of both Duse and Bernhardt. In his opinion, she was merely a promising debutante who lacked acting technique. Also, he criticized her looks: "Her face is not beautiful, nor very impressive, and she has the bad habit of grimacing to such an extent that some of the closeups are repulsive."[14] One wonders if her appearance in a *German* film was the real root of such antipathy. Baughan added that she still had a long way to go before she could be compared with the Gish sisters or Constance Talmadge in terms of acting talent.

Some small-town exhibitors complained that *Passion* made them no money. The manager of the Majestic Theater in Reedsville, Wisconsin, called it "a big picture, but not what small towns want. A historical costumer play. Lost money and did not please."[15] The picture also disappointed at the Liberty Theater in Florence, Colorado: "Did not please many. Not the kind of picture for a small town. A picture for the classes and not the masses."[16]

A German film was, of course, bound to attract much resentment. The manager of the Merit Theater in Hartford, Arkansas, told *The Exhibitor's Herald* that the picture was a bust for him: "Lost money. Foreign history does not appeal to our folks."[17] Another theater manager took issue with critics, complaining that they "rave about the wonderful productions of foreign stars, but very few of your audiences do."[18] A letter to *Motion Picture Magazine* from reader Francis K. Beckwith said, "I don't see why people rave so much about Pola Negri. Yes, she is wonderful, but I don't care for those foreign plays!"[19]

Motion Picture Magazine tried to ease some of the concern about the so-called "German invasion" of the movies, stating that they would provide a fresh viewpoint and hopefully broaden the audience's interest and knowledge of silent film. They warned, "[L]et us guard against provincialism."[20]

Calling it "provincialism" significantly understated the issue. A large segment of America's population in the early 1920s wanted nothing to do with anything *foreign*, be they intellectual notions, cultural influences or, for sure, moving pictures. Xenophobia tightened its suffocating grip on the national character. America had sent its men "over there" to fight a war and was horrified by what had followed them back home. Cultural shifts challenged the long-dominant values of rural life. Immigrants fled war-shattered Europe and arrived in droves at Ellis Island. They quickly found themselves unwelcome in America. Prejudice was rampant amidst industrial upheaval and political paranoia. In 1921 with the war still fresh in everyone's mind, exhibiting a German movie amounted to an act of treason. Some theater screenings for foreign films were met with hostility and violence from so-called "patriots."

Witness the events at a Los Angeles theater playing Robert Wiene's surrealist masterpiece *The Cabinet of Dr. Caligari* on May 8, 1921. Outraged to find a German-made picture being exhibited at Miller's Theater, the Hollywood Post of the American Legion organized a parade to protest. They were joined by several hundred sailors from the Pacific fleet and a crowd of over 2000. When the mob reached the theater, they pelted it with rotten eggs while the Shore Patrol and local police stood by helplessly. The manager of the Miller had little choice but to withdraw the picture.

The Venice City Council responded to the incident by passing a law requiring a special license costing $500 nightly to exhibit any German-made picture within its city limits. The *Los Angeles Examiner,* the local Hearst paper, undertook a campaign to have the picture banned locally.[21]

Ironically, the so-called "German invasion" of the movies started out as an "American invasion" of postwar film markets in Germany, Austria and the Balkans.[22] Expecting little in the way of native competition for American pictures, Ben Blumenthal, Famous Players–Lasky's talent agent in Europe, was astounded to discover a flourishing German film industry that had grown during the war and met domestic expectations. The American film companies realized that in order to open the German market to their films, they would have to open America to German movies. Hence the sudden importation of so many German films at once and the signing of first-rate artists like Lubitsch and Negri to American contracts.

Hollywood itself, however, was a hotbed of xenophobia. Would foreigners supplant them at the studios? Film critics, manifesting a popular rather than a highbrow mentality, closed ranks and denounced European films as un–American.[23] Tinseltown rolled up the welcome mat and drew the blinds. Actress Rubye De Reymer spoke for many when she railed against European stars coming to America: "Think of our actresses who have made pictures what they are today! Think of Mary Pickford and Pauline Frederick! To hear the remarks going the rounds about these foreign players you'd imagine they were responsible for all the good acting in the world!"[24]

Foreign players? De Reymer herself was of Norwegian extraction.

In short, most Americans would have none of it. They wanted their country to stay as they remembered it and were unwilling to tolerate anything that threatened the established order of things. No foreigners. No foreign films. It is telling that the use of words such as "floods," "deluge" and "tidal waves" was applied to both the sudden glut of European movies and the postwar influx of immigrants.[25]

If *Passion* cracked the gate open for German pictures, *Gypsy Blood* knocked the gate off its hinges. If critics were astonished by Negri's acting in *Passion,* they were stunned by her performance in *Gypsy Blood,* the re-titled *Carmen,* also imported by First National. "This Negri is amazing," *Variety*'s reviewer wrote. "She can do more with her face than most people can do with a subtitle. That is art in acting."[26]

"Pola Negri is a natural La Carmencita," said *The Exhibitor's Herald*. "No actress has portrayed that character more convincingly for the camera. The demands of the story are admirably met. From emotional heights to the depth of depression the transition frequently is abrupt. The Polish star demonstrates rare artistic ability in retaining complete poise throughout."[27] The *New York Herald* called her "the most genuinely seductive actress seen in years on the screen. She put a meaning in every line of her lithe figure." The *New York Sun* declared that *Gypsy Blood* had "amorous scenes so fiery that the film seems in danger of spontaneous combustion." The *New York Journal* said she was "all that could be desired and at times more." The *New York News* declared:

> Pola Negri is a beautiful, vehement and volcanic Carmen. She is a very flame of energy; she flings herself into the part with a turbulent and a brusque beauty that are extraordinary. She makes the illusion a perfect one, being at all times Carmen, not an actress trying to be Carmen.[28]

Theda Bara and opera star Geraldine Farrar had played Carmen in previous American film adaptations of the opera and Farrar was still thought by some to be the quintessential gypsy seductress. Marion Wilson of *Billboard* considered Farrar's interpretation unforgettable and thought that Pola's portrayal lacked daring, subtlety, refinement and imagination. She did add that Negri's acting was "remarkable in many ways."[29]

The Photodramatist asked readers to "[c]ompare *Gypsy Blood* and the American

Carmen, with Farrar. Farrar is unquestionably an artiste—but an operatic artiste. A vivid figure to be sure, but not the Carmen of the cigarette factory. Negri, on the other hand, was the Carmen of Mérimée's rather than Bizet. She was unkempt, dirty, lazy, insolent and faithless—but was she not Carmen? How many of our insipid ingenues have the courage to so portray a role when occasion requires?"[30] For *Photoplay* there was only one true Carmen: "And then came Pola Negri in *Gypsy Blood*.... It took courage and a high capacity to portray so real and unadorned a Carmen; but Negri's art was equal to the task ... because she subordinated herself—and her beauty even—to the demands of an unlovely but compelling truth."[31]

In some quarters *Gypsy Blood* was more of a foreign fiasco than a work of art. The trade journal *Wid's Daily* complained that Negri's Carmen was boorish and unfeminine. Manager Jack Cairns of Detroit's Brooklyn Theater called the picture "the biggest frazzle the First National has turned out. Lay off buying a franchise, take this tip, until the First National gets wise and eliminates some of their so-called stars ... wait until they weed out this trash."[32] An exhibitor from McGehee, Arkansas, called it "a picture that the blue law advocates can hold up to the people and get judgment. No good for small towns."[33] "Like all the foreign pictures ... a lemon," said another theater manager. "The made-in-America pictures, by American directors and American actors, are good enough for me and my patrons."[34]

The "German invasion" rolled in like high tide. *Variety* complained about the dumping of 46 German films in New York theaters in one week.[35] Yet most of the European productions were ignored by audiences outside of the major cities. Noting the meager returns on pictures like *Caligari* and Lubitsch's *Deception*, *Photoplay Magazine* attributed their failure in America to the German character and inappropriate subject matter. "The Germans are class-ridden, racially prejudiced, patriarchal, sexually immoral, and non-philanthropic; they have a taste for obscenity, enjoy horror and suffering on the screen, are cynical, sadistic and pessimistic ... and revel in watching other people's emotions put in a test tube ... with a residue of nastiness left in the bottom."[36] "Demand for German pictures, there is none," *Picture-Play Magazine* declared. "The Negri is a drawing card because she is a curiosity. She doesn't get admiring letters from the girl fans, and there is little interest in her home life or her favorite flower."

Variety went so far as to declare that there wasn't anything special about Negri, and that there was nothing she could do that American stars couldn't do just as well. The hubris and vitriol just about drips off the page:

> There is a tendency among the highbrows who have seen German pictures exhibited here to deprecate the acting of American stars and their support. Where else, they ask, save in these imported pictures can such acting be found as shown by Pola Negri? To point out the fallacy in this comparison is neither to slur the illustrious foreigner nor to praise unduly our home talent.
>
> Those who have attempted to answer these aspersions have said: Surely such exhibitions as given by Lillian Gish in *Broken Blossoms* and *Way Down East*, by Norma Talmadge in *Panthea* and Mary Pickford in any number of productions are not to be despised. Of a certainly they are not, but that is not the root of the matter. The root of the matter grows down into fundamentals, takes into account the attempt to meet American taste and explains at once differences that are differences, not the contrasts seized on for argument by those praising foreign artistry unduly.
>
> The reason no American actress has ever given a performance comparable to Pola Negri's accomplishments in *Passion* and *Gypsy Blood* is because none has ever tried. Reverse conditions and you have your answer. Could Pola Negri appear in and make an American picture popular? She could not. She has been trained in another school for another purpose and brings about entirely opposite results than those aimed for here. Nor could Ernst Lubitsch produce a *Pollyanna*. In fact, he would fail where an American, if there were any object

in doing it, such is American adaptability, could do such pictures as Lubitsch is doing, for the world trade. The point rests, typed large, in the fact that we could, if we would, produce along foreign lines.[37]

In other words, Americans had never given a performance like Negri's because they simply didn't have to—and that was the entirety of their explanation.[38] So there. *Variety* was willing to call her acting exceptional, but only because it was "unusual and Americans do not attempt it."

Negri, however, had already made an indelible mark on the cultural landscape. *Motion Picture Magazine* printed a full-page photograph of her, depicting her in modern dress, and captioned it: "Presenting Pola: Who has brought a Continental flavor to the shadow-screen. Her characterizations are both vivid and subtle."[39] In the same issue, a joking response to an anonymous reader's letter stated, "You say 'Pola Negri' means 'Very Dead' in Greek? Are you sure about this? She doesn't appear to be so in pictures."[40]

Sumurun, the third of First National's trio of imports, opened in New York in September 1921 after a brief dispute with Famous Players–Lasky over the American distribution rights delayed release of the picture. It was issued in a heavily edited version retitled *One Arabian Night* with its erotic charge severely diminished by cuts to please the censors. *Variety* described the picture as "colorful … the atmosphere of the east being perfect in detail" and called Negri "tremendous! This is the one word that describes her performance most fittingly. She has fire and an allurement that is essential to the role assigned her, she also displays the fact that she is a dancer of exceeding cleverness."[41] Another reviewer called the picture "exceptional," applauding both its dramatic intensity and "unusual" comic relief. The reviewer added, "The acting of Pola Negri may be said to be the finest and most convincing of her career before the American public."[42] *The Des Moines Capitol* said: "Mlle. Negri is the inspiration of at once desire and disgust, the reactions which her part demands."[43] The best observation came is a response to a reader's question in the April 1922 *Motion Picture Magazine*: Who designed the costume for Pola Negri in *One Arabian Night*? What costume; I didn't see any."

One Arabian Night was neither as profitable nor as acclaimed as its predecessors. "Miss Negri fails to be the convincingly licentious person she is supposed to represent," wrote *The Educational Screen*. "The strength of her Carmen, her DuBarry is somehow lost."[44] *Screenland Magazine* said the picture was "unfortunately based on a moral plane abhorrent to American picture-goers," but called Negri "voluptuous, fascinating."[45] A letter from S.C.F. in *Picture-Play Magazine* summed up the native attitude towards foreign pictures in general:

> I have been surprised at the general approval of the Lubitsch picture, *One Arabian Night*. To me it was like looking at a pretty girl's skin through a powerful microscope—so coarsely ugly. One well-known reviewer said it "had movement." It had, indeed. Such waving of arms, rushing about, writhing of features, and popping of eyes I have never seen outside of a gala performance by an All-German company. The manhandling of the presumably dead body of the poor old hunchback seemed questionable comedy, but perhaps my sense of humor is deficient. Pola Negri's vivid performance seemed hardly sufficient compensation for so much unpleasantness. Too often in the foreign mind, realism is used as a synonym for ugliness.[46]

The *Davis County Clipper* echoed a similar sentiment, reluctantly recognizing that there was a demand for pictures of Negri's type: "Let us sincerely hope the majority never leave shows of the class in which this actress have appeared or others of like nature," the writer added in obvious disapproval. "Without feeling that the time spent in viewing has been lost and there remains a very unpleasant 'taste' as a reminder for some time."[47]

Despite such reactions, distributors raced to cash in on Negri's name by importing a number of her other German-made pictures. The Howell Sales Company offered *Vendetta* and *Intrigue* (a re-titled *Das Martyrium*) to independent exhibitors. According to *The Daily Star* of Queens, New York, *Vendetta* had "strong indications pointing to the fact that it must have been made in the days before Pola Negri became as celebrated as she is now, for it lacks the fire and the power that have characterized her other impersonations."[48] *Billboard* called *Vendetta* "sleep-producing" and "repetitious" and found Negri unsuitable in the role of a high-class Corsican. "The actress requires roles in which she can rant, pant and gnash her teeth and suffer miserably. Then she can be depended upon to give a very vivid interpretation."[49] The picture didn't do much for the box office at the Rialto Theater in Allentown, Pennsylvania, according to its manager: "The star was the main point of interest used in appealing for patronage. Showed, as usual, that an European actress has her own following but can't break in with others. Many go to see her, others won't respond to the appeal for pictures in which she is starred."[50]

Variety thought *Intrigue* was poor: "The picture reeks with sex stuff, ponderous in a German way and silly rather than risqué." They complained that the flat photography made Negri look like a middle-aged woman and said her acting was of the "vamp type stilted and absurd beyond the worst offenses of our own Theda."[51]

Late in 1921, independent exhibitor Joseph A. Levinson announced he was selling *The Polish Dancer,* a re-titled *Slave of Sin,* Negri's first picture, on a state's rights basis: "Already a number of territories have been disposed of for this picture, which has been praised by all who have seen it as one of the most exceptional pictures reflected on the screen. The star is seen to advantage in *The Polish Dancer* ... which calls for the best there is in Mme. Negri, who responds successfully and meets the every requirement of the role."[52] One wonders if he even allowed exhibitors to *see* such a poor picture before bidding on it. One cheeky wag noted in response: "Pola Negri's next picture will be 'A Polish Dancer.' And she can't dance!"[53]

Famous Players–Lasky added to the glut of Negri pictures on the American market with their release of *The Carousel of Love,* which they retitled *The Last Payment.* "Miss Negri shines in role depicting her as a woman of no morals—an unmoral rather than immoral screen female.," said *Variety*'s reviewer. "Hers is not the doll type of beauty we worship in this country, and her acting is the kind that demands 'strong' roles visualizing women of the people. This limits her characterizations and debars her from enacting modern society women; and, as everyone knows, the pictures that draw the most money in America are those portraying our heroines residing in mansions."[54] *Picture-Play Magazine* thought the Germans incapable of handling a modern setting and found the leading lady hopeless miscast. "Pola Negri is badly out of place in this stereotyped story of *A Fool There Was.* She is just as fearfully and wonderfully in earnest as ever, but her background won't support her—the same story has been done so much better over here—and even then, it wasn't worth doing."[55]

Her German imports were primitive-looking, poorly made and showed their age. A *New York Morning Telegraph* reader wrote in to say that while he thought Negri was the perfect film star, *The Last Payment* had caused him to lose considerable faith in her. The picture looked "old" in its furniture, costuming and its ballroom dancing. Had it been an American picture, it would be laughed off the screen. The writer wondered why the studio would let such a picture injure Negri's popularity.[56]

The next Famous Players–Lasky release was *The Red Peacock,* the retitled version of 1920's *Arme Violetta*. *The Exhibitor's Trade Review* described the plot, which is very reminiscent of *Camille*:

> Violette lives in Paris with her drunken stepfather. She is a flower girl. One stormy night outside a theater she is selling her wares, when Alfred Germont, a young playwright, Gaston Roy and Florette Lavalle emerge. Violette, trying to sell her flowers, falls from the running board of their auto. They take her to Florette's apartment, where she is revived. Florette gives her a fashionable wrap to wear and a bottle of brandy to take home to her stepfather. On her return, her parent becomes violent and casts her into the street. She again meets Alfred who takes her to his rooms. They fall in love. He is compelled to leave for his home in the south, owing to his sister's illness, but induces Gaston to give Violette a place as maid. Gaston becomes enamored of her. Florette, jealous, discharges the girl. Violette accepts the protection of one of Florette's guests, Count Girey, and lives with him. Alfred has a play accepted and it becomes a success. On the opening night at the theatre he sees Violette in Girey's company. She implores her to take her away with him and he does so. The two are happy, but Alfred's play fails and he becomes financially embarrassed. Alfred's father and sister visit Violette secretly and beg her to give up Alfred, alleging she is ruining his career. For love of him she consents and goes away with Gaston to Monte Carlo. In the finale Alfred learns she is dying and his sister tells him of the sacrifice made by his mistress. Alfred seeks her out, she tells him of her love and dies in his arms.[57]

"Considered solely from an artistic viewpoint," said *The Exhibitor Trade Review*, "[*The Red Peacock*] is worth looking at on account of the star's magnetic personality and dramatic talent. Otherwise, it cannot be listed among the better grade of foreign productions recently imported to this country. Its box office value depends entirely on the strength of Miss Negri's name as a drawing card."[58] *Variety* thought Negri's personality distinguished her in mediocre productions, but doubted that she could "get over" with American fans who generally preferred the "sweet n' pretty heroine...."[59] In his "That's Out" column in *Motion Picture Magazine,* gossip columnist Tamar Lane was satisfied that American girls "will continue to hold first place in our heart" after seeing Negri's recent pictures.[60] The German film invasion had proven to be nothing more than a sputtering firecracker.

Famous Players–Lasky's next German retread was *The Yellow Ticket,* re-titled *The Devil's Pawn* for the American market. *Variety* called it "trashy" and said, "Pola Negri does not shine in the sweet simplicity roles." The *New York Herald* thought there should "be a law against putting Miss Negri in modern society plays." According to the *New York Tribune,* "Pola Negri is always interesting to watch and probably you will forget about the story." The *New York Sun* concluded that the only thing remarkable about the picture was her acting.[61] By now, anyone new to the Pola Negri phenomenon must have wondered what all the fuss was about. When *The Eyes of the Mummy*, a retitled *Die Augen Der Momie Ma,* was released, *Motion Picture Magazine* could hardly believe that such a poor picture could even be made. "Even with Pola Negri and Emil Jannings in the cast, the production is unable to soar above a mediocre level," the magazine said. "The story is wildly improbable and concerns Egyptian hocus-pocus. Capable players as Pola and Emil are, they cannot lift this story into the class of entertaining subjects."[62]

According to *The Exhibitor's Trade Review*, "Pola Negri emerges from this picture with considerably less praise than she usually receives. It is, however, entirely the fault of the material that has been used and not because of her own acting."[63] Her work in *Passion* and in those first few films seen in America made so strong a mark that Negri almost always received the benefit of the doubt from the critics. A bad film was never her fault. If a picture was inferior, it was because the material was unworthy of her talents.

Seeing the poor reviews afforded *Intrigue* and *Vendetta, Famous Players–Lasky* purchased the rights to seven of her remaining Ufa pictures and locked them away to ensure that no one else released them and lessened Negri's marquee value as a star.[64]

Negri was famous in America now—but who was she? Was she German? Polish? Russian-Polish? Hungarian? What had she done before getting into movies? What was her real name? The air of mystery about her made her a Rorschach test for moviegoers to imagine their wildest fantasies. The first mention of her in *Photoplay* came in response to a question by "Helen from Connecticut," and briefly states that *Passion* made Negri an international star, that she was Polish, and her matrimonial status was unknown. A newspaper item from the same month provided a very different thumbnail sketch: "Born in Poland. Twenty-eight. Single. On stage as soon as she could walk. Ballet dancer. Violinist. Toured in Spoken drama in France, Italy, Austria, Germany and Russia. Black hair. Flashing brown eyes."[65] Huh?

"Pola Negri is a Jewess and was born in Vienna where she attracted Max Rinehart's [sic] attention," *Variety* wrote a month later. "Her name was Pauline Schwartz. This means black and her stage name was easily thought out. The pictures in which she has been appearing here were made five years ago."[66] And if that wasn't in itself totally wrong, the same piece also states that German-born Ernst Lubitsch was Polish.

"Pola Negri's real name is Pauline Irgen," said another newspaper writer. "In Germany she is known as Pauline Schwartz. Pola Negri is simply the Polish version of her German stage name."[67] The piece goes on to say that while she has *some* Polish blood, she was actually born in a part of Germany that was given to Poland after the war. According to a 1921 issue of *Cinemundial,* a Spanish-language movie magazine, "They say that Pola Negri is Polish.... I suspect she is a compatriot of Wagner." She wasn't German. *British Vogue Magazine*, on the other hand, said she was Russian.[68]

As for her life before getting into the picture business: "She had been working as a sales clerk in a Berlin department store," according to *Picture-Play Magazine*.[69]

The author of the *Photoplay Magazine* article "She Delivers the Goods" dismisses Negri's dramatic experience prior to entering movies as negligible. "She was a dancer and a pantomimist, learning thereby the rudiments of gesticulation. Now at the age of 27, she is a meteor flashing through the heavens, a product of the screen, and not a transplanted stage actress."[70] That "negligible" dramatic experience entirely omits her successful stage careers in Poland and Germany. Negri, he adds, is highly emotional in both her acting and private life, her restlessness accounting for the fact that she looks much older on screen than in person.[71] "Restlessness" or bad lighting?

A *Filmplay Magazine* writer allegedly went to Berlin to get the facts and apparently came back with someone else's life story.[72] After determining that she was indeed Polish, he delivered the news that "Pola Negri" was actually Paula Negri, formerly from Posen, Poland; that before she went into the picture business, she sold decorative ribbons at a store in Berlin's Leipziger Platz; and when the Armistice came, she was one of the first to apply for a job at the Lubitsch Studio as an extra. *Passion* made her famous and landed her a titled husband, a "Count Dimorski."[73]

Picture-Play Magazine's Helen Klumph took a crack at deciphering the enigmatic Negri in her July 1922 piece "What About Pola Negri?" She determined that Pola was between 25 and 30, that her parents were poor, and that when she was young she found a job at Wertheim's Department store in Berlin while living on her own in a rooming house.

Then, she says, Negri took up the violin and performed in concert halls. A trip to Russia earned her a spot in the Imperial Ballet. After a year of that, she returned to Berlin, spent some time in Vienna and then went on the stage. After a while he married a count from "one of those kingdoms near Romania."[74] Where did Pola find the time to do all that?

They built her up. They made her colorful and enigmatic ... made her just what people would want her to be. *As you like her.* They told their readers about her good looks, fashionable style and personal magnetism, but mostly overlooked her acting talent—a problem considering her reputation as Europe's greatest dramatic actress.

One *actual* Negri interview appeared in *Movie Weekly* in July 1922.[75] In response to questions, she denied all of the rumors of her being German—although some wouldn't believe her—and all that nonsense about her real name being Paula Schwartz—although some wouldn't believe her. Then, much to this author's own surprise on first reading the interview, she dropped a puzzling reference to a maiden name of "Apolonia Haluska"—which isn't mentioned again in any other interview, article, biography or film history to date. She also denied ever having been a cabaret dancer and, no, she had never been a Russian Imperial ballerina—a "fact" that still gets repeated today. All of those dizzying rumors and contradictions should raise a compelling question: Was Pola Negri really *ever* who she said she was? Contrary to what you might assume, the more you read about her—the more you find out about her—the *more* enigmatic she becomes.

No one—and everyone—knew the truth about her. The idea of a *Polish* actress starring in "German films" was unbelievable to at least one moviegoer who asked in the September 1922 issue of *Photoplay,* "Where do you people get that stuff about Pola Negri being Polish, because she married that Polish *no count?* Her right name is Pauline Schwarz, born and reared in Hamburg, if anyone should ask you. Give the devil his due, even if he is *German.*"[76] A similar sentiment was shared by actor Joseph Schildkraut, then appearing in a New York play. He had performed with Pola in Reinhardt's *Sumurun* in Berlin and according to him, the stories about her being a Polish countess, a concert violinist and a lead ballerina for the Russian ballet were press agent creations. She was actually "Fraulein Schwartz," late of Wertheim's Department Store. As for being the greatest actress in Europe, he accorded that honor to Henny Porten, who he said was Germany's favorite actress.[77] Several months later, Schildkraut refused to answer questions about Pola during another interview, stating he had received an indignant letter from her wondering why he had said things about her that "weren't true."[78]

Every actor returning to America from Germany had their own impression of Pola Negri for publication. "She is in every sense an artist," said Ivan Neede. "It was an experience to observe her at work. She is full of spirit and quick to speak her mind. But she is never unreasonable, never coarse, never spiteful. She has poise, but not arrogance."[79] Actor James Kirkwood said audiences would be attracted to her: "Pola Negri will always be popular with men patrons of motion pictures because she is an unusual combination of two qualities particularly enjoyed by the masculine element, vitality and vivacity, these two softened by truly feminine traits which keep her from the air of masculinity which men resent. At the same time she is not a clinging vine. In other words she steers a splendid middle course which should build and retain for her the admiration of both men and women."[80]

Whenever Negri's acting ability was actually mentioned, it was hyperbole at its finest. "There is no make-believe about her characterizations," Helen Klumph said of her. "There is no flinching at realism. She vibrates. She is a magnet. Her passion is swift and torrential and relentless, and her gaiety is spontaneous. Crude and coarse she may be at times, but she is always convincing."[81] The *New York Tribune* said it best: "Pola Negri is filled with fire, magnetism and genius."[82]

At the time of her signing with the Lasky Studio, Jesse Lasky announced that Negri would be the first of many foreign stars to be imported to make pictures stateside. That migration would be slow in coming. Adolph Zukor, president of Famous Players, advised in a telegram: WOULD BE VERY BAD FROM ALL ANGLES BRING OVER MORE THAN ONE AT A TIME. SHOULD LEAVE REASONABLE PERIOD BETWEEN TO AVOID PROPAGANDIST CRITICISM AND BE SURE MAKE NO PROMISES.[83] Negri would have to lead the way and show that she could impress the natives. The title of her first American picture was announced as *Bella Donna*.[84]

She set sail from France and arrived in New York on the S.S. *Majestic* on September 13, 1922. News reports from the ship had her mostly remaining in her first-class cabin during the trip, studying English and appearing in public only to dine one evening at the captain's table. Famous Players–Lasky, awaiting her New York arrival, arranged for a grand reception complete with musicians and singers (to serenade her with Polish folk songs from floating barges), flowers galore and a large crowd at the pier to witness her landing.[85] Author Norman Zierold described her arrival:

> Fabulous Pola Negri, the temperamental European actress, lived up to her elaborate advance publicity.... Pola herself stood in regal splendor, ringed by admirers, and sputtered forth exclamations of joy in her native Polish. She wore a stunning Cossack dress. High Russian boots and a turban made her appear taller than her actual five feet, six inches. When for a moment she lifted the turban in a gesture of salute to New York, everyone saw the lustrous jet-black hair, which fell in bangs almost to her eyebrows. Her luminous dark eyes were framed by heavily made-up brows and lashes, while her skin was startlingly white by contrast. A small sequined mole at the corner of her left eye served as a beauty mark.[86]

The press thought she was absolutely stunning. "Just picture for yourself a delicately chiseled beauty, so blue-white in her pallor that she looks as though had been cut from Carrera marble," said *Picture-Play Magazine*. "Frame her face in inky-black hair. Add to that the magnetism of Geraldine Farrar, the fire of Priscilla Dean, the smoldering depths of Theda Bara's eyes, some of the finesse of Corinne Griffith, and the clear-cut movements of Mae Busch. Over it all throw a consciousness of power and an amazingly sensuous and selfish mouth, and you have a general idea of what Pola Negri looks like."[87] The *New York Morning Telegraph* said, "Pola Negri's smile, her charm, and her beauty are worth the most extravagant language, for she is as one enthusiastic youth said, a thousand times lovelier off the screen than on.... Bets are being made that in a few months she will be the most talked-of motion picture actress in America and the odds are all in her favor."[88]

Originally she was scheduled to work out of the Famous Players studio in Long Island. Yet as soon as she arrived, it was announced that she would be shipped to Hollywood to begin work on her first American picture. It was a terrible disappointment for Negri, who had hoped to live in New York. According to one newspaper piece, upon hearing that she was to leave almost immediately for California, she gasped and asked, "How are operas in Los Angeles, please?"[89]

She spent a total of eight days touring New York City and meeting the famous and influential. The day after her arrival she was feted at Sherry's Restaurant at a luncheon hosted by Famous Players–Lasky for the benefit of a crowd of 100 journalists and exhibitors. During other outings she was introduced to celebrated stage luminaries and literary intelligentsia including Ethel Barrymore, Jascha Heifetz, George Jean Nathan, Alexander Woollcott and Geraldine Farrar.[90] As an opera fan, she was delighted to attend a performance of *Tosca* by the New York Metropolitan Opera Company. Another evening saw her at the *Ziegfeld Follies* where she was invited to stand and take a bow during the show by its cowboy star, Will Rogers. She also made a sensational personal appearance at the Cosmopolitan Theater during the premiere of the Marion Davies film *When Knighthood Was in Flower*. It was said that she received more applause than Marion, who was in attendance along with her family.[91]

At the end of the week, she was whisked away to the West Coast. In *Memoirs*, she claims she fell ill during the train trip to Los Angeles, suffering from the intense heat while passing through the Mojave Desert; arriving in California with its much cooler climate was a relief. It would be years before she'd dare make the trip cross-country again. She disembarked from the train in Pasadena. Thousands were waiting to greet her in downtown Los Angeles, but it was thought prudent for her to disembark beforehand to avoid a mob scene. She was met instead by a small group of studio representatives and a crowd of the curious who had come to gawk at her as if she were something entirely beyond their understanding."[92]

5

The Paradox of Publicity

Men beware. Wives, watch your husbands. Girls, get ready to take a few lessons in sirening! Pola Negri, the screen's greatest, has arrived in this country to make a series of pictures. —Daisy Dean in *The Sheridan Enterprise*, September 13, 1922

During her maiden voyage to America, Pola's studio-appointed escort, Ben Blumenthal, complained she was spending too much time in her cabin studying English. He told her she should get out and walk around the decks and be seen for publicity's sake. Negri politely informed him that she *was* thinking about publicity. The less she was seen aboard the ship, she said, the more people would talk about her.[1]

Talent brought her to America. Publicity would kill her career.

There were so many questions once she arrived. Everyone wanted to know: Did Pola Negri have true "star" quality? Talent? Beauty? She didn't *look* like an American actress was supposed to look—no blond kewpie doll here. She was a bit older than the usual ingénue and in her German pictures she wasn't always attractive. *Motion Picture Magazine* said, "[I]n some of her finest pictures she is downright ugly; and at times she appears old enough to be her leading man's Godmother."[2] Granted, the flat and stark lighting used in those early German features was unflattering, but the criticism of her looks ignored the fact that in both *Madame DuBarry* and especially in *Carmen,* the point was for her *not* to look beautiful. Negri played real women on-screen, not glamorous movie characters.

The Famous Players–Lasky press machine fed newspapers and magazines every detail concerning her past, present and foreseeable future. Of course she had star quality! She was so many things rolled into one: a "beautiful orchid," "a hot-house flower," a colorful Continental personality and a "tiger-woman" of fierce emotional temperament. Pola Negri was sold to the public as an exotic personality.

Moviegoers were assured that in Pola they were getting one of the most beautiful women in films. According to one movie magazine, "The first thing that impressed the American film producers, when they saw Pola in the flesh, was her marvelous beauty, the likes of which never had been in an American studio before. They saw at once that she had never been properly photographed."[3] She was described in another article as "a beauty, but of a vital, almost barbarian sort."[4] It's hard to think of Negri, a sophisticated woman who spent most of her time in Berlin and Paris, as a "gypsy," the most common description of her in magazines when they needed a short-hand description for her fiery and passionate persona.

Pola Negri arrives in America on September 13, 1922 (photograph by Paul Thompson).

Every detail about her was meticulously examined and debated in newspapers across the nation. Was she five-foot-six? Five-four? Five-five? And her eyes, what color were they really? She was described as "of medium height and slightly built. Her hair is raven black and her skin is smooth as velvet. Her eyes are dark blue and her beauty is further enhanced by a wonderfully red mouth and small white teeth."5 One writer said, "[H]er hair is heavy, jet black, as also are her intriguing eyes. In alluring contrast, her skin is white and unblemished."6 Another writer described her eyes as "greenish-gray and hard as nails."7 "Miss Negri is a brunette, with gray-blue eyes that twinkle behind long lashes," proclaimed the *New York Evening Telegraph*. "Her hair is dark and her skin white, so white that Dolores (a famous Ziegfeld showgirl) is no longer in the running."8 A *Casper Herald* newspaper article called her skin "remarkably fine and soft, as was evident even through the conventional flour-barrel makeup affected by Europeans. Evidently her cheeks have a translucency which gives a glow to her countenance under the studio lights and enables her to express emotions which would otherwise be smothered by a coarse skin."9 Harriette Underhill of the *New York Morning Telegraph* described her this way:

> She is not very tall ... and she is quite slender; she has beautiful white hands with lustrous pink nails.... Miss Negri's hair is jet black and her skin is like white velvet. She has very dark blue eyes with long black lashes, a bright red mouth and perfectly even, small white teeth.... [A]dd to this description that she is the smartest looking woman we have seen in a very long time and you'll have a fair idea of the way Pola Negri looked to us.10

The movie magazines trained a microscope on her attributes, as if they might somehow clue them in to her personality. Her nose: "Pola Negri possesses a nose which reveals a strong, domineering, vital and somewhat wild nature."[11] Her smile was "seldom a full smile. Nearly always it veils a mocking at the thing or person smiled at. Even in tragedy it hides a humorous levity. It is her subjective subtlety, her sense of the contradictions of life that gives Pola Negri her power."[12] Her handwriting contained "all the fire and passion, all the refined sensuousness, all the allure which is both exotic and deliberate, all the assertiveness which so paints this personality with the aura of the Chief Figure."[13] Her signature was "a broad ruthless sweep that looks as if it had been made with a brush, shows that she is extremely sensuous, even sensual. Whimsical, but not sentimental, brutally willful, despotic, passionate, she courts flattery and will brook no opposition."[14]

Journalists waxed eloquent on Negri's beauty and regal poise. Herbert Howe, a writer for various movie magazines, was her principal cheerleader during the silent era. His description of her allure is perhaps the best written:

> I herewith solemnly proclaim Pola Negri a Divinity....
> A Goya woman. Frost white skin with blood scarlet lips. The luminous blackness of eyes.[15] Matched with her hair, the raven is a dull mulatto.
> —Night and countries of the moon—Nights of Baghdad, nights on the Nile, Venetian nights with tiny red and amber lights turning water into wine.
> But someone else will have to write a Sonnet to the Supreme Coquette. I'd grow hysterical.
> I only know that every enchantress of man in history is credible when envisaged as her. Queen of Sheba, Queen of the Nile, Helen of Troy, yea the Venus ambrosial.
> Here is the altar of femininity. The charm of sex in essence.[16]

For others she was "imperious" in her beauty and had a "primitive instinct" that made her desirable. One writer noted: "Her appeal to men is not a subtle one—it is entirely direct." Her charisma had a sensuality that was startling and smoldering. A new kind of sexual competition, she made prissy women fear for their marriages. *Screenland Magazine* said: "A Pola Negri consumes and is consumed with the blood-heat of a supreme and persistent passion, sex-lure in primitive grandeur."[17] In the same issue, a letter from reader Eleanor Barnes declared: "Pola Negri symbolizes the primitiveness and dormant passion of all woman. She is the poppy, enticing in her pure suggestiveness, a nature so plain that it is complex. A 'gypsy' girl."[18] In her essay on Negri, author Diane Negra notes, "[She] was consistently associated with a discourse of erotic and cultural aggression that seemed to challenge American morality."[19] Just glimpsing her film performances, it was obvious Negri knew all about sex and liked it—without the benefit of marriage. She didn't possess the "cool" sensuality of an indifferent beauty like Garbo, who was faking passion anyway. No, her allure was red-hot like a Clara Bow, although Clara's characters were always just sweet kids underneath it all. Pola had clearly *done* what Clara's eyes and smile only suggested should happen.

Beauty, of course, is in the eye of the beholder. Reader Alva M. Joesting asked *Motion Picture Magazine*, "[W]hy, with her square shaped face, does she wear her hair sticking out in bunches at the sides? It is anything but attractive that way. She also uses too much makeup around the eyes."[20] "Miss Negri makes up so badly that nobody can tell what she really looks like," said painter and moving picture director Penrhyn Stanlaws. "Her facial faults can be summoned up in one expression: her face is too square."[21] He later changed his mind, listing her as one of the most beautiful women in the world, crediting her with "vibrant, magnetic physical charm" and calling her eyes "finely colored pools of emotion, containing the lurking hit of mysticism—the spell of the occult."[22]

To become an American movie star, Negri underwent the studio glamor treatment. They straightened her long, unruly hair, which for this author was her most magnificent feature. Her sparkling gray eyes were emphasized by shaving off her eyebrows and remaking them with black lines to make her expression "wistful and tragic."[23] Negri gets the credit for using dark lipstick before anyone else in pictures and started the vogue for painted fingernails and toenails. The story goes that at a Hollywood party, another female guest spotted Negri's red-painted nails through her open-toed shoes and cried out in horror that her toes were bleeding. Her white makeup was much copied by young girls, turning them, as one writer remarked, into "silent white mysteries with tragic faces gashed with scarlet lips."[24]

She was hailed as one of the best-dressed women in Hollywood. She favored high Russian boots and headscarves[25] and was credited with making the turban an essential fashion accessory.[26] She arrived in America with a profound cosmopolitan fashion sense that appealed to female moviegoers. Never a fan of color, she preferred to wear all-black or all-white clothing. Instead of the latest fashionable coiffure, she chose to wear her long hair loosely drawn back from her forehead.

Occasionally, there was a newspaper item about her such as: "Paris and Hollywood have suddenly decreed that shoulder blades are once again in style after several years of spinal modesty.... Paramount is willing to back the lovely Pola Negri as having the only perfect back on the screen."[27]

From time to time her studio released beauty and health tips attributed to her, but most likely the product of publicity department flacks. One was: "A beautiful skin is every woman's birthright. While lotions, massages and cosmetics are good remedies, a healthy skin does not need a remedy. I keep my skin well by a method inexpensive enough for everyone. It is, in fact, free as the air."[28] Another: "Every week I set aside at least one day which I devote to exercise.... I make sure, whatever it is, that I exercise thoroughly and use all my muscles."[29] Sometimes her health tips were not quite the truth. One, written under her byline, detailed the evils of tobacco: "Tobacco destroys beauty—I know, I have watched its effect in too many cases not to have a wholesome dread of it." She also stated that in scenes requiring her to smoke, she made sure it was no more than a puff or two and assured the reader that she "never finishes" a cigarette.[30] In reality, Negri smoked like the proverbial chimney.

She never gave much indication that she cared about any of these things. Herbert Howe quoted her: "I do not care about the—*schonheit*—the beauty. I want that the people shall feel," her fingers clutched intensely at her breast, "to feel—to *be* me."[31]

Her adoring fans were amazed by her realistic acting and bewitched by her charms. "She does more acting in one scene than the American actresses do in five reels," wrote one of her admirers. "To me she is far better looking and has much more personality than any of our actresses."[32] "She is the most natural woman on the screen, for she never saves herself for closeups or cares how she looks," said one letter to *Picture-Play Magazine*. "I think she is marvelous. She makes a lot of these limp, lady-like so-called 'stars' look like jellyfish. You can't say her acting is vulgar, because it is true to life, and the real facts of life are, by no means, all perfect and beautiful."[33]

Negri's publicity painted her as unique—and she was a true Renaissance woman by comparison to her contemporaries. She spoke six languages: French, Polish, Russian, Italian, German and English. Famous Players noted in an October 1922 newsletter, "She only knows 107 English words and 80 of them are American slang."[34]

She painted, sculpted and played the guitar, organ, harp and violin. She was an accomplished horsewoman and looked rather fetching in a riding habit. She enjoyed operas, orchestras and museums—and getting people to see things her way. Although she liked company, she was just as happy with solitude and a good book. She was used to champagne and fine wine and had just arrived in a country that had banned them in the name of morality. Los Angeles, in fact, had *none* of the things she adored about Berlin. Hollywood, she said quite bluntly, was a backwater town by comparison. By saying so, she earned the resentment of the parochial movie colony and the Hollywood Chamber of Commerce.

Her relentless studio publicity emphasized her foreignness as part of her appeal. With her Slavic looks she would never pass for an American, but her Polish accent was often played up for maximum effect in print. In fact, Negri was probably the only actress of the silent era ever regularly quoted *phonetically* in her interviews. Here she is quoted on whether she is happy playing the "bad woman" in her first American-made picture, *Bella Donna*:

> No. When zey meet me at ze steamer and say, "Madame Negri, you are to do *Bella Donna*, I felt like cry.... I don' like to play ze bad woman all ze time.... Someday I play ver' good woman. Maybe she leetle unhappy and she suffer, but she very good.[35]

On the subject of acting, she said:

> I theenk always of audience, people everywhere, all, sorrowful weeping wiz me. I poot my whol' heart, my whol' soul into my art, my expression, my tars, so zat zey may feel wiz me what I feel, so zat zey perhaps suffair what I suffair.[36]

Publicity also gave her an aura of menace and danger. Woe to those who stood in her way when it came to matters of the heart! She was portrayed as a huntress, a siren, a woman capable of getting any man she wanted. Sexually, Negri was positioned as a woman of destructive potential—as the vamp, the enemy of conformity.[37] She knew the dangers of passion. She told *Photoplay*, "Love is ruthless. In pursuit of its desires it will destroy that it may achieve. That it may lavish upon one its largesse, it will crush a thousand who stand in its way."[38] Early interviews with her recount her tragedies in love: her tender first love, a painter, who allegedly died in her arms from consumption; of the high price paid in heartbreak for her success; and even her sense of fatalism about forever being alone. Her sensual allure was contemplated as "inevitably fatal."[39] At the end of a *Motion Picture Magazine* article by Gladys Hall and Adele Whitley-Fletcher, one of the authors muses that she wouldn't want Negri as an "enemy."[40] Men were supposed to flock to her. Women were supposed to loathe her.

The movie magazines might be forgiven for indulging in exaggeration as their job was to give their readership exactly what they wanted in an exotic movie personality. Yet those early magazine articles unfairly portray her as intimidating and indifferent, unlikable even—not exactly the best qualities for a bankable box office star.

Negri cherished art and acting and she was very serious about her craft. One of the first quotes attributed to her upon her arrival in America was, "My art. That is all I live for."[41] Sometimes she could be pretentious and self-aggrandizing about it; for example, the quote attributed to her in movie producer Sam Goldwyn's autobiography: "I consider my work great, as I am a great artist."[42]

Most of her imported German films didn't exactly support her opinion of herself. *Picture Play Magazine* called *The Devil's Pawn* "about as bad as they come except for the always interesting acting of this extraordinary star."⁴³ *Photoplay* added: "Pola Negri is as big-eyed as ever, but not quite so alluring as formerly."⁴⁴ Pola was said to "deeply regret" the pictures that had followed *Passion* to America and hoped that the public would understand that they had been made earlier in her career.⁴⁵ Yet while she was apologizing, Famous Players kept her German pictures in circulation.

The old pictures tarnished her reputation. Her publicity left some with a bad taste in their mouths. In a 1922 article discussing who might be considered the "Sarah Bernhardt of the Screen," *Picture Play Magazine* discounted her on the basis that "Negri is a foreigner."⁴⁶ (And Sarah Bernhardt wasn't?) The author of the piece wrote:

> When it came to selecting the two most eminent screen actors among the women, there was no disagreement. Lillian Gish and Norma Talmadge were universally acclaimed. Pola Negri was not considered, because as one of our correspondents pointed out, quoting from Sarah Bernhardt: "It is the spiritual, keen-edged humor of refinement and sorry akin to the divine that test the artist, not the coarse, vulgar or animal."
>
> Strangely enough, there was little mention of Pola Negri. Some spoke of her as a future possibility, some passed her by with saying that they could never consider such an unsympathetic personality truly great. "She has to act hard," one correspondent wrote. "To hide an indifferent manner that almost betrays boredom. She seems to me cruelly polite when the action calls for real warmth and cordiality.⁴⁷

The passage confirms the belief that movie audiences wanted their heroines sweet and sympathetic, the All-American girl who would be compliant, colorless, peaceable and cuddlesome as a kitten. Negri would never be any of those things and, as it would turn out, largely unsuccessful in America.

The Goldwyn Company, arriving late to the party, acquired the American distribution rights to *Sappho*—re-titled *Mad Love*—and issued it with a letter of endorsement from Negri stating that the picture's success in Germany had been unparalleled, even by *Passion*.⁴⁸ Famous Players must have loved that boost for their competitors! But the American reviews it got were lukewarm at best. The *New York Times* called her "the same vibrant, vivid, virtuous Pola who has made DuBarry, Carmen and Camille live on the screen as real people whom you might like to know, or if you are wise, keep away from."⁴⁹ There was that hint of danger again. The *New York Daily News* said, "All that saves *Mad Love* is Pola Negri,"⁵⁰ and summed the film up as "just another vampire picture … and it is not a very notable vampire picture either."⁵¹ *The Educational Screen* didn't care for the film at all: "This is not a notable picture…. Not even an interesting picture. It is frequently overacted and the unrelieved tragedy will hardly appeal to the general American public."⁵²

Famous Players' publicity for *Bella Donna* made it clear that this was to be Negri's first *American* picture; advising exhibitors to "not be fooled by imitations." She would be better in American films, they predicted. *Variety* reported:

> The Famous Players believe an altogether different Pola Negri will be seen upon the screen when appearing in its American-made productions. Upon Miss Negri reaching Hollywood, she was taken in two poses, one with her German makeup and the other with her American makeup. It is said the pictures look like two different girls. It is also claimed her German direction held back a great deal that is in the girl and has been brought out for the screen under American direction. This will be easily believed by anyone seeing Negri this week in *Mad Love* at the Capitol, New York. Including Negri, all that German-made film has is its title.⁵³

The studio claimed her acting style was innovative genius. Rather than rely on facial mannerisms to convey feelings, she was unique in expressing as many emotions as possible with hand movement—a technique learned during her early days in theater pantomime. According to one publicity piece, she played an entire scene of *Bella Donna* without a single change of expression. Then, as soon as her leading man left the room, "Miss

Above: **From German style hair and make-up ... to (*right*), glamorous Hollywood movie star, 1923 (both photographs by Donald Biddle Keys).**

Negri remained standing in the doorway, one hand raised above her head on the door frame. With a single motion of that hand she told the entire story of her desolation and her decision to make use of this man for her own ends."54

The studio's press machine heralded her as ethereal, a force of elemental nature. In keeping with such ballyhoo, columnist Harry Carr said she was a "wild wind from the Russian Steppes" and "a bucking bronco." Carr also gets the credit for being the one to call her a *tiger-woman*. "She has the same soft and beautiful ferocity.... She has the same silken relaxation that springs into claws and teeth without warning.... And she has the tiger's magnificent disdain. You can't help loving her for her disdain."55

Of course, on the set, her domain, she was the queen and the center of attention—an artist with a relentless, single-minded pursuit of perfection. The "tiger-woman" cared nothing about others. Edwin Schallert wrote in *Picture-Play Magazine*:

> Those who had appeared in her pictures have confessed to me their absolute inability to cope with her. They accuse her, in fact, of not giving a single thing. She rules the set absolutely as its mistress, and this is something that can well be understood after one watches her and realizes how much of herself she literally hurls into her acting.

> She has been known to stand for minutes before a mirror, pretending to be making up her lips or her eyes. In reality she was not making up at all. She was going through her preparations for the next episode. She tested every expression of her face, studied it from every angle, endeavored to get over some undreamed of nuance of feeling, some absolutely new light of eyes, curve of lips, engraving of forehead, to eliminate, if possible a spoken title, which titles, she frankly admits, and with a positive venom in her voice, "I hate."[56]

Publicity insisted her attitude, her artistic selfishness and idiosyncrasies made her a great actress—and as a great actress she could be forgiven a few "eccentricities of temperament."[57] Then, of course, when she was criticized for being temperamental, the studio neither said or did anything to defend her or downplay the incidents, making things worse for her. *Temperamental*—the one word forever associated with Pola Negri. Today we would call it "passion," and she was very passionate about fighting for whatever she thought it would take to make her performance work. Perhaps it was too impossible a task at a studio determined to standardize everything from the plots of their pictures to an actress's look on the screen, yet fight she did against them with all of her "tiger-woman" ability. The "temperamental" label, however, as in being temperamental for no reason other than her own ego, stuck to her unfairly and killed her as a relevant actress.

Harold Zierold catalogued her alleged "tantrums" on the set of *Bella Donna*. She was appalled by the Chinese decor of her studio bungalow, formerly belonging to Mary Pickford. She fled from the set in terror whenever a black cat appeared—being from "gypsy stock" she could not be persuaded that it was anything but a bad omen, and would not come out of her bungalow until she was assured that every cat on the lot had been caught. Distracted by passersby, she demanded that a wall be built around her set.[58] Negri would not agree to change her white facial and black eye makeup and raged at the studio's insistence that she soften her portrayal of her character to make her less "vicious." She complained about the music on the set, insisted on having champagne available in her dressing room between takes or she could not work, that she had to have a Polish cook for Polish dishes or she could not work, and if anyone dared disagree with her, she would angrily let out her bloodcurdling cry of, "In Poland, we kill!"[59]

Reports of her "temper tantrums" made the magazines and filled the newspaper headlines. In one magazine article about "temperament" among Hollywood stars, an "unknown actress" tells a story she'd heard about how Negri had become distracted by the noise of carpenters at work on an adjacent set. She became upset, clutched her hair with both hands, let out a torrent of profanity in French and deliberately sat down in a pool of grease, ruining her dress and halting production until a new identical dress could be created. The *Perth Sunday Times* claimed she held up production on *Bella Donna* because the first day of filming was scheduled for Friday the 13th. Being superstitious, she simply *could not* appear in front of the camera that day.[60] A *New York Times* article, "Queen of the Vamps," reported on Pola refusing to budge from her dressing room until everything from the lights to props to the camera and all of the crew were set perfectly. She hated waiting on anybody or anything when filming a scene. According to the article, her emissaries—her personal maid and assistant—would inspect the set like Marine drill instructors checking the barracks and report back to her when everything was a go. Then Pola would emerge, "imperiously, sometimes with a smile, sometimes with a scowl.[61]

Her *Bella Donna* co-star Conrad Nagel defended her, calling her "a regular fellow and a genuinely interesting woman." He didn't deny her being "temperamental" on the set, but suggested it was merely for publicity and a case of Pola "living up to the stories that preceded her."[62]

"Every artist has good days and bad days," Negri once said about her fabled temperament:

> Sometimes it seems to me that I won't be able to work, but I never let that feeling get the better of me. I believe in temperament, but not in letting temperament overcome you. When I don't feel in the mood for working I depend on the music that accompanies the scenes. I let it bring me into the mood and then everything is all right.[63]

Acting demands a high emotion. Silent film acting required every nerve of her being to create her character and sometimes those nerves frayed due to demands of the role or because of fatigue and frustration. There is no doubt that Negri could be imperious and impulsive. She had to be if she wanted to be true to herself. To subsume one's self into a character is to abandon self-control, and sometimes the intensity of the drama becomes overwhelming. Yet while Pola was demanding, publicity exaggerated her demands, making them seem outrageous and self-serving. For that, one article called her the "most hated woman in Movieland" and a "prima donna" who makes "capital of her temperament." One newspaper poll awarded her "the cut-glass pacifier as the most temperamental woman star in the movies."[64] A dubious honor.

A 1938 newspaper item blamed her volcanic temperament on feelings of insecurity upon arrival in America. According to the story, friends in Germany told her she would be at a disadvantage in Hollywood since American girls were more beautiful than she.[65] Some said her volatile behavior came from bad advice from comedienne Mabel Normand, who advised her during her voyage to America to "upstage them and they'll give you everything you want."[66] The newspaper item concluded that Pola "deliberately decided on temperament as a weapon—and by virtue of it achieve a glamor none of her competitors could match."[67]

"There is only one excuse I can see for ever holding up production," said Negri. "If a scene does not appeal to me and I do not feel I can give it my best work, I stop to discuss it with my director. If that is temperament, then I am temperamental."[68]

A *New York Morning Telegraph* letter writer wondered why there was such an uproar regarding her fits of pique. "I've no doubt that she's temperamental, but does this distinguish her from any other actor or actress or from any other human being of any consequence? ... There's hardly a cinema star that shines who couldn't learn something about acting from Pola."[69]

Perhaps the Famous Players–Lasky press department truly believed that exaggerations of Negri's temperament made her more interesting to movie fans. This can be the only rational explanation why they paradoxically allowed her to be cast in a bad light as a way of making her "interesting."

Negri had problems upon arriving in California. Call it a case of culture shock compounded by loneliness and insecurity in a studio system far different from her German experience. According to writer Juliet Harpman, her faltering English caused her to be misinterpreted. All of the publicity over her arrival in the U.S. caused jealousy among American women.[70] Instead of being welcomed by the Hollywood acting colony, she was treated with suspicion and resentment. She did not mingle or accept dinner invitations, as she found social affairs dull when she didn't know any of the guests. At first she had no friends so she kept company with her books and music. People misinterpreted her discomfort for indifference and she wound up criticized for being haughty and snobbish.[71]

Herbert Howe theorized that she was resented because she was competition and because she ignored those who would curry her favor.[72] Because she didn't do what was expected of her, the press painted her as arrogant and difficult. Harry Carr claimed that on her first visit to the studio she demanded a dressing room just as big and prestigious as the one occupied by Gloria Swanson. As the story goes, Gloria had the only private dressing room on the Lasky lot. Pola took one look at it and decided she had to have one as well. The only other structure comparable in size was Mary Pickford's old bungalow that then housed the studio scenario department. According to Carr, the writers and editor were evicted without warning to meet Negri's demand.[73]

Variety, on the other hand, reported that her reaction to her first studio visit was a hushed, "So quiet, so complete."[74] Nothing about demands. In another version of the bungalow story, Pola didn't like the Oriental decor installed by Pickford during her time there. The news that she wanted to change it set off howls of outrage. Why wasn't something that had been good enough for "our" Mary good enough for her? Who did she think she was? The issue was quelled when Pickford graciously "allowed" her to make changes. It's all a lie. She never asked or changed a thing.

Perhaps it would have been much kinder of the studio had they allowed Negri, who had never seen anything like California or had much in the way of contact with ordinary Americans, some time to acclimatize herself. They should have demonstrated the American method of making pictures to her first instead of instantly expecting her to "get it" without experiencing some growing pains.

At the time of her arrival, California was in the middle of an oppressive week-long heat wave.[75] She was not used to the hot climate and it sickened her. She was unfamiliar with American cuisine and there didn't seem to be anyone in Hollywood who could cook the Polish dishes that might have alleviated her terrible homesickness. Worse for her, she knew absolutely no one in Hollywood apart from Charlie Chaplin and she was under intense pressure from an intrusive press. She was maliciously referred to as "the competition" behind her back at the studio and she balked at answering personal questions from the press—not knowing that every actor was asked them. She thought it was something personal.[76]

She hated making *Bella Donna*. It was a poor choice of film for her and she'd had no say in its selection. The director, George Fitzmaurice, was serviceable at best, most likely chosen for her by the studio because they both spoke French. She recognized that the script by Ouida Bergere, Fitzmaurice's wife, was weak and her leading role had been radically altered from the original conception in Robert Hitchens' novel. The studio deemed the titular character too pathological a specimen of vamp and, fearful of local censorship boards, attempted to make her more sympathetic. This was a disastrous decision, forcing Negri to play a character removed from the dictates of the plot, resulting in a fantasy caricature rather than a real woman. They signed her for her talent; told America she was a great actress; and then gave her nothing to display her prowess, all but assuring the failure of her Paramount debut.

Perhaps Pola naively believed that she could change the script as needed during production, that the studio that had imported her would be as concerned as she was with quality and artistry. While making pictures in Germany with Lubitsch, she had been allowed a great deal of input into her characterization. In America, however, an actress was expected to play the role as written in a minimum amount of takes and not question or attempt to change the shooting schedule to allow her time to understand her character. No one at Famous Players was interested in her input. From the beginning of the production, she was lost as to what to do or how to play the role.[77]

"Every time I expressed my opinion contrary or made an objection of any sort, I was heralded as 'temperamental,'" she wrote in *Photoplay* a few years later.[78] There were many distractions during filming. She didn't like the studio's wheezing organ, which was supposed to inspire an actor's emoting on the set. Music was part and parcel of filming a picture. She requested something better. It was immediately reported in the newspapers that she had demanded that an entire orchestra be hired. She found passersby and onlookers distracting and asked that something be done about them. A high wall was built to close her set, which didn't sit well with a press suddenly denied easy access to her and a public that considered this another high-handed and arrogant gesture on her part. According to the *New York Morning Herald*, those "who want to gaze on the beauty of the Polish star will have to satisfy themselves with her picture instead."[79]

She was convinced that *Bella Donna* would fail and the stress took its toll on her. Newspapers regularly reported on her "fits," how she would announce (in that phonetic way) "*I feel seeck*," flee the set and refuse to return to the studio for a week or more. In truth, she sank into a black depression and was scarcely able to rise from her bed in the morning.[80] Her frequent absences from the studio were satirized in the *Screenland Magazine* article "From AM to PM in Hollywood"[81]:

> 9:45 a.m.: Lasky office boy sent in search of Pola Negri
> 11:00 a.m.: Lasky assistant director sent in search of Pola Negri
> 12:06 p.m.: Lasky director sent in search of Pola Negri
> 2:00 p.m.: Lasky studio manager sent in search of Pola Negri
> 3:15 p.m.: Jesse L. Lasky starts in search of Pola Negri
> 4:15 p.m.: Pola Negri reports for work
> 4:30 p.m.: Pola Negri quits work

Even though her problems with scripts and directors were mostly confined to her first two pictures, movie magazine writers again and again rehashed her early problems in Hollywood for the rest of her career. Negri handled her baptism by fire in America with a great deal of dignity, but it cost her dearly. She confessed to one magazine, "I cried day after day and night after night behind closed doors. When I went out my head was high. It will always be high.... Although I am very sensitive, criticism cannot make me turn aside. I am not discouraged."[82]

As if exaggerating Negri's "tantrums" weren't enough, the folks in the Famous Players–Lasky publicity department had something else up their sleeves to foist on her. In what can only be considered a bizarre turn, they concocted a now-legendary feud between her and fellow studio star Gloria Swanson in a grab for headlines and the box office. In reality there was no feud, but it is still one of central "myths" about Negri.

This major Hollywood studio set two of its own contract players against each other for over two years with insinuations of bad blood generated solely by the press department. In her autobiography, Swanson explained that she and Negri had the same sort of screen image and attracted most of the attention, so press agents conjured up a story that the newcomer, Pola, intended to put Gloria down and take over as "Queen of the Studio." At the time it happened, Swanson did not appreciate the ploy:

> Next to being actually misquoted, I don't mind having little things exaggerated. The papers have made it appear that Pola Negri and I indulged in a common row over the cats at the studio. We were pictured as squabbling little vulgarians. It would have seemed more fair if they had also remarked that Miss Negri had been a guest at my house and that I think that her little foreign ways are fascinating. Her accent is delightful.[83]

The truth, she wrote in her autobiography, is that they felt no rivalry and, in fact, didn't even know each other.[84]

The start of the "feud" can be traced back to one of Negri's first public appearances in Tinseltown at an Actors' Equity charity event at the Hollywood Bowl. Film stars were invited to dress as historic figures and Negri went in costume as Theda Bara playing Cleopatra—sort of a symbolic passing of the torch from one vamp to another. The studio's publicity department let it be known to the press that as Negri was being presented as the guest of honor at the event, Swanson would not be attending. Therein was the feud's central precept: Gloria hated Pola and would have nothing to do with anything she was involved in.

At the center of the feud are the cats. According to legend, a construction superintendent on the Famous Players–Lasky lot had taken to feeding the stray cats roaming the grounds, the feline population had multiplied to about 100 and they had become pests. "Pola Negri does not like cats," one newspaper wrote. "She is afraid of them…. So Pola, who knows well what is due a star, simply announced that she would work no more until the cats were killed. 'Ze cats, ze must go!' … 'Eet ees zey or I!'"[85] According to the story, Swanson put the imperiled pussycats under her personal protection, leaving her rival with no choice but to find a way to co-exist with them.

Negri denied any malice towards the cats and blamed the story on someone from the press who disliked her and spread the rumor that she had ordered the cats killed. In 1930, she admitted to being superstitious and genuinely afraid of cats, but insisted she had an enclosure made at her own expense to keep them out of her way. She added, "It did not make any difference to the cats."[86]

The book *The Paramount Pretties* turns the dusty myth on its ear, claiming it was *Swanson* who didn't like cats. An alternative version of the myth has Pola and Swanson throwing cats at each other!

The press cheered Swanson's victory over the arrogant interloper. She had vanquished the foreign upstart and showed her who was the true queen of the lot. Yet this was only the first salvo of the "war." At stake was studio pre-eminence and the right to choose the best stories, the best directors, and the best studio personnel. Both stars wanted to win and so the feud was on.

Over the next two years they allegedly battled over who had the better dressing room (as noted earlier, Negri "demanded" to have a bungalow like Gloria's). They battled over music. Pola hated loud music, so Gloria allegedly hired an entire brass band to play just to annoy her. Actually, that was Gloria's director Allan Dwan's doing.[87] The fake feud climaxed in the supposed proclamation from Gloria that she would never again step foot on the Famous Players lot as long as Negri was there and then made good on her promise by being wheeled around the studio in a wheelchair. The story was, of course, bunk. The reason for the wheelchair was Gloria's unwillingness to risk tripping over all of the electrical cables strewn across the studio floor between her dressing room and the set.[88]

According to Swanson biographer Michael Shearer, during the production of *The Coast of Folly* Gloria was carried from her bungalow and back by footmen holding aloft a sedan emblazoned with her husband Henri De La Falaise de la Courdaye's coat of arms. Shearer adds that the studio orchestra was instructed to play "La Marseillaise when she entered and everyone in the cast and crew was requested to bow."[89] In his autobiography, long-time Famous Players–Lasky Paramount Pictures chief Adolph Zukor cites several of Gloria's own incidents of temperamental behavior such as refusing to do retakes, criticizing her studio wardrobe, scenery and dressing rooms.[90] Yet it's Negri who is the one remembered chiefly for her temperament.

Even after Swanson left Hollywood to make pictures exclusively at the company's Astoria, New York, studio (a "retreat" briefly seen as a triumph for Negri), the press still harped on the "feud." Harry Carr, with his penchant for comparing actresses to animals, pitted them against each other, Swanson as a friendly white bull terrier, willing to get into scraps and coming out on top no matter the odds, Pola as the dangerous tiger who accepts her losses and goes down to defeat in a "gesture of great despair."[91]

Plainly put, Gloria is the plucky and tenacious All-American girl, the friendly and personable star—the sweet girl from Chicago playing dress-up in exquisite clothes. Pola is aloof, dramatic and demanding. She does not possess the traits of *our* Gloria. Pola is different and ... *temperamental*, although still a great actress. Any way you look at it, Pola loses the round.

Negri was troubled by the whole idea of a feud with someone that she really didn't know, yet she never said anything publicly to end the ploy. She admits in her *Memoirs* that the feud was so well engineered that both actresses began to believe it themselves. At an exhibitor's dinner in downtown Los Angeles, Gloria, apparently upset at the amount of publicity that Negri had been getting, sent word that she would not appear first; Pola, the lesser star, should be the opening act. Pola, furious at the suggestion that she play second fiddle to Gloria, refused to go on first. So, according to the story, both ladies sat fuming in their dressing rooms, unwilling to go out. Negri says that after an hour she became bored with such nonsense and made her grand entrance into the hotel ballroom. Gloria then made her own entrance and they were both shocked to find that they were wearing the exact same gown. They had gotten their dresses from the same designer. Negri wrote that while she was received with great applause, Swanson's subsequent appearance was met with "minor amusement."[92]

The "feud" ended with Swanson's departure from Famous Players at the expiration of her contract in 1925. As a publicity gimmick the feud has few rivals in the history of the movies, but what good did it do Pola Negri? It made her seem small and fussy. Her purported "fits of temper" made her an unsympathetic prima donna. She was portrayed as the outcast—detested within her own studio and hated by the rest of Hollywood. Instead of disarming small-town America with a colorful off-screen persona that would fascinate and intrigue them, the studio unbelievably handed them reasons to dislike and resent her.

In time, publicity did her in. Negri became who and what they said she was, resulting in a loss of popularity that ultimately doomed her movie career in America. In hindsight, none of what was said or written about her would have mattered much had she received more of an opportunity to display that top-notch acting talent that had made her famous in her films for Lubitsch.

That, alas, was not to be.

6

Pola Negri in Paramount Pictures

Pola Negri's American movie career was a case of unfulfilled expectations. Her triumphant performance in *Madame DuBarry* aka *Passion* set an impossibly high bar she was unable to reach again in her Paramount releases. Not that her acting was ever bad. She was praised by movie critics even in a dud like *The Crown of Lies*, but she never matched the brilliance or intensity of her German roles. She repeatedly failed to be the brilliant actress she could be. Of all of the major players of the silent era, Negri was held to a higher standard than any save Charlie Chaplin, and was given material unworthy of her talent. During her Paramount tenure she was saddled with a stream of mediocre pictures, and moviegoers lost interest in her. Exhibitors complained about the low grosses and losses and critics mourned her "squandered talent." By the expiration of her contract in 1928, she had worn out her welcome here and was blamed for not achieving what had been predicted for her upon arrival on these shores.

After all of the publicity, Famous Players-Lasky had no idea what to do with her after the public's initial excitement wore off. As Diana Negra theorizes, they created two Pola Negris "fundamentally at odds with each other."[1] Off-screen, she was the "tiger woman" who loved fiercely and dangerously and was a temperamental creature of incredible passion and talent. On-screen, however, her frothy persona was diluted to weak tea to make her more palatable to the public and local censors. Her first two American features, *Bella Donna* and *The Cheat*, presented her as a glamorous vamp, capable of subverting the normal domestic order with her vivid sexuality. Her subsequent roles deliberately neutered this "erotic aggression" and tried to tame her, to no one's satisfaction. In her best German pictures, *Madame DuBarry*, *Carmen* and *Sumurun*, Negri played to her strengths in portraying lower-class women who used guile to climb to the top of the social order; unconventional women behaving in realistic fashion. Time and time again, Famous Players cast her as a conventional, inoffensive heroine caught in highly implausible situations not of her own making, the exact opposite of the kind of roles that made her a powerful and intriguing actress. The studio dared not translate Pola's real-life persona into pictures out of fear of controversy; but a "safe" Pola was just another actress stripped of everything that made her interesting in the first place. This paradox turned her into a contradiction, into a woman who, Negra suggests, was literally at odds with herself. The studio never solved this conundrum of their own making and the end result was defeat.

Negri headlined in pictures that failed to attract the interest of moviegoers. The box office value of her name quickly plummeted. She was *never* much of a draw in small-town America. She couldn't catch a break. When the stories were chosen for her, there were complaints from the critics that she was not the fiery and passionate actress that she had been in German pictures. When she won the right as part of her contract to pick her own stories and directors, the exhibitors complained that the stories were too sophisticated or too foreign to appeal to the American public.

By the end of her contract with Lasky, she was reduced to starring in programmers such as *The Woman from Moscow,* pictures meant to do nothing more than fill the slate for the studio's "block-booking"[2] sales to exhibitors. Her popularity vanished. Exhibitors wouldn't even put her name on the their marquees. The "tiger woman" was hunted to extinction. Pola Negri left America, unmourned and unwanted.

Her meteoric rise ended with a brutal fall. Where once she had been one of the most memorable stars, she wound up as a mere footnote in film history. With most of her pictures lost, we can only read the surviving synopsis compiled from information from the *American Film Institute Catalog of Motion Pictures* and other sources, look at the photographs, and imagine what should have been.

Bella Donna

Famous Players-Lasky
Distributor: Paramount
Released April 1, 1923

STATUS: Prints of this movie exist in several European archives. No DVD is available.
CREDITS: *Director:* George Fitzmaurice. *Scenario:* Ouida Bergere. *Story:* Robert Smythe Hitchens. *Photographer:* Arthur Miller.
CAST: Pola Negri (*Bella Donna*), Conway Tearle (*Mahmoud Baradi*), Conrad Nagel (*Nigel Armine*), Adolphe Menjou (*Mr. Chepstow*), Claude King (*Dr. Meyer Issacson*), Lois Wilson (*Patricia*), Macey Harlam (*Ibrahim*), Robert Schlable (*Dr. Hartley*).

STORY

While honeymooning in Venice, Ruby Chepstow becomes involved in a scandal that results in her husband killing an admirer. She attains notoriety under the name Bella Donna and is saved from suicide by Nigel Armine, a young engineer from a wealthy American family. Mistaking her interest in his family fortune for love, Nigel abandons his fiancée Patricia, ward of Dr. Issacson, and marries the beguiling adventuress. They journey to Egypt, where he has a contract job with a local firm. While in Cairo, the bored Bella Donna falls under the spell of wealthy Egyptian Mahmoud Baradi, who seduces her on his houseboat. Upon learning that Nigel will not inherit the family fortune, she quarrels with him. She goes to Baradi's tent and he persuades her to poison Nigel so they can be together. The Egyptian provides her with fatal drugs that she puts into her husband's food and drink. Nigel is seriously ill when Dr. Issacson and Patricia pay him a visit. Issacson diagnoses the case as poisoning and finds an antidote. Accused of attempted murder, Bella Donna defiantly declares her love for the Egyptian. She goes to Baradi, and finds him with another woman. When he casts her off, Bella Donna, rejected by all, wanders into a desert sandstorm to await death.[3]

Portrait of Pola for *Bella Donna*, Paramount, 1923. Directed by George Fitzmaurice.

REVIEWS

The Exhibitor's Trade Review:

The brilliant work of Pola Negri in this, her first American-made picture, is warranted to satisfy the most exacting critic and swell the ranks of the foreign star's large army of admirers. The film presents one of those rare instances in which a leading lady's talents rejuvenates a withered plot, transforming it into life aglow with passion, honeycombed with sinister intrigue and terminating in somber tragedy. In order to achieve this feat the star had to overcome the rooted dislike of American audience to unhappy endings and encounter the handicap of the well-worn situation made painfully familiar by a long series of "sheik" pictures—the infatuation of a white woman for a tawny-skinned son of the desert. That she succeeded is a tribute to her genius. Take Pola Negri out of the feature and it would be relegated to the oblivion which awaits commonplace productions.

According to *Variety*, Negri's acting was "like a taxi clock, either too fast or not at all. Her schemes for anguish appears to be a line drawn across her cheek and a drop of glycerine under the left eye. One-eyed criers are new over here." They were sure the picture would give her a big start as a movie star, but advised the studio to "allow her to follow her own notions in acting."[4] The *New York Times* reviewer called her acting "compelling," and noted: "There may have been other vampires of the screen, but none possessed of the art of Pola Negri."[5]

Most opinions of the picture, however, were harsh. The *New York Globe* said of Pola: "She plays for no sympathy and presents a thoroughly unwholesome woman—but no one can make literature out of yellow journalism and that is what this part amounts to."[6] "Pola Negri's first American-made picture does not fit her as well as those tailored in Berlin," wrote the *Photoplay* reviewer. "Pola is more beautiful but less moving.... The picture is thoroughly artificial."[7]

Exhibitors also expressed their displeasure. "This is not good entertainment," the manager of the Rex Theater in Wahoo, Nebraska, wrote to *The Exhibitor's Herald*. "Patrons expressed their opinion strongly 'negative.'"[8] The manager of the Lincoln Theater in Pittsburgh, Pennsylvania, noted, "[T]he screen is not benefitted by this sort of an offering. Too much vamp and sex stuff."[9]

Movie magazine readers weighed in with laments of their own. Mrs. EML from Washington, D.C., wrote *Photoplay* to say, "If we must have vamps of the snaky type, why not remain loyal to our All-American Theda Bara.... I am sure she was far more acceptable than Pola Negri is in her first American production."[10] A reader from England poetically mourned what had been done to his favorite actress:

A Brickbat

And is this—Pola? She who charmed
us all in other pictures,
and by her acting quite disarmed
the critic's usual strictures?
Is this the girl who made us thrill
to all her moods and passions?
is she henceforth to simply fill
a role for frills and fashions?

Oh woodman, woodman spare that tree
and don't be so exacting
Oh, Paramount let Pola be
allowed to do some acting!
Her beauty, passion, charm, caprice
are wholly wasted on a

> deplorably directed piece
> of mush like *Bella Donna*
> —*Bardolph*, Manchester, England[11]

No amount of publicity spin could save *Bella Donna* from box office failure and Negri's reputation as a great dramatic actress was hurt by her limp American debut. Stills depicting her in moments of emotion do seem to give the impression that her performance was a bit over the top. Even her main Hollywood cheerleader, columnist Harry Carr, called her acting "wretched" and blamed it on her being forced to play "a society woman of artificial conventions ... a *Pollyannized* imitation of the original character."[12] *Motion Picture Classic* laid the blame for the picture's "artistic failure" on Pola, stating that she "began figuring out what to do instead of plunging right in as she has done when she had a director she knew and trusted."[13]

Exhibitors and the public complained about the "sex stuff" in the picture and the realistic, downbeat ending. They didn't want realism. They wanted to go home happy.

Pola's defenders blamed studio interference, claiming executives had gotten cold feet after showing an uncut version of the picture to a group of exhibitors. Would Negri's performance make it past the local censor boards? Would her malefic character be banned in small towns? Would that downbeat ending be scorned by the "tsk-tsk" brigade? Rather than risk it, the studio insisted on cuts, toning down her character to make her "censor proof." The weak result doomed the picture to failure. *Screenland Magazine* wrote, "[A]ll the fans who had been looking to see the widely advertised Pola Negri in an American film and all the critics who feared that Pola was being 'conventionalized' came to pray and remained to scoff."[14] *Picture-Play Magazine* aptly noted that perhaps Negri "could only appear to complete advantage in pictures made in a country where there are no censors and where grown-up characters are allowed the privilege of displaying grown-up emotions."[15]

Negri didn't think much of the picture either, calling it "*teerible*," according to *Photoplay*, and confessed that neither she nor director George Fitzmaurice knew what the picture was actually about.[16] "My imagination of the role was so different! But I allowed myself to be persuaded. They said to me, 'Ah, but American audiences are different! You will not succeed unless you adapt yourself to our ways.'"[17]

She had disappointed her first time up, and it was unforgivable. *Photoplay* ran a full-page photograph of her in all of her studio-created elegance with this caption: "The Countess Dombski of Poland has become an ordinary citizeness of Hollywood. With plucked eyebrows and a pet dog, Pola is not the 'Bella Donna'—the pretty lady. Will we ever again see the bedeviling DuBarry or the vivid, seductive Carmen?"[18]

Screenland's verdict was that Pola had "flopped": "Had her first American-made picture approached the qualities of artistry shown in the work she did abroad, she might have continued to hold the scepter in her white, ruthless hand. And if Pola had had tact—!"

But Pola and tact were not twin sisters, nor even distant cousins. The attention paid her by worshipful officials, the flattery of the press, the ogling to which she was submitted everywhere she went, made an impression on Pola. She began to believe she was as great as they said she was.

Then came her first American-made picture. Her Bella Donna lacked the fire, the flashing genius of her DuBarry and her Carmen. She was swaggering, gauche, sometimes unlovely. Her heroine, who was supposed to be a wicked, passion-ridden thing, was only lukewarm and didn't seem to know herself what it was all about.

"Lubitsch is Pola Negri," said the wise ones. "Can Pola come back? Will another vivid performance such as her gypsy dancer in *One Arabian Night* restore her to her wobbling throne? I doubt it. Pola has been rubber-stamped."[19]

Negri's disappointing debut seemed to have impacted at least one member of the public. A newspaper item from 1923 reported on a woman's lawsuit against Negri for substantial damages on the grounds that the actress had "alienated" her husband's affection. The wife admitted to the court that her husband had never actually met Negri, but he had seen the comely Polish star in *Bella Donna* and afterwards, she complained, became "totally indifferent" to her.[20]

According to author Tom Rice, the Ku Klux Klan launched protests against *Bella Donna*, resulting in the picture's ban in the state of Texas. They complained that the picture was "coarse, degrading and insulting" as well as "an insult to the white race." And that fervid romance between a Westerner and an Arab? That was "open propaganda for social equality."[21] It could only lead to dreaded "miscegenation" and the Klan was having none of that.

Between *Bella Donna* and her next production, *The Cheat*, Negri made a cameo appearance in Paramount's *Hollywood*, released in July 1923. It concerned an ingénue's rise in the picture business and featured cameos by Douglas Fairbanks, Mary Pickford, William S. Hart, Ben Turpin and Leatrice Joy. In one scene, the hapless heroine attends a banquet at Negri's Hollywood residence. That would have been interesting to see. It is a shame that this is a lost picture.

According to a 1934 *Silver Screen Magazine* article, the "temperamental" Pola didn't want to do the picture at all and made herself as difficult as possible on the set, hoping to get fired. As the story goes, right in the middle of a crucial scene, she pretended to faint, knowing it would hold up production. Director James Cruze, tired of her "constant temper tantrums," responded by pouring a bucket of ice water over her head to "revive" her. According to the article, the impromptu shower "ruined her makeup and ran all over her dress. Pola came to instantly and for five minutes hurled epithets in five languages at Cruze and individual Paramount executives."[22]

The Cheat

Famous Players-Lasky
Distributor: Paramount
Released August 27, 1923

STATUS: Lost
CREDITS: *Producer-Director*: George Fitzmaurice. *Adaptation*: Ouida Bergere. *Photographer*: Arthur Miller.
CAST: Pola Negri (*Carmelita De Cordoba*), Jack Holt (*Dudley Drake*), Charles De Roche (*Claude Mace, known as Prince Rao-Singh*), Dorothy Cumming (*Lucy Hodge*), Robert Schnable (*Jack Hodge*), Charles Stevenson (*Horace Drake*), Helen Dunbar (*Duenna*), Richard Wayne (*Attorney for Defense*), Guy Oliver (*District Attorney*), Edward Kimball (*Judge*).

STORY

Carmelita De Cordoba, the daughter of a wealthy South American, arrives in Paris for her wedding to her father's elderly business partner. Her beauty attracts the attention of a swindler, Claude Race, posing as an Indian prince, Rao-Singh. Young American

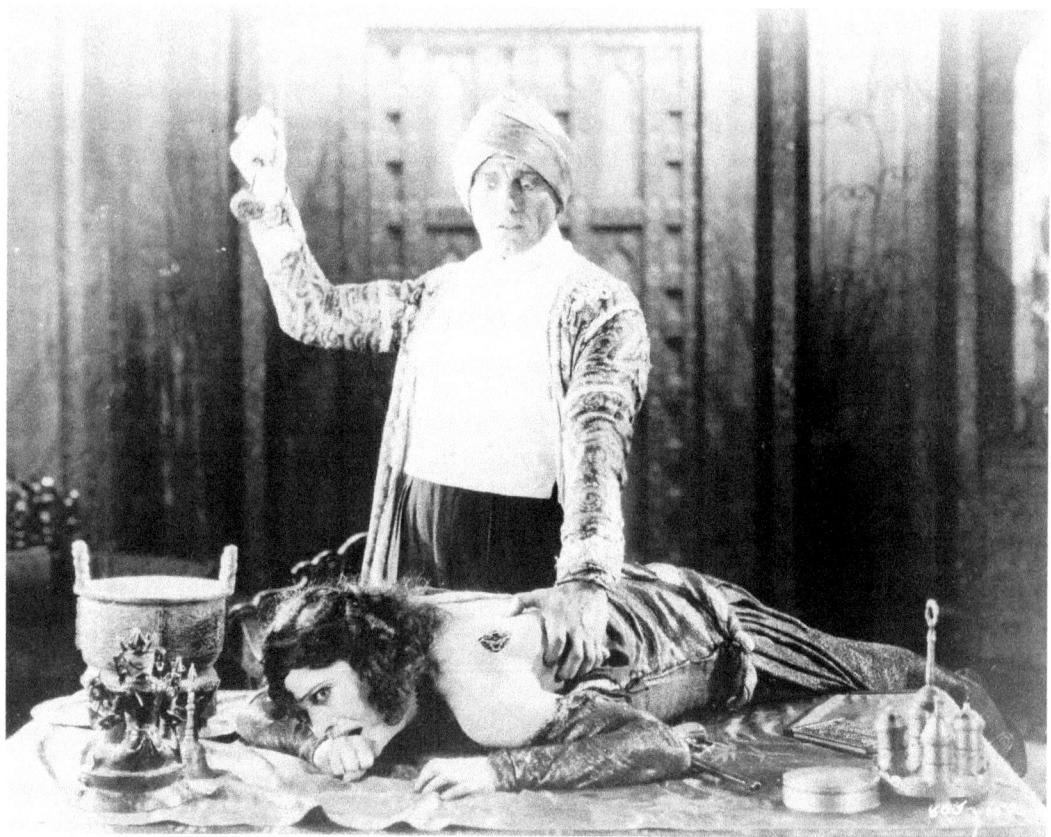

Miss Negri and Charle De Roache in a scene from *The Cheat*, Paramount, 1923. Directed by George Fitzmaurice.

Dudley Drake falls in love with Carmelita and she marries him instead. Her father disowns her for her disobedience. The newlyweds move to New York where Dudley begins work on a project that he hopes will pay off lucratively. Carmelita makes the acquaintance of socialite Lucy Hodge, who invites her to her country home. There she again encounters Rao-Singh, who takes her out gambling. She runs up a $10,000 tab to the casino and he agrees to cover her losses in return for an evening alone with him with his apartment. When Dudley's project comes up big, Carmelita repays Rao-Singh, denying him his pleasure. Decrying her as "a cheat," Rao-Singh brands her shoulder with his personal mark. Fighting him off, Carmelita gets hold of a pistol and shoots in self-defense, wounding him. To protect her from scandal, Dudley takes the blame for the shooting, stands trial and is found guilty. Then Carmelita tearfully exhibits her branded shoulder in court and tells all. Dudley is acquitted and Rao-Singh is exposed as a fake and taken to jail. Husband and wife are reunited.

Reviews

Variety

> Another mark for Paramount so far as production is concerned, but it doesn't mean a thing for the star. Pola Negri fails to convince in her characterization of a South American.

> The willful, thoughtless and spoiled characterization Miss Negri was given would seem to have been somewhat beyond her registering powers. Where the role should create a sympathetic atmosphere there is none, with just the opposite becoming more true than otherwise. Miss Negri throws upon the screen a distinctively hard personality, which, when she is vamping, is fool-proof, but when it should create pathos there is a direful lack of that in roles of this sort.[23]

The *New York Times* called her a "graceful and artistic mistress of the screen."[24] The *New York Mail* said she was "at her wildest and best in this picture" while the *New York Herald* called *The Cheat* "the dullest, cheapest and most asinine movie we have seen in months." "Pola Negri is surprisingly bad as the branded heroine of the now familiar story," said *The New York American*. "She not only looks like, but acts like a conventional movie star."[25]

Once again the studio had tampered with her fiery screen presence to make her palatable to a bland public. The *Exhibitor's Trade Review* wrote, "[E]vidently the revamped Carmelita was designed to show Miss Negri in a mildly pleasing light, as opposed to *Bella Donna* and other ladies of doubtful chastity whom she previously impersonated."[26] In a letter to The *New York Morning Telegraph*, a reader lamented, "I saw her in *The Cheat* and there is every indication that she will join the great army of stenciled stars.... Here's a woman with ... all the qualifications ... to make up a successful actress, but all this is ... submerged so that she may 'wear clothes pretty.' Can't someone save her?"[27]

Motion Picture Magazine said it was a shame "that she must be burdened with the type of stories which have marked her American appearances. The Negri of *Passion* is a different personality entirely."[28]

A picture titled *The Song of the Shadows* was originally announced as the follow-up to *Bella Donna*,[29] but someone at Famous Players decided that remaking *The Cheat*, a box office smash from 1915 directed by Cecil B. DeMille, was a good choice for her. It wasn't. Negri told *Photoplay* that she initially refused to do the picture. The first draft script had her performing a series of stunts like jumping from an airplane into the water and then jumping from a motorcycle onto a moving train. Negri "politely" informed the studio she was not a stuntwoman.[30] Her reaction was, of course, exaggerated in typical Hollywood fashion. "As for Pola's demonstrations in Hollywood, one of the most celebrated of her pyrotechnic picnics occurred when she was handed the script of *The Cheat*," wrote Herbert Howe. "She read it and gently tore a hole in the roof with it."

Negri subsequently agreed to do the film, but still protested that she was not suited to the role.[31] Perhaps she feared the role was too similar to the one she had played in *Bella Donna*. Paramount, unfortunately, refused to listen to her and dealt her another losing hand at the box office.

Tales of her fiery temperament continued unabated in the press. Describing her preparation for the courtroom scene at the climax of the film, *Photoplay* told its readers:

> Pola spent most of her time with her makeup. She powdered, lip-sticked, patted her hair and adjusted her clothes every time the camera stopped grinding. Watching her proved ... uninteresting in the extreme and Director Fitzmaurice was literally sweating in his effort to get something convincing out of her.[32]

Unhappy about the constant criticism, Negri longed for the simpler days of moviemaking in Germany when all that mattered was the heart she put into her work. Here in America she had to please the exhibitors, the financial people, the censors and the public. "Here you become so tired arguing, arguing, arguing, that you almost give up," she told one magazine.[33]

She was once again stuck with the pedestrian George Fitzmaurice even though she did not believe him to be the right director for her.[34] Fitzmaurice himself made news during filming by walking out on the picture with *Variety* describing it as pulling a "Von Stroheim."[35] He insisted that he had been given permission to leave the picture by Jesse Lasky because delays in shooting *The Cheat* (caused by Pola's stormy romance with Charles Chaplin) conflicted with a previous commitment to helm a Goldwyn picture.[36] One writer speculated that Fitzmaurice's real reason for leaving the company in a hurry was having to say "yes" to Negri too many times.

According to her autobiography, Pola originally sought out actor Wallace Reid to be her leading man in the picture. He was in a debilitated state from the ravages of drug addiction and although he was game, it was evident that he was not up to the task.[37] She ended up with granite-jawed one-dimensional Jack Holt instead.

Stills from *The Cheat* capture the 26-year-old Negri at the height of her beauty, clad in a variety of swirling capes, stylish headbands and slinky gowns. The film's press sheet notes that it gave her the opportunity to "wear the greatest array of dazzling Paris gowns that ever delighted the eyes of the ladies in your audiences."[38] Gone is the great untamed mane of hair and kohl-ringed eyes of her German films, replaced by a cardboard cut-out of a rich man's wife more pleasing to American moviegoers. It's comical that Famous Players would try to turn her into a copy of Hollywood's most famous "clothes horse," Gloria Swanson, when they already had them feuding in the press.

The Cheat was an overripe melodrama in which her character was driven *by* the plot rather than *driving* the plot—unlike her women in *Madame DuBarry* and *Carmen* who took matters into their own hands. She was the standard heroine in need of rescuing and that meant sacrificing her vitality and fire. Pola's acting strength was portraying characters with emotional and logical realism. It was a fool's errand to continue to turn her into a fantasy character dressed in beautiful costumes and put in improbable situations.[39] Every time the studio tried to fit her into the mold of a "glamor girl," the mold broke. As the UK publication *Pictures and The Picture-Goer* put it, "Pola Negri, smooth and Paramounted, is a Pola astray."[40]

"We brought Pola Negri to America because there was a universal appeal in her elemental fires and passions—We hailed her as a great actress," wrote *Motion Picture Magazine* in a quiet indictment of how the studio had already compromised Pola for public consumption. "Then we proceeded to temper her abandon—to whitewash her passions … and then make her neither the emotional, sophisticated woman nor the simple, trusting Pollyanna."[41]

The Cheat was her second straight failure. According to the press, Negri recognized what had gone wrong and announced that for her next picture she was "going to stop being beautiful," meaning she was aware that all of the studio's focus on her looking glamorous was hurting her work. "There are enough beautiful women in Hollywood without me."[42] She vowed she would do her next picture, *The Spanish Dancer*, her way.

Yet she was already on the verge of being written off as a relevant actress. *Shadowland* wrote, "Pola Negri has gained nothing by invading America and is nowhere nearly as important a personage in Hollywood as she was in Berlin."[43] *Motion Picture Classic* said of *The Spanish Dancer*, "Pola must come through this time or suffer oblivion."[44]

During production of *The Cheat*, Negri underwent emergency surgery for tonsillitis, delaying shooting for a few extra days. And there was also that engagement business with Charlie Chaplin.

Interlude: Negri and Chaplin—
A Spectacle in Three Acts

Chaplin's *My Autobiography*, published in 1964, devotes just two pages to Pola Negri. In his telling, she made a nuisance of herself by constantly calling to demand his attention. After his repeated refusals, she lost interest and quit calling him. He makes no mention at all of their relationship. He does state that at one point he was approached by a Lasky studio representative who begged him to announce his engagement to Negri as her "obsession" with him was causing her "temperamental fits" on the set of *The Cheat*. Chaplin says he saw no reason to do Famous Players any favors.

Negri spends about 30 pages of her *Memoirs of a Star* on her relationship, engagement and breakup with Chaplin shortly after her arrival in America in September 1922. In her version, Chaplin doggedly pursued *her*.[45] Although his omission of their relationship does seem a sore point to her, Negri blames Charlie's "fact-free" recounting on his "total lack of a sense of humor about his private life."[46]

As previously noted, they first met at a party at the Palais Heinroth in Berlin in 1919. Chaplin was touring Europe for the first time since before the war and Negri was being celebrated for her role in *Madame DuBarry*. Al Kaufman, Famous Players' representative in Berlin, introduced them and, according to a pair of Charlie's biographers, they got along famously. "From their first meeting, they were inseparable," wrote authors Peter Cotes and Thelma Nicklaus in *The Little Fellow*. "She opened for him the great houses of Berlin, and he achieved the same social distinction he had enjoyed in London and Paris.... Later, when she announced her intention of taking up film work in Hollywood, he was able to arrange considerable advance publicity for her...."[47] Chaplin's actual contribution to her publicity remains unknown.

As the story goes, Chaplin asked Kaufman to tell Negri she was "divine." Kaufman spoke to her in German and a startled look came upon her face. She slapped Chaplin's hand and reputedly said in her best English, "Naughty boy." Apparently for the sake of a joke, Kaufman had translated his compliment of her as "You're terrible."[48] Negri recalled it a bit differently:

> I squandered all of the English I knew upon him in one magnificent outburst. I called him "little jazz boy Charlie." Wishing to pay me a compliment in German he asked Mr. Kaufman how to say "I adore you." But what he really said to me was "I think you are a piece of cheese."[49]

With Famous Players' announcement they were importing her to America, gossip columnists wondered whether Pola and Charlie would be taking up where they had left off in Germany.[50] On the eve of her departure for New York, Herbert Howe, interviewing Negri in Berlin, asked about her feelings for Chaplin and if she intended to marry him. She said yes but then claimed to have misunderstood the question. She said she liked Chaplin, but had no time for marriage. "The next five years," she said, "are for work."[51]

In a different interview, she singled out Chaplin as one of the people she was hoping to see in California: "He is ze great artist. And he is just ze man—he is great, too. When I get to California, I see him again."[52] Yet when she got to California, Chaplin did not call her. She took it as a snub. Charlie would later say (through a press agent, of course):

> It began in Berlin a year and a half ago. I fell in love with Pola the instant I met her and the only reason I didn't tell her so was because I was too bashful to confess it. I did tell her she was the loveliest lady I had ever met and I'm sure she must have guessed the secret of my heart.
> But for nearly a year the ocean separated us—and an ocean is an awful bar to a successful love affair.

> I have purposefully avoided her when she first arrived in Hollywood for I felt it would result exactly as it has. Isn't it strange how we instinctively feel the fate that is about to overtake us?[53]

According to Negri's autobiography, they met again at a charity costume pageant at the Hollywood Bowl in September 1922. Ironically, the car she was riding in collided with Chaplin's automobile on the way to the function. No one was hurt, but Chaplin wound up canceling his other commitment to follow her to the gala. When she scolded him sharply for not calling her before, "he giggled merrily." She found that "the more witheringly sarcastic I was, the more pleasure he derived out of being with me."[54] Publicity, however, offered a different take on this story. According to Pola and *her* press agent:

> Strangely enough we missed each other at rehearsals—it was not until the actual performance that I saw him wielding the baton. As I walked towards him I looked in to his face.
>
> It was then that I realized I had been in love with him for more than a year—without being aware of it. I could hardly wait until the pageant was over to see him. And later he confided to me that he had experienced the same feeling at exactly the same time.
>
> Of course, after the performance we met. The following day he called me at my home and since then, except when business or social duties prevented, we have been inseparable.
>
> We understand each other perfectly, and I am sure we will be happy. For my Charlie is not only the dearest boy in the world, but the cleverest. He is a genius.[55]

Charlie's press agent's response to Pola's press agent:

> [W]hen I saw Pola in all her glorious beauty as she swept toward me, that fateful day of the great pageant, I could not resist her any longer. Something I can't describe surged all over inside of me. I felt like a drowning man—yet excited as I had never been before.
>
> And it was not long before I confessed my love and, to my happiness and surprise, I learned that Pola felt the same way about me.[56]

None of this is remotely true, but it sold a lot of magazines and newspapers.

A few days after the gala, according to *Memoirs*, Chaplin sent a troupe of Hawaiian singers to serenade her at her home. She considered it a charming and thoughtful gesture, even though they kept her up all night, making her too tired to report to work the next day on *Bella Donna*. They were soon dining together regularly and, in Negri's version of the story, it was Chaplin who brought up the idea of marrying. She was hesitant, being more concerned with her first American picture.

Rumors of their engagement began to swirl in December 1922. There was speculation in the press that Charlie always intended for Pola to follow him to America—and then marry after a discreet period of time in order to avoid suspicions from the "bluenoses," the morality groups who kept close watch on the private lives of movie stars after the Roscoe Arbuckle scandal. Others were convinced their relationship was strictly for publicity. It was a game that Chaplin had played before, as this witheringly sarcastic gossip item describes:

> It was quiet in Hollywood, Charlie Chaplin didn't have anything to do over the weekend and his name had not appeared in any of the papers in months, so he started to dope out something that would get him a little publicity. Finally he hit on an idea. He knew it was good because he had used it five or six times in the past and it had never failed, and, in addition, it doesn't cost anything. So Charlie decided to let it be "rumored" that he was again engaged to a picture actress.
>
> This time it was Pola Negri, the Polish star, who was to be the "other end" of the engagement. Pola is a foreigner and not acclimated to inside Hollywood details.
>
> So the LA daily papers, which just love to play up picture stuff on their front page, fell for the story.
>
> To date the story stands about 50–50 as far as the principals are rumored. Neither party will affirm or deny the rumor. Charlie is or isn't going to marry Pola Negri, whichever way you want to look at it.[57]

Douglas Fairbanks and Mary Pickford may have been Hollywood's Golden Couple during the silent era, but Charlie and Pola were the first celebrity romance to really command headlines during an age when the truth didn't exactly matter. The press stalked them incessantly, staking out their homes, intruding on their private dinners, and following them around in caravans of automobiles wherever they went, nearly running them off the road on a couple of occasions. When Pola and Charlie went on vacation together to Santa Barbara in January 1923 and booked a room at the Samarkand Hotel—known as Santa Barbara's "Honeymoon Hotel"—the press were sure that news of their engagement was imminent.

Much to their consternation, Pola would neither confirm nor deny anything. "I cannot say whether Charlie and I have been married—I cannot answer your questions pertaining to my personal affairs, especially concerning Charlie. It is true he drove me here, but I have a very good reason for declining to answer any questions." A reporter reminded her that all they had to do was check the marriage license register to confirm a marriage and asked, "Now, why won't you tell us?"

Pola's answer? "Because."[58]

The next day's newspapers reported she had booked a small cottage at Pebble Beach under the name of "Countess Dombski" and had been sighted wearing a diamond solitaire ring of "gigantic proportions."[59] Asked where she had gotten it, "she wouldn't say.... She wouldn't tell anyone anything."[60] According to reports, "letters, telephone calls, telegram and flowers, all bearing the name of Charlie Chaplin, continued to arrive—but the burning question of whether they are from Miss Negri's intended husband or merely from 'a friend' went unanswered."[61]

Despite denials, the rumors reached a fever pitch. Negri went to Del Monte, California for a two-week vacation. When Chaplin unexpectedly arrived to visit her, the press wondered whether this was it. In front of the assembled reporters, Pola announced their engagement. When asked to comment on whether this was true, a nervous-looking Charlie simply gulped and said, "Yes." When asked when the wedding might take place, she said, "We are to marry—when I do not know. Perhaps after my contract is finished, perhaps before. We do not know and have not decided. We have been engaged for a long time, but we decided to say nothing about it. We felt it was our affair and not zee world's."[62]

The next morning Chaplin returned to Los Angeles alone. Negri lingered in Del Monte one more day, then packed her bags and also headed back to Los Angeles to begin work on *The Cheat*.

Their engagement announcement played like a bit of magnificent theater and some thought it just that. Anonymous sources reported them already married, but were keeping it quiet for personal reasons or for publicity's sake. Other eager-to-be-quoted "friends" declared that two "temperamental" artists like Pola and Charlie would never marry.[63]

In his autobiography, actor Adolphe Menjou, who co-starred with Pola in *Bella Donna*, wrote:

> Pola may have been responsible for the popularity of what Hollywood calls "the fighting romance"—a love story in which boy and girl meet, immediately detest each other, fight bitterly for eight reels, and then suddenly end up in each others' arms. Pola's battle with her boyfriend were some of the most spectacular ever waged. In one historic clash of temperaments between Pola and Chaplin, Pola climaxed the stormy scene by fainting gracefully on a bearskin rug. While others rushed for water to resuscitate her, Chaplin refused to be outdone and fainted dramatically at her side. Pola was so infuriated that she immediately broke off their engagement.[64]

They fought incessantly. Pola got mad at him when a reporter quoted him as saying he thought *Bella Donna* was "rubbish." Charlie got mad when Pola mocked his tendency for picking random words out of the dictionary and deliberately working them into social conversation to make himself seem more intellectual. Furious after something Chaplin had said or done, Pola would storm out of his house cursing at him in her usual multilingual tirade or throw him out of her house. Every argument between them made Pola "feel seeck," causing another delay on the set of *The Cheat*. He wanted her to leave Famous Players, quit pictures and marry him. She scoffed at that notion, wondering why his career should be more important than hers.

Whenever the press asked them to confirm a wedding date, the enigmatic bride and groom gave nothing. Pola, in particular, played the enigmatic Sphinx. *Photoplay* reported. "Time and again she has drastically refused audiences with impatient reporters either at the studio or at home. She simply reinstates and reiterates, "*I have nuzzing to say.*"[65] *Motion Picture Magazine* expressed a wish for Chaplin to "come out with an engraved statement answering such questions as: are Pola Negri and he married, if they haven't been married secretly, when are they going to be married in the presence of their enemies and friends?"[66]

The movie magazines, desperate for material, indulged in the speculative fiction that a marriage was definitely imminent and even reported on whether a Ouija Board considered them astrologically compatible (the Ouija Board wasn't sure).[67] The press photographed them together at parties, film premieres and on the golf course. The invasion of privacy became so intense that Negri bitterly complained to her studio that an army of reporters had encamped on her front lawn. Famous Players did nothing to help her. They were unhappy about her involvement with well-known ladies' man Chaplin, yet they milked the relationship for all of its publicity value, even announcing to the press that she couldn't marry Charlie because her studio contract forbade it. "I would not be so foolish as to sign a contract which would forbid my marrying if I wished," was Negri's cool reply.[68]

Some movie fans were put off by the very idea of Chaplin marrying Negri. During an interview after the failure of his first marriage, Charlie had expressed a wish for a "restful wife." Why then, went the question, would he marry someone as tempestuous and high-spirited as Pola? For Mrs. MLM of Carlisle, Pennsylvania, it was clear that the nefarious foreigner was only using poor Chaplin for her own advantage. "I am not surprised to read of Pola Negri's engagement to Charles.... I bet she will lead him a merry dance.... It is enough to make any right-minded American sit up and rave to see anyone put it over the way 'The Negri' has done."[69]

Act One of this drama ended with Famed Polish painter Tadeusz Styka arriving in Los Angeles for an exhibit of his work. Negri once sat for a painting by him in Paris and agreed to sit for another one now. Both of her portraits were put on display. The press immediately called him Chaplin's "rival" for Negri's affections. Styka returned to Poland after gifting her with the paintings. If he had sought to somehow win her heart during his stay, he must have been cruelly disappointed to hear that Pola presented Chaplin with one of the paintings of her as a gift for his 34th birthday.[70]

Act Two opened with a Los Angeles newspaper article quoted Chaplin declaring that his marriage to Pola would have to wait because he was "too poor" to marry. It was probably a spontaneous jest on his part, but she took it as a thinly veiled comment that she was only marrying him for his money. Furious, she called off the engagement. Their break-up was page one news, with the headline a "POLA NEGRI JILTS CHAPLIN. "I consider

I am too poor to marry Charlie Chaplin," Pola was quoted as saying. "He needs to marry a wealthy woman and he should have no difficulty in finding one. Therefore, I release him from his engagement. I wish him the best of luck and I will always be his devoted friend."[71]

For all of the theatrics, the break-up lasted anywhere from two hours to six hours, depending on the newspaper doing the reporting. According to most reports, Chaplin hurried over to Negri's house to persuade her that he had never said anything about being too poor to marry her. At first she would not even see him, but he gradually wore her down. Later, a relieved and smiling Chaplin went home and Negri told the reporters still present at her home, "I have taken him back and we are quite reconciled and engaged again. He swore to me that he had never said he was too poor to marry me."[72]

Chaplin, with further assistance from his ever-quotable press agent, declared:

> I have always wanted to be married, to have a real home, with children. I have wanted this more than anything in the world. And for years I had hoped that I would meet the right woman—a woman with sympathy, understanding, affection and at the same time possessed of beauty, charm and intelligence.
>
> Until I met Pola, this ideal woman remained a dream. Today she is a reality.
>
> I can understand my love for Pola, for she is everything I have ever dreamed of. But why she would love me is something I will never understand. I lack the physique, the physical strength that a beautiful woman admires. However, perhaps it is best that I do not question the gifts of the Gods.
>
> I will be a difficult husband to live with—for when I am at work I give every ounce of myself to my task. My wife will have to show great understanding—great sympathy. And my wife must trust me—there must be mutual trust, mutual freedom from suspicion, or there can be no happiness. Understanding—that's the great thing in married life. And that is what Pola and I have in common.[73]

Lovelorn hearts fluttered and romantics let out a sigh. All was right in the world again, courtesy of some first-class press agent malarkey.

Meanwhile, the couple had still not set a wedding date. *Variety* wrote:

> Those who are anxious to hear the wedding bells of Charles Spencer Chaplin and his bride to be or not to be, Pola Negri, will have to wait at least six months, according to reports. Miss Negri put to rest all rumors that Charlie and herself were to be married on April Fool's Day. From the outlook the film couple may be engaged for a long, long, time.[74]

But then this, reported by a London Newspaper: "*Neveraire* [sic] shall Charlie Chaplin marry Pola Negri—she is my wife. A divorce? I know nothing of it.... [I]f I find that Charlie Chaplin would marry my wife—ha!... A duel it shall be. The man who takes my wife shall answer to me with my sword."[75]

Those were the words of Count Eugene Dombski, when asked about the engagement between Chaplin and his ex-wife. The idea of Charlie facing a "wild-eyed" Polish count in a duel tickled the fancy of imaginative feature writers. Would Charlie be adept enough with his Tramp's cane to fend off his sword-wielding challenger?[76]

Pola was quoted as denying she was still Dombski's wife, that she had a proper divorce decree and she was "free, free, free" to marry the man of her choice."[77] She defiantly declared she would marry Chaplin in spite of anyone who came between them. Again, this was all a fabrication by the tabloids.

Mildred Harris, Chaplin's ex-wife, got some much-needed press for her own stalled film career by affirming that the engagement was a headline-grabbing stunt, cooked up a press agent in Berlin (with Chaplin's consent) to give Negri a big dose of publicity. She predicted that Charlie and Pola would never actually marry. Pola reputedly replied with a healthy dose of vitriol: "I do not care a snap of my fingers for Miss Harris' opinions, nor for her.... Her opinions are ridiculous—preposterous. My only concern is that she shall not annoy Sharlie. He is very busy and must concentrate upon his pictures unbothered by petty announcements.[78]

Act Three began when, according to Negri, Chaplin became jealous of her male co-stars in *The Cheat*. After he accused her of cheating on him with French co-star Charles De Roche in the presence of two reporters he'd brought along to see her response, Pola decided she'd had enough drama from him and broke off their relationship for good.

Yet it is also possible that the end really came after what was called "The Marina Vega Affair." In April 1923, there was a report of a possible suicide attempt at Chaplin's Beverly Hills home. A young Mexican, Marina Vega, allegedly infatuated with Charlie, broke into his house with the intent of persuading him to marry her. After being twice ejected by Charlie's valet, she turned up a third time and calmly announced she had taken poison. Chaplin had her put in a car and taken to a hospital for examination. No trace of poison was found in her system. It was believed that Vega had simply swallowed some hand lotion. She was committed to a psychiatric ward for further observation.[79]

What went unreported, according to lore, was a physical altercation between Pola and Vega—kicking, scratching and hair-pulling—that ended only after Charlie poured a bucket of cold water over them. Pola became so angry, goes the story, that she literally fainted from rage and then, for a laugh, Charlie pretended to faint and fell to the floor right next to her. Furious, Pola got up and stormed out of the house, telling a startled Chaplin that she didn't want anything more to do with him.

It wasn't until five weeks later that the world found out that Pola and Charlie were finished. She was at a Hollywood nightclub in the company of tennis champion Bill Tilden. Coincidentally, Chaplin was seated nearby with actress Lenore Ulrich. "I cannot possibly marry Charlie," she told a reporter. "He is too temperamental. He dramatizes everything."[80] (It's fair to say this calls to mind something a pot once said to a kettle.) She added, "Mr. Chaplin should never marry—he is lacking in all matrimonial requirements."[81] Pola then said she was glad it was over.

Rumors subsequently arose linking Pola with Tilden, who had just won the California championship. One newspaper even identified him as her new lover.[82] Pola would only say that she admired Tilden very much and, typically, refused to answer any questions about their "relationship." Tilden said there was nothing to the rumors and complimented her: "Miss Negri is very charming and a great artist and it has been a pleasure to meet her."[83] In truth there was nothing romantic between them, but the press needed a culprit for the Chaplin-Negri breakup. Tilden fit the bill.

If her engagement to Chaplin was indeed all for show, it was a grand production worthy of the ticket. It was also the first instance of what would become a running joke over the next few years: Who was Pola Negri engaged to *today* and how long would it be before she moved on to the next engagement?

Years later, when Chaplin was appearing on-screen in *City Lights*, there were rumors that he would fight back against the talkies by creating a new movie production company to continue making silent pictures. According to the rumors, one of the first artists he planned to sign was Pola. The story is highly unlikely.

In face of all of the evidence, why did Chaplin ignore their engagement in his autobiography? Well, Charlie did not consider it gentlemanly behavior to speak ill of his various wives and girlfriends and, like most narcissists, he preferred to talk about himself.

Did Pola really love him? Probably not. After their breakup, she was quoted as saying, "Charlie appealed to my mother complex. And his personality interested me. I study—

I study—and then I study too much!"[84] She later added, "Love inspires me in work or it must go." And, most tellingly: "I am a fatalist. I believe in my star. It is my fate to be unhappy in love."[85]

She had no idea how true that pronouncement would become.

The Spanish Dancer

Famous Players–Lasky
Distributor: Paramount
Released October 7, 1923

STATUS: The original version of this picture no longer exists. A five-reel public domain version, about half of the length of the original, can be purchased on DVD. As of 2011, a Dutch archive had assembled a nine-reel version using discovered outtakes and alternate shots, but it is not currently available on DVD.

CREDITS: *Producer-Director:* Herbert Brenon. *Adaptation:* June Mathis, Beulah Marie Dix. *Photographer:* James Wong Howe.

CAST: Pola Negri (*Maritana, a Gypsy Dancer*), Antonio Moreno (*Don Cesar de Bazan*), Wallace Beery (*King Philip IV*), Kathlyn Williams (*Queen Isabel of Bourbon*), Gareth Hughes (*Lazarillo, a Prisoner*), Adolphe Menjou (*Don Sollustre, a Courtier*), Edward Kipling (*Marquis de Rotundo*), Dawn O'Day [Anne Shirley] (*Don Balthazar Carlos*), Charles A. Stevenson (*Cardinal's Ambassador*), Robert Agnew (*Juan, a Thief*).

STORY

Unable to pay his creditors, Spanish nobleman Don Cesar recklessly throws a farewell party at his castle before he loses all his possessions. He hires the renowned troupe of Maritana and her gypsy dancers as the entertainment. During the party, Maritana convinces him to let her tell him his fortune in the tarot cards. She predicts that he will find poverty, yet also love—and death. Shaken, Maritana keeps the last prediction to herself.

Reduced to poverty, Don Cesar runs again into Maritana and her troupe on the streets and rescues her and a young boy from an attacker, wounding the attacker in a fencing duel. Arrested by the king's guards for violating a royal proclamation against dueling, he is sentenced to death. Maritana, in love with him, has an admirer in Queen Isabella, so she goes to the palace to beg her to spare Don Cesar's life. The kind-hearted queen intercedes with King Philip and obtains his assurance of a pardon for the former nobleman.

Don Sollutstre, the king's scheming advisor, plots against the French-born queen. When the king sets his lustful sights on Maritana, Don Sullutstre convinces the monarch that if the gypsy girl married a nobleman, an affair between them would be more acceptable to the royal court. The king, determined to have Maritana for a mistress, agrees to the plan. Sollustre goes to the imprisoned Don Cesar and tells him that the young boy he saved will be spared his ears if Don Cesar agrees to a marriage of convenience before his death. Maritana is told that if she marries a masked nobleman, Don Cesar will be spared. That night, Don Cesar and Maritana are unknowingly married to each other.

Maritana is whisked away to the king's hunting lodge to be seduced. Don Cesar escapes from the prison firing squad with the help of the boy and goes off in search of his bride. Arriving at the lodge in time to save her honor, he challenges the startled king to a duel to the death—but jealous Queen Isabella, having been told by Don Sollustre of her husband's infidelity, arrives and instead finds her husband giving his blessing to Maritana and Don Cesar's union. The couple kisses.

Reviews

"Pola Negri comes back to her own in this picture," said *Photoplay*. "She is again La Negri of *Passion*. She has shed the veneer of sophistication and has reverted to the primitive woman type...."[86] The *New York Times* reviewer, on the other hand, thought her performance "appears to suffer from an overdose of direction."[87]

The *New York Sun* wrote, "Pola is more lustrous than ever as the Gypsy Dancer," and the *New York Tribune* said the picture offered "the old, flaming, glorious, gorgeous Pola Negri, a gypsy girl almost as untamed as Carmen." *The Washington Times* said, "Restraint has apparently been removed from La Negri's method of expression—with excellent results for all concerned."[88]

Screenland Magazine gave the picture a passing grade. "True, the Negri displays a little more vitality than in either of her previous American efforts. But her abandon is calculated and the old spark isn't there."[89] The *New York Post* disliked *The Spanish Dancer*, noting that bringing Negri to America "has meant artistic death."[90]

The most interesting observations came from disgruntled exhibitors. The manager of the KP Theatre in Pittsfield, Illinois, wrote in *The Exhibitor's Herald*: "All right, Pola, as far as patrons of this theater are concerned, you can pack up your traveling bag and head back to the 'Fatherland.' Failed to please."[91] Jack Cairns, manager of the Brooklyn Theatre in Detroit, Michigan, told the *Herald*, "I always lose plenty when I play this lady. I also ran *The Cheat* and took a nice flop again. I am off of costume plays."[92]

Negri's third picture was originally to be a version of the hit play *Declasse,* but the underwhelming reception to her first two films persuaded the studio to accede to Negri's demands to do a big romantic costume drama. Ironically, *The Spanish Dancer* was originally meant as a picture for Rudolph Valentino under the title of *The Spanish Cavalier* before he walked out on his contract with Famous Players–Lasky, complaining that the studio didn't understand his need for more artistically satisfying projects. The script was rewritten as a starring vehicle for her. She begged the studio to borrow Ernst Lubitsch, who seemed to be drifting aimlessly under contract to Warner Brothers, to direct her. But before Negri could retain Lubitsch's services, Mary Pickford signed him to direct her in a version of the same story: *Rosita* (1923), released by United Artists. The Pickford picture was more critically praised than *The Spanish Dancer,* though it was not as financially successful.

Spanish Dancer director Herbert Brenon said of his star, "Pola is not easy to direct.... She belongs to the type that allows situations to take complete control of the emotions.... If the camera is started at the moment of her complete surrender to the tide she gives what no other screen actress has ever done before."[93]

Negri suffered two black eyes when, during a mob scene, co-star Antonio Moreno accidentally hit her in the face with a carelessly thrown boot.[94] It left a small permanent scar over her right brow. She also incurred a painful bout of "Klieg eyes," suffering from burned retinas due to the bright carbon-powered lights used in filming pictures during the silent era. According to a newspaper article, Negri worked on 39 scenes in one day—12 was the norm—and "before the last scene was completed she was obliged to bury her head in her arms and rush blindly from the set."[95]

The Spanish Dancer was a big hit according to *Memoirs*. Yet from what remains of it in the public domain print, it seems to have been a vast costume spectacle that overwhelms its by-the-numbers love story. The edited print—almost half the original movie is missing—deletes most of Negri's scenes. Also, what were probably once elaborate dance numbers are reduced to a mere glimpse. In the early sequences in which she plays the "untamed" gypsy girl, her performance is all fire and zest, yet when she is all made-up and dressed to the nines in the wedding scene she looks entirely artificial and miscast. Again the studio had her playing the "good girl," the inoffensive and self-sacrificial heroine no one would find even the least bit controversial. What saves her portrayal from being completely bland and mediocre is the spirit she radiates and the sincerity of her passion in the romantic moments. Nevertheless, the picture comes across as something of a boring affair.

Portrait for *The Spanish Dancer*, Paramount, 1923. Directed by Herbert Brenon.

Despite the fact that her first three pictures had been awkward affairs, Negri still retained her ardent fans. Frances J. Barclay of New York City wrote to *Screenland* to say:

> It has become the habit of some of the movie scribes to condemn Pola Negri. She is an artiste. Polish or not, temperamental or not, she has *genius*. And genius knows neither nationality nor disposition. Who does not remember when *Passion* was first shown on our American screens? Never before had such warmth, such roguery; such stark human nature, both good and evil, been portrayed on the screen. Even in her other foreign-made pictures (the ones that were widely shown to the American picture-going public) she was the portrayer of sheer personality.
>
> And now, while *Bella Donna* and *The Cheat* were not the complete frosts some people have labeled them, still, they did not achieve the success expected. Why? Because of censorship. One could almost hear the director coaching this silver sheet flame, dampening her ardor, holding her back, checking her, and all for fear that some moron in Podunk, who has had something to do with the framing and enforcement of the censorship laws in his particular community, might take offense and condemn an expensive, beautiful picture.[96]

As far as the studio was concerned, Negri was "back" where she was supposed to be. Jesse Lasky announced that all future studio productions would center around her, Gloria Swanson and Tom Meighan, while other contract players would appear without major billing in "all-star" productions—in effect separating "A" players from "B" players.[97] In reality, this was the studio's attempt to curtail spiraling production costs by reducing player salaries. It also meant the end of expensive "super spectaculars" like *The Spanish Dancer*.

Shadows of Paris

Distributor: Paramount
Released February 17, 1924
Alternate Titles: Mon Homme, My Man

STATUS: About 20 seconds of this picture survives in the 1936 Paramount compilation film *Fashions of Love*.
CREDITS: *Director:* Herbert Brenon. *Scenario:* Fred Jackson. *Story "Mon Homme":* Picard and Carco.
CAST: Pola Negri (*Claire, Queen of the Apaches*), Charles De Roche (*Fernand, an Apache*), Huntley Gordon (*Raoul, Minister of the Interior*), Adolphe Menjou (*Georges de Croy*), Gareth Hughes (*Emile Boule*), Vera Reynolds (*Liane*), Rose Dione (*Madame Boule, a Café Owner*), Rosita Marstini (*Madame Vali, a Poetess*), Edward Kimpling (*Pierre, a Roué*), Maurice Cannon (*Robert, a Taxi Driver*), Frank Nelson (*Le Bossu, the Hunchback*), George O'Brien (*Louis*).

STORY

Claire, formerly the Apache Queen of the Paris criminal underground, has infiltrated French high society masquerading as a grieving Polish widow. Believing that her Apache lover Fernand was killed in the war, she meets Police Chief Raoul de Gramoni. Enchanted by Claire, he asks her to marry him. She agrees, although her only reason is to use him for information that will benefit her band of thieves. De Croy, Gramoni's secretary, learns about Claire's secret criminal identity and threatens to expose her unless she yields to him. Fearful, she retreats to the underworld and finds Fernand alive. Her joy is short-lived when Fernand reveals himself to be in De Croy's service and tries to force her to surrender a diamond necklace given to her by De Gramoni. De Croy double-crosses Fernand and kills him in her boudoir. When confronted, Claire tells her lover the truth about her criminal past and he forgives her for her deceit.

REVIEWS

"*The Shadows of Paris* gives Pola Negri a far better opportunity to display her histrionic talent than any of her other productions made in Hollywood," wrote the *New York Times* reviewer. "She is … really quite effective both as a brazen girl in an Apache den and as the mistress of an Avenue Marigny mansion."[98] The *Exhibitor's Trade Review* commented:

> Paramount has a sure box office winner in this—the best made American film in which Pola Negri has appeared. That widely advertised and deservedly popular star is seen to great advantage in a role which suits her exotic, magnetic personality in every detail and will appeal tremendously to the legion of Negri admirers.
> Pola Negri acts with the tempestuous fire and polished art which distinguished her work in *Passion*.… [W]hether clad in the rough garments of an Apache or the brilliant trappings of a society leader, she is equally impressive and alluring.[99]

Negri and unidentified actor in a scene from *Shadows of Paris*, Paramount, 1924. Directed by Herbert Brenon.

Pola finally had a big hit on her hands. The *Detroit News* said, "A good many of those admirers of Pola Negri who were alienated by *Bella Donna* and *The Cheat* may be won back by the fiery performance of the European star in *Shadows of Paris*." The *Film Daily* said the picture "puts Pola Negri back in one of those 'Tiger Woman' roles that she does so well."[100] The *Chicago Post* said, "Pola Negri will fascinate you as she never has before.... She is in a class by herself." But the *Los Angeles Times* called *Shadows of Paris*, "the worst picture in which Miss Negri has ever appeared.[101]

This was a picture and role more suited to her talents. She seemed to have her regained her old confidence after the debacle of her first two pictures. A fiery and swaggering Pola Negri was a good thing and it appeared that she was learning to trust others and enjoy herself on the set. One newspaper piece noted, "[F]or the first time since her arrival in Hollywood she laughed spontaneously and moved with easy camaraderie among her associates during the filming."[102]

This picture, a Michael Arlen–scripted picture and another massive costume spectacle, *Madame Sans Gene*, were meant to fulfill her three-year Famous Players contract. Britisher Arlen was a hot writer with a hit Broadway play called *The Green Hat*. Imported to Hollywood, he received $40,000 from Famous Players–Lasky to write an original screen story for her. It was announced in the trades as *Crossroads of the World*.

Pola, however, never made the Arlen picture. *Madame Sans Gene* was supposed to be shot in Paris, but the star of that picture was Gloria Swanson when it was released in 1925. Curiously, just as Mary Pickford had rained on Pola's parade by releasing *Rosita* before *The Spanish Dancer*, Gloria made a very similar picture to *Shadows of Paris* titled *The Humming Bird* and the studio released it a month ahead of *Shadows*. The fact that Gloria's picture made more than Pola's further fed "the rivalry" between them.

According to the press, Negri appeared to have learned something from the bad publicity surrounding her reported "temper tantrums" on her first two movie sets. *Motion Picture Classic* reminded readers she'd been rather off-putting when she had first come to America. Things had changed. Pola "had torn all of the 'Ritz' out of her soul" and removed the wall around her set. According to the magazine, she was now acting like "a regular fellow" and working out in the open "with the rest of us folks like a nice girl."[103]

There again is that condescending attitude, the suggestion that Pola thought she was better than the rest of us and needed to be taken down a peg or two. Once she had eaten crow, she'd be just another regular person, another nice girl. Yet if anyone in the press still believed that Negri was a "regular fellow," they were sadly mistaken. She was too strong a personality to ever be conventional and there was still a lot of fire inside her. In one interview, she made clear her unhappiness with the way that the studio and exhibitors had tried to change her screen persona in her first two pictures. They wanted her to be beautiful and sympathetic? She would not be. She was not going to be a slave on the auction block for "stupid little exhibitors." If they would not let her tell "real stories" or be a "real person" on the screen, she would leave moving pictures and return to the stage.[104]

Shadows of Paris also had to compete with the belated American release of *Die Flamme,* her last German production with Ernst Lubitsch, re-titled *Montmartre* and also released by Paramount. *Variety* called *Montmartre* "weak," but praised Negri's performance as "convincing proof she belongs in the very top rank of our screen emotionalists."

The *St. Louis Star* stated, "this is by no means Pola Negri's best picture."[105] The *Exhibitor's Trade Review* predicted that Negri fans would go away disappointed, calling *Montmartre* "very poor entertainment. Made abroad, and to all appearances, many moons ago, it ranks easily as one of the worst specimens of foreign output.... Even Pola Negri's talents are unequal to the task of 'putting the picture over' but she still registers as the great artist she has ever been."[106]

Movie magazines like *Photoplay* continued to cover her prominently, calling her a prime example of screen attraction and calling her "a woman of elemental naturalness.... She is a blend of sophistication and utter *naiveté*. Her emotional naturalness bursts through all control. She is incapable of sustained pose."[107]

For some, however, she had been over-exposed. In the very same *Photoplay,* a letter from Fern Blair of Elvin, Missouri, stated that while she liked Negri, she felt the magazine had printed far too many photographs of her. *Pictures and the Picture-goer* wondered if her "notoriety" had not robbed her of her dramatic powers.[108]

During this time, Negri submitted her papers for American citizenship. According to reports, her permanent residence in this country would entitle her to become a naturalized citizen by 1927.[109]

Men

Distributor: Paramount
Released: May 4, 1924

Status: Lost
Credits: *Director-Writer:* Dimitri Buchowetzki. *Adaptation:* Paul Bern. *Photographer:* Alvin Wyckoff.
Cast: Pola Negri (*Cleo*), Robert Frazer (*Georges Kleber*), Robert Edeson (*Henri Duval*), Joseph Swickard (*Cleo's Father*), Monte Collins (*Francois*), Gino Corrado (*The Stranger*), Edgar Norton (*The Baron*).

Story

Cleo, a lonely café waitress, is lured from Marseilles to Paris by a procurer with promises of stage stardom. She is instead seduced and abandoned by a lascivious baron. While grieving over her disgrace, she is approached by George Kleber, whom she rejects despite his gentlemanly willingness to help her. Years pass and Cleo is now a famous dancer who fascinates banker Duval, but she rejects his love like she has with all men. During an elaborate costume party George again appears. Cleo cruelly toys with him and laughs in disdain when he tells of his passion for her. Determined to prove his loyalty despite her rejection, he recklessly steals money from Duval's bank where he is employed and gives it to her. Threatened with arrest, George is saved when Cleo, who now loves him for the honesty of his feelings for her, offers herself to Duval in payment of his debt. Duval turns her down, but forgives the crime and brings the lovers together.[110]

Reviews

The Exhibitor's Trade Review said the picture "affords Pola Negri manifold chances to display her emotional ability in tempestuous scenes of passion, of which that noted star takes full advantage."[111] *Variety* called it "a picture the fans are going to flock to and like immensely."[112] The *New York Times* reviewer described Negri's acting as "exhilarating"[113] while the *Montreal Gazette* said the picture "gives Miss Negri full opportunity for exercising those gifts of twin-six emotionalism and 18,000-volt love for which she is justly famous."[114]

A reader complained to *Photoplay* that the picture was "really the worst I have seen in a long time. The story is a typical dime novel, and Negri's acting was of the old-time stock company soubrette type."[115]

This picture's director Dimitri Buchowetzki had previously directed her in *Sappho* a.k.a. *Mad Love* at Ufa. He wrote *Men* with her in mind and waited four years to work with her again rather than make the production with any other star.[116] A *Motion Picture Magazine* article declared that the Russian knew how to handle the star. He would discuss the role with her until he saw in her eyes that her interest had been won. "In other words, Pola's genius was throwing out sparks. If possible, he sent her out in front of the camera at that instant; for that instant was the divine moment.... Handled in that way, there is no finer actress than Pola Negri—living or dead."[117]

In her article "The New Pola," writer Eunice Marshall stated that Pola's trust in her director made her "temperament-free." "Buchowetzki is no Pollyanna, nor does he wish

Pola to be one. Her point gained, her attitude towards her fellow workers changed. She no longer treated them like something she slipped in when the door was left open. She is gracious ... and gives praises where it is deserved."[118]

While some segments of both the public and press seemed to now like her because she "had seen the light," there were many who never would, based on the exaggerations written about her.

Publicity for the picture cited her utmost dedication to her craft, relating a story how she arrived on the set of *Men* one morning only to find that filming had been called off for the day (the director was at home, ill). She retreated to her dressing room and did not emerge again until five p.m. When asked what she had been doing in there all day, she replied that she had been practicing her expressions in a mirror.[119]

Her co-star in *Men*, Robert Frazer, told *Photoplay* he had never worked before with an actress of such "sublime dramatic talent."[120] "She ignores all stage technique, all camera angles. She is just a mighty, vital rush of human power."[121]

Actress Alice Terry put the lie to all the tales of temperament being told about her: "She is charming—but after all the wild things you heard about her temperament you expect her to do a somersault or something. Of course she doesn't so naturally you're a little disappointed."[122] In the same issue of *Photoplay*, there was a vote of confidence for her from a reader who praised Pola for putting "her whole heart and soul into playing" and concluded, "[T]here can be no argument as to her supremacy among movie stars."

Still, what was Pola without a little display of that famous temperament? *Motion Picture Magazine* obliged, quoting her renewed threat to quit pictures for the stage if she was forced to continue to make what she called "pussy-cat stories."[123]

Variety noted that Negri and Famous Players had expressed a mutual dissatisfaction with her output and concluded that the problem was not poor and implausible scripts and situations, but "too much *continentalism*."[124] In other words, American moviegoers were simply too unsophisticated to grasp her European style, so her popularity would be better served by simpler stories. This false conclusion overlooked the real problem: An "unadulterated" Pola Negri was too passionate in person, too intense in her acting, and too challenging for the average American moviegoer. She needed to be "dumbed-down" to succeed.

The studio's cure for continentalism was to put an American in charge of her productions. Director Robert Cruze—who had allegedly poured ice water over Negri's head on the set of *Hollywood*—was picked to oversee her pictures. It was announced he would also direct her next film, *A Woman Scorned*.[125] Nothing, however, came of this misconceived arrangement and the studio never really found a way to improve her box office standing. As much as Famous Players–Lasky might wish it, she was never going to be a "popular" star.

According to the rumor mill, Negri would become the bride of handsome actor Rod La Rocque. Gossips noted that they had been seen together in public on a regular basis. Pola steadfastly denied the rumor and said that she and La Rocque "were simply victims of circumstance in having attended a series of Hollywood parties to which each had been invited."[126] *Variety* reported, "[T]his may or may not mean anything, but Pola Negri and Rod La Rocque are vacationing at Del Monte Beach with him calling her 'Dear' and she cross-firing with 'Rudy.'[127] Pola also gave a dinner at the resort in La Rocque's honor Sunday night."[128]

6. *Pola Negri in Paramount Pictures* 79

Pola in costume for *Men*, Paramount, 1924. Directed by Dimitri Buchowetzki.

Lily of the Dust

Distributor: Paramount
Released August 24, 1924
Alternate Titles: *Compromised*; *The Passionate Journey*

STATUS: Lost.
CREDITS: *Director*: Dimitri Buchowetzki. *Scenario*: Paul Bern. *Photographer*: Alvin Wyckoff.
CAST: Pola Negri (*Lily Czepaneki*), Ben Lyon (*Richard von Prell*), Noah Beery (*Colonel von Mertzbach*), Raymond Griffith (*Karl Dehnecke*), Jeanette Daudet (*Julia*), William J. Kelly (*Walter von Prell*).

STORY

Poor but honest Lily works as a clerk in a bookstore near a German military garrison. One day she meets Von Prell, a young officer, and they fall in love. Von Prell's brutal commanding officer, Mertzbach, steals her away to become his wife. Despite her abusive marriage, Lily continues to see Von Prell, who risks his military career to be with her. Discovering her betrayal, Mertzbach wounds Von Prell in a duel and then casts her out into the streets. Destitute, Lily accepts the kindness of Dehnecke, an industrialist, and becomes his mistress. Von Prell recovers from his injuries and declares his love for her, but his uncle refuses to bless their relationship. Rejected again, Lily decides to remain with Dehnecke.

REVIEWS

Variety didn't think that the picture or Pola's performance were very good.[129] The *New York Times*, however, called *Lily of the Dust* her best American picture to date, stating she would win admirers with her "sincere performance."[130] *The Exhibitor's Trade Review* sounded a note of caution regarding the picture's theme:

> This combination of a good-looking title and popular star should draw the crowds wherever *Lilly of the Dust* is shown. It gives Pola Negri ample opportunity to shine in tempestuous passion scenes where the emotional ability of the Polish actress is demonstrated to the utmost. It is however, a picture essentially suited to sophisticated audiences only. The big theaters should find it a paying attraction, but in houses catering chiefly to the family trade, there is every reason for believing that many patrons will resent its frank parade of immorality. For the story merely deals with love affairs of a woman of easy virtue, false to her marriage vows, abandoned by her husband, becoming the mistress of another man, welcoming back her first lover; and when fate separates her from the latter, turning for consolation to the chap with whom she lived after hubby cast her aside.[131]

Translation: Lily is a whore. Small-town America won't go for it.

Critical reaction to the picture was mixed. The *Boston Globe* called Negri's acting "by turns, tender, wistful and cyclonic,"[132] while The *New York Daily Mirror* stated, "She is the same sparkling, flashing actress that took this country by storm."[133] The *Cleveland Press* observed, "The problem is that Pola is too sophisticated to play the naively helpless victim of circumstances in *Lily of the Dust*,"[134] and the *New York World* opined, "[S]he is far more attractive and important than the things she is trying to express in pictures. She needs a good play and the need is quite urgent."[135]

Her fans felt the same way. "Pola Negri is always wonderful," one fan wrote to *Pictures and the Picture-goer*:

Miss Negri and Ben Lyon in *Lily of the Dust*, Paramount, 1924. Directed by Dimitri Buchowetzki.

In my opinion she is the only one to portray life as it is. To make an audience forget the actress and remember only the character she is portraying. I can see a soul there that a director fails to bring to light. The result is a sadly disconnected offering. I refer to *Lily of the Dust*.... The themes selected for her are not appropriate, and she is not placed in the correct moods and situations. I wonder whether she will ever have a director who has as much ability to direct as she has to perform. If Pola Negri ever does, we will have perfection in motion picture entertainment.

Lily of the Dust marked Buchowetzki's second American picture with Negri. At five reels, it was also her shortest picture to date—and what ever happened to all of the controversy about "unhappy endings"? This film's modest success established the plot template for most of Negri's future pictures: Her character finds a doomed love; denied happiness by fate, she takes up with a man who desires her only as a possession; and then she is rescued or redeemed by an unexpected opportunity. Eerily, this plot would mirror her real-life romances. Yet in film after film it was a device used in a mechanical fashion, undercutting her dramatic ability and ultimately draining the public's good will towards her acting.

Negri's co-star, actor Ben Lyon, wrote about her in a fanciful article, "Vampires, I Have Known," for the February 1925 *Photoplay*. He called her the kind of woman with whom you would want to indulge in a "purely pagan, Continental romance." Then, years, later when you have married some nice girl, you would think of her fondly and sigh deeply—remembering Pola with a red rose behind her ear.

Negri, increasingly frustrated with American film production methods, spoke out about it. She told writer Myrtle Gebhardt she thought she had been brought to America as an actress, but discovered she was brought "as a personality for exploitation, to be remade by the American pattern." She complained of being held back by American producers afraid of innovation and realism. The unrealistic characters and situations in her pictures pained her. She said, "Only when you portray true impulses, what comes from the heart, can you impart realism to any work." The studio's attempts to standardize her had "crushed her," yet she was the one being blamed for the artificiality of her pictures.[136]

Gebhardt acknowledged that because of Pola's versatility and temperament, she could not be standardized to a one-size-fits-all actress. Her heroines were primitive and physical—unreceptive to audiences "cramped by inhibitions." Gebhardt also wrote that at work, when Pola was interested, she was ready and eager with her "deep, harsh voice exclaiming, her eyes flashing, pulsed with something far more real and brutal than I ever felt before on a movie set." She had also seen Pola, when she wasn't in the mood, "sit inched in a chair, smoking furiously, sulking."[137]

Despite repeated denials, rumors of a possible wedding linked Pola to Rod La Rocque, particularly when it was announced that they would be working together in her next picture, *Forbidden Paradise*.

Forbidden Paradise

Distributor: Paramount
Released November 16, 1924
Alternate Titles: The Czarina; The Wages of Virtue

STATUS: A complete copy of this picture exists in two American film archives. A fuzzy and incomplete copy with Czech subtitles and no music is on the Internet.
CREDITS: *Director:* Ernst Lubitsch. *Screenplay:* Agnes Christine Johnson, Hans Kraly. *Photographer:* Charles J. Van Enger.
CAST: Pola Negri (*The Czarina*), Rod La Rocque (*Alexei*), Adolph Menjou (*Chancellor*), Pauline Starke (*Anna*), Fred Malatesta (*French Ambassador*), Nick de Ruiz (*General*), Madame Daumery (*Lady-in-waiting*), Clark Gable.

STORY

The imperious Catherine rules a small European kingdom by whim. Lonely for romance, she takes as a lover any man, usually one in uniform, who catches her eye.

Miss Negri and Rod La Rocque in a scene from *Forbidden Paradise*, Paramount, 1924. Directed by Ernst Lubitsch.

Alexei, a young officer, wins Catherine's favor when he foils a plan by revolutionary conspirators to topple her from the throne. He is loved by Anna, the queen's faithful lady-in-waiting, but he readily deserts her for Catherine's affections. When Alexei discovers that he is only the latest in a long line of lovers, he turns against her and joins the revolutionaries within the army. The attempted revolution fails and Alexei is arrested for treason. Catherine shows her kindness and sets him free to be with a forgiving Anna. In the meantime, she embarks on an affair with the handsome new French ambassador.

REVIEWS

The reviews were the best of Negri's American film career. *The Exhibitor's Trade Review* said, "Pola actually is the Czarina—no one will deny it."[138] "No one who enjoys Pola Negri's acting should miss her in the part of the great Catherine," wrote the *New York Bulletin*. "She is delightful, subtle, humorous and mistress of every situation."[139] *Photoplay* was enchanted by Pola's czarina, calling her both good and bad, and stating that her "wickedness is done gorgeously and regally. And her goodly actions are done in humanly and womanly fashion. The combination cloaks her with a rare quality of diplomacy that leaves her always in command of any situation that arises and that trait denotes genius."[140]

Here is the long overdue reunion between Negri and Ernst Lubitsch, resulting in her best American picture. This is how she should have been presented by Famous Players–Lasky from the very beginning: sympathetic and sexy, fiery yet lovable. The leading role was custom-made by Lubitsch for Negri's talents. Catherine is beautiful, charming, funny, devious, spoiled rotten, passionate, petulant and positively regal. Pola plays her to perfection. There isn't a false note in her performance and for once she was given a role that matched her real personality.

Adolphe Menjou, however, playing her devoted chancellor, nearly steals the picture; he is a great deadpan comic foil to her impetuousness. On the strength of this performance, Menjou rose to leading man status at Famous Players. Yet all eyes will and should be on Pola Negri, who on this role alone merits inclusion in the Silent Film Star Hall of Fame. It's a shame that she didn't get to play more roles like this one while at Famous Players–Lasky and it proves that with a great director and a script that played directly to her strengths, she was the greatest actress in silent pictures. If you ever get the opportunity to see this picture, do so.

There is a sequence in the first reel of the picture where the czarina has her hair cut. Pola wore a wig for the sequence. Just as well, since a mishap with a permanent wave machine ruined her hair and forced her to cut it "short as a boy's," according to one press account. The same account also alleged that her natural hair color was brown and that she had been dyeing it black for years.[141]

During negotiations on her new contract, Negri threatened to quit Famous Players unless she was given the right to choose her directors. The studio asked her why she was so concerned about directors as long as her pictures were making money. Negri astutely answered that she couldn't keep making money if she was in bad pictures. The studio got the point and she finally got Ernst Lubitsch.[142]

Negri also reportedly demanded that Lubitsch direct her in one picture a year. She didn't win on that point, however; *Forbidden Paradise* would be their last collaboration. Pola would never get such inspired direction again.

Yet there was some consolation for her in the short run. *The Reel Journal* (January,

24, 1925) reported that Negri had finished third behind Harold Lloyd and Gloria Swanson in a poll of the most popular screen stars. Also during this time, she moved out of her rented Hollywood house and purchased a Beverly Hills mansion that had belonged to actress Priscilla Dean for $100,000.[143] According to Negri, it had

> tennis courts and a swimming pool ... rose gardens and Italian gardens and vegetable gardens; a four-car garage and a patio with a magnificent fountain; there was even a private projection room downstairs. To run the place efficiently, it took a staff of six.... My enormous sunken black marble tub resembled nothing so much as a Cecil B. DeMille set.

One of the first purchases for her house, according to *Motion Picture Magazine*: 2,000 books for her library. Reading, she said, suited her better than pursuing pointless romances.[144]

A letter by "Sharpshooter" from *Pictures and the Picture-Goer,* January 1925:

> There are all sorts and sizes of smiles to be seen in Filmland. Some positively give you the creeps; some remind you of the dental chair; some make you feel thoroughly pleased with yourself and everyone else.
> But there's only one like Pola Negri's—her own!

East of Suez

Distributor: Paramount
Released January 12, 1925

STATUS: Lost.
CREDITS: *Director:* Raoul Walsh. *Scenario:* Sada Cowan. *Story:* W. Somerset Maugham.
CAST: Pola Negri (*Daisy Forbes*), Edmund Lowe (*George Tevis*), Rockliffe Fellows (*Harry Anderson*), Noah Beery (*British Consul*), Kamiyama Sojin (*Lee Tai*), Mrs. Wong Wing (*Amah*), Florence Regnary (*Sylvia Knox*), Charles Requa (*Harold Knox*), E.H. Calvert (*Sidney Forbes*).

STORY

Daisy Forbes, returning to China to visit her father, discovers he has died. She becomes a social outcast among the local British society after it is revealed that the Chinese nurse who raised her is actually her mother. Daisy falls in love with George Tevis, and then is devastated when George, persuaded by his uncle, the British counsel, parts ways with her to protect his promising diplomatic career from scandal. A Mandarin white slaver, Lee Tai, kidnaps Daisy and enslaves her through drugs and hypnotism. She is rescued from a life of prostitution by roguish Harry Anderson, who marries her in the mistaken belief that she comes from a wealthy family. On learning she is a penniless half-caste, he treats her brutally. Meanwhile, George, regretting his uncle's advice to leave her, locates her and discovers that she is a married woman. Daisy is still in love with him, and when Harry finds out, he threatens to kill her true love. Yet before he can harm George, he drinks wine poisoned by Lee Tai and dies. Tevis takes Daisy back to England to be his wife and Lee Tai is executed for his crimes under Chinese law.

REVIEWS

Variety said, "There is glamor and lure about the title that will appeal and the fact that it has almost an all-star cast should prove of value to the box office. Miss Negri as

Pola Negri as Daisy Forbes in *East of Suez*, Paramount, 1925. Directed by Raoul Walsh.

Daisy Forbes ... proves that she can troupe with a repression and still get over all the fire of dramatic intensity."[145]

The *New York Times* called her performance "interesting."[146] *Motion Picture Magazine* called it "something of a come-down" and the *Exhibitor's Trade Review* lamented, "It seems too bad that this bright particular star should be burdened with such a weak and tedious story."[147] The *Brooklyn Daily Eagle* complained Pola changed outfits too often: "Why did they tell us we were going to see the movie version of *East of Suez* and then give us a fashion show[?]"[148]

During her tenure with Famous Players–Lasky, Negri portrayed Spaniards, a Frenchwoman, Americans, a South American, Austrians, Russians and Poles. This was her only attempt at playing an Asian and a half-caste at that. Mary Pickford also tried to pull it off during her time at Famous Players and couldn't do it either. Publicity photos of Pola in *East of Suez* reveal a very uneven makeup job. In some photos she looks passably Asian, in others entirely Caucasian, and in some she looks God-only-knows-what.

Variety's review entirely ignores the picture's subtext of racism. Daisy is ostracized by her fellow Englishmen as an inferior and the hero's uncle considers such a "half-breed" as unsuitable marriage material. Love wins out in the end, but there was a serious message in the original Somerset Maugham story that was lost in its translation to the screen.

Some of the picture's fluff publicity concentrated on Negri's wardrobe and hair: "Pola's new headdress is Chinese, a style in which the hair is fashioned and then drawn tight so that it seems carved in ebony.... Pola's blue-black dresses lend themselves to the smooth perfection of the Oriental style."[149]

The Charmer

Distributor: Paramount
Released April 20, 1925

STATUS: Lost.
CREDITS: *Director:* Sidney Olcott. *Scenario:* Sada Cowan. *Photographer:* James Wong Howe.
CAST: Pola Negri (*Mariposa*), Wallace McDonald (*Ralph Bayne*), Robert Frazer (*Dan Murray*), Trixie Friganza (*Mama*), Cesare Gravina (*Senor Sproutt*), Gertrude Astor (*Bertha Sedgwick*), Edward Davis (*Mr. Sedgwick*), Mathilda Brundage (*Mrs. Bayne*).

STORY

Mariposa, a beautiful flamenco dancer, is discovered performing in a cheap Seville café and is taken to New York by Señor Sproutt, a prominent theatrical producer. Billed as "The Charmer," she becomes a much sought-after stage star in café society. Two of

Negri and Robert Frazer in *The Charmer*, Paramount, 1925. Directed by Sidney Olcott.

her most ardent admirers are millionaire playboy Ralph Bayne and his handsome chauffeur Dan Murray. Mrs. Sedgwick, hopelessly smitten with Bayne and jealous of his interest in Mariposa, invites her and her mother to a weekend party at her estate, intending to humiliate the beautiful dancer. Despite her efforts, Bayne, determined to make Mariposa his mistress, persuades her to accompany back to his room for dinner. Mrs. Sedgwick also goes to Bayne's hotel suite, closely followed by her suspicious husband. The gracious Mariposa selflessly saves the society woman's reputation from scandal and divorce at the cost of her own good name. Murray, disgusted with his employer's shameful treatment of her, attempts to force Bayne to marry her at gunpoint to restore her honor, but Mariposa will not to be told what to do. She chooses Murray instead to be her husband.

REVIEWS

According to the *New York Times*, "[T]he idea of appearing as a Spaniard evidently appealed to Miss Negri, and there is no doubt that the costumes she wears in this production, together with a touch of freakishness in the dressing of her hair, are suited to her type."[150] *Variety* advised: "Although this picture is off Negri's hunting ground, in so much as she does no vamping or sophisticated female stuff here, it demonstrates a versatility which extends to the playing of sweeter and more sympathetic roles.... *The Charmer* is excellent first-run material, will fit any program and give good entertainment. Just because it has Negri in a different sort of a role—don't get frightened. Apparently the change is well advised."[151]

"Pola renders an excellent characterization of the Spanish dancing girl. She actually lives the part and is thoroughly at home in it," reported *The Exhibitor's Trade Review*.[152] *Photoplay* said, "Pola Negri gamely tackles a poor story and plays it as gallantly as though it were a masterpiece."[153] *Motion Picture Magazine* concluded, "Pola Negri is still in need of a story that can do justice to her emotional whims and fancies."

This is one film this author wishes were still possible to see. Pola looks fantastically lovely here as a Spaniard and it is proof of the natural beauty she could be beyond all the fancy clothes and affectations. A dramatic comedy should have been right up her alley, allowing her the opportunity to be both smart and sexy. Unfortunately, even the synopsis betrays an unfortunate tendency towards forced situations. It's a "standard" story and just about any actress could have been shoehorned into the leading role. *The Charmer*, with a little more imagination and less formula in its scenario, could have been a big hit for her. After all of the good will earned via her performance in *Forbidden Paradise*, it is disappointing to read about the continuing mediocrity of her film vehicles. She needed far stronger material and a gifted director to inspire her.

After completing *The Charmer*, Negri decided to go home to see her mother for the first time since leaving Germany in 1922. While waiting in New York for the departure of her ship, *The Leviathan*, she told a *New York Times* interviewer that she was headed to Europe in search of good stories to film. She planned to visit Paris and Berlin and speak with Max Reinhardt about acquiring the movie rights to one of his recent plays. She added that she hoped to visit New York more often in the future, particularly for the theater and opera. When asked the inevitable question about her aborted engagement to Chaplin, she would only say, "[P]rofessional people should not marry" and "[J]ealousness [*sic*] and ego ... make happiness impossible."[154]

The very charming Miss Negri, c. 1925.

There was also news of another alleged engagement: POLA NEGRI ENGAGED TO RICH AMERICAN was the headline making the rounds. Pola, playing cat-and-mouse with the press, refused to name her prospective husband; "I want to tell my mother first."[155]

The man in question was identified as Crane Gratz from Pasadena. They had been spotted together in several Hollywood nightspots. His mother denied there was any truth to an engagement, telling reporters that Negri and her son had known each other "a little less than a week."[156]

That denial didn't stop Pola from still claiming to be engaged to *someone*. She acted like it was now somehow expected of her. According to the *New York Times*, she told a group of reporters meeting her on one deck of her ship that she was not engaged, and then told a crowd on another deck that she *was* engaged and showed off an eighteen-and-half carat engagement ring. When it was pointed out to her that she was wearing the ring on the wrong finger, she calmly explained that she hadn't had time to have the ring properly sized and that she would name her fiancé on her return.[157] This clever woman had learned quite a bit about working the American press.

After she sailed for France, there were rumors of her engagement to a Dr. Daniel Corson, who had just divorced actress Alma Rubens.[158] It wasn't true. Pola's experience with Chaplin had taught her the value of keeping her name in the newspapers and the "engagement" ploy was a guaranteed headline-grabber.

Back in Poland, she sold her real estate holdings in Bromberg and, being the dutiful daughter, purchased a villa at Cap Ferrat on the French Riviera as a place for Eleonora to reside with Casimir De Hulewicz as her live-in companion. She also purchased an 18th-century chateau in Seraincourt, France, as a potential future home. She hoped on the expiration of her Lasky contract to live in Europe and travel back and forth to Hollywood to make a couple of pictures a year.

While overseas she nearly lost all of her possessions in her Beverly Hills estate when an antique furniture firm got a writ of attachment on her property on a claim for $2,260. The seizure was forestalled by an indemnity company that floated a $3,000 bond with the sheriff to give her lawyers time to appeal the judgment.[159] This was the first of several instances where Negri either "neglected" to pay her bills or foolishly ignored lawsuits, resulting in civil judgments against her.

Upon returning to America on May 1, 1925, aboard the S.S. *Berengaria*, she ran into trouble in New York when she was caught with trunks containing 16 bottles of French wine in violation of Prohibition laws. She was fined $5 for each of the bottles, which were smashed on the spot. An embarrassed Negri claimed that her maid had "accidentally" stashed the bottles in a trunk while packing for arrival.[160] More serious than a minor case of bootlegging, however, was the accusation that she had tried to smuggle $35,000 of jewelry, including four diamond bracelets, through U.S. customs. Her explanation was that she "had forgotten she had declared her intention of becoming an American citizen and therefore could not bring in jewelry as a visitor anymore."[161] Although she was eventually cleared of attempting to smuggle in the jewelry, she was still assessed a whopping $57,000 fine for not declaring them. She paid up and her confiscated jewelry was returned to her in June.[162]

This indignant editorial ran in *The Educational Screen* after the incident:

> It seems strange to us that the government finds the power to stifle such a man as Count Karolyi and refuse him the right to free speech in America, but that it allows foreigners like Pola Negri, von Stroheim, Michael Arlen and others to come over here and pollute the minds and hearts of our growing boys and girls. And Pola just now comes back from Europe and attempts to smuggle in her jewels and her liquor and still be considered a fit subject to become an American citizen, and is now taking out her papers. Methinks there were certain requirements for becoming an American citizen. Surely the greatest of these should be a fine moral character and particularly in the case of a person in the public eye, he or she should be one whose life and ideals are an inspiration to the youth of America.[163]

Flower of Night

Distributor: Paramount
Released October 18, 1925

STATUS: Lost.
CREDITS: *Director:* Paul Bern. *Screenplay:* Willis Goldbeck. *Story:* Joseph Hergesheimer. *Photographer:* Bert Glennon.
CAST: Pola Negri (*Carlotta y Villalon*), Joseph Dowling (*Don Geraldo y Villalon*), Youcca Troubetzkoy (*John Bassett*), Warner Oland (*Luke Rand*), Edwin J. Brady (*Derek Bylandt*), Eulalie Jensen (*Mrs. Bylandt*), Cesare Gravina (*Servant*), Gustav von Seyfferitz (*Vigilante Leader*), Helen Lee Worthing (*Josefa*), Thais Valemar, Manuel Acosta, Frankie Bailey.

STORY

Don Geraldo y Villalon, owner of the Flor de Noche (Flower of Night) gold mine, is swindled out of it by some unscrupulous Americans in a gambling den. His daughter, Carlotta, falls in love with John Bassett, the mine's new assistant superintendent, and defies her father's prohibition to go to a local dance with him. At the dance, she is accosted by Derek Bylandt, the brutish mine supervisor. She struggles to fend off his sexual advances and he dies of a heart attack. When the incident brings disgrace to Carlotta's family, her father commits suicide. Guilt-ridden, Carlotta becomes a dance hall girl in San Francisco. While on business, Bassett runs into her there, but rejects her after seeing what she has become. Heartbroken, she becomes involved with Luke Rand, who promises to help her get the mine back for her family. Upon hearing his plot to kill Basset, however, Carlotta goes to her love's aid. Basset kills Rand in self-defense and he and Carlotta are reunited.

REVIEWS

Variety declared the picture an out-and-out flop, warning that another like it would kill her career.[164] The *New York Times* called Negri's performance "brilliant," the best acting she had ever done before the camera.[165]

The *New York Daily Mirror* cleverly said *Flower of Night* "does not bloom. It wilts. And it's a darn shame to thrust such a story on an actress of La Negri's fine ability." The *New York Morning Telegraph* called it "curiously uninteresting and trivial" and the *New York World* labeled it an "unimaginative third rate melodrama."[166] "*Flower of Night* ... is hardly a vehicle for the brilliant Pola Negri," the *Milwaukee Sentinel* reviewer wrote. "For one I'd like to protest against the thrusting of a such a story on an actress of Miss Negri's ability."[167]

The picture fared no better in the eyes of the fans. Cecile Newman of Newark, New Jersey, wrote to *Photoplay*, "If this picture is supposed to be art—then give me death.... The acting was terrible. Ye gods!... Pola's acting verges on maudlin sentimentality. Ridiculous, silly and very disgusting—I would say."[168] "Pola Negri could act once, but her American films have all been washouts," wrote a *Pictures and the Picture-goer* reader. "She tries to ape Gloria Swanson and look lovely, but it won't do. She's miles above Gloria as an actress, though, she's not strictly beautiful, and if she stops posing and being a fashion plate she can do great things."[169]

Portrait for *Flower of Night*, Paramount, 1925. Directed by Paul Bern (photograph by Eugene R. Richee).

Originally, *Flower of Night* was supposed to be filmed at the Famous Players studio in Astoria, New York, and Negri went East to make the picture. At the last second, however, studio executives decided that the production could be more cheaply done in Hollywood, so Negri immediately returned to California.¹⁷⁰

Written by the acclaimed Joseph Hergesheimer, it was intended as a "prestige" feature, but in the end it fared no better than the average program picture Paramount routinely offered exhibitors. Go back and read the synopsis' for *Lily of the Dust* and *East of Suez*: *Flower of Night* has the same basic plot. The use of the same story in a succession of films is evidence that she had already been reduced to "standard heroine" roles. The result here was another awful picture and it appears Famous Players was rapidly losing interest in her. There can no other possible explanation as to why they insisted on saddling her with cardboard cut-out roles that sought to give her a different look, but did little in the way of letting her act.

Her "look" in this picture doesn't help matters much. Negri may have been promoted as an exotic "flower" herself, but it doesn't justify the weird outfit she wears or the incomprehensible haircut that she sports in the picture. She is hopelessly miscast. There was no chance she could ever pass for Mexican.

She still couldn't catch a break. The *Film Daily* reported that *Flower of Night* and most of her other films had been banned in the Soviet Union "for their portrayals of lives not looked upon as favorable by Soviet authorities."¹⁷¹

Movie star romance cropped up again with another reported engagement, this time to Metro-Goldwyn contract player William Haines. Gossip columnists revealed that the two met at the Coconut Grove nightclub in the Ambassador Hotel where Pola kept a bungalow. According to *Variety*, Eleonora Chalupec, Pola's mother, recently arrived from Poland, was to formally announce their engagement.¹⁷² According to another item, Haines' mother, on hearing the news of the engagement, told him, "You have one mother, why annex another woman old enough to be your mother?"¹⁷³

Haines was gay—openly gay in defiance of Metro studio head Louis B. Mayer, who had "ordered" him to acquire a wife for the sake of his heterosexual image. It is often-gossiped that a Los Angeles magazine ran a spread showing Negri and her fiancé checking out beds for their future home, but no such article has ever surfaced.¹⁷⁴ Like Bill Tilden before him, Haines received a great deal of publicity from being matched up with Pola and in later years referred to himself as a "graduate from the Pola Negri Finishing School" for everything that he learned from her about being a movie star.¹⁷⁵

Miss Negri in a scene from *Flower of Night*, Paramount, 1925. Directed by Paul Bern.

No sooner had the Haines story

faded than Rod La Rocque made a return appearance in her love life, although Negri insisted publicly she had no intention of marrying him. She did, however, admit "that La Rocque is in her company nearly all of the time and that he has been a regular visitor at her Beverly Hills home."[176] In *Memoirs* she recounts how he tried to surprise her by climbing up to her open bedroom window one night with a birthday gift for her. Thinking he might be a burglar, she nearly shot him with the pistol she kept under her pillow.

One odd newspaper report from this era concerns a sanity hearing for Justine Valse, who claimed to be Pola's film double. She wasn't. Arrested for attempted extortion, Valse insisted she had been duped into participating in a scheme to blackmail Negri with a series of "compromising" photographs that Valse had posed for. A court judge declared her insane and committed her to the state asylum.[177]

Between *Flower of Night* and her next picture, *A Woman of the World*, Negri turned up in photographs with severely bobbed hair. Perhaps it was the "flapper influence," but it was a look which, frankly, she was a bit too old to model; it gave her a touch of the grotesque. She looks very thin with huge eyes that dwarf her head, and her face has a harshness to it that makes her practically unrecognizable. There is no mention in any articles of the time or in her autobiography of an illness, but she does not look healthy. These photographs cast her in an unattractive light and depict a women struggling to keep up with fashion changes instead of setting them. The "new" look didn't last long.

A Woman of the World

Distributor: Paramount
Released December 28, 1925
Alternate Titles: The Tattooed Countess; A Countess in Iowa

STATUS: A public domain DVD is available.
CREDITS: *Director:* Malcolm St. Clair. *Scenario:* Pierre Collins. *Photographer:* Bert Glennon.
CAST: Pola Negri (*Countess Elnora*), Charles Emmett Mack (*Gareth Johns*), Holmes Herbert (*Richard Granger*), Blanche Mehaffey (*Lennie Porters*), Chester Conklin (*Sam Poore*), Lucille Ward (*Lou Poore*), Guy Oliver (*Judge Potter*), Dot Farley (*Mrs. Barebauer*), May Foster (*Mrs. Fox*), Dorothea Wolbert (*Annie*).

STORY

The Italian Countess Elnora tattoos her wrist with her lover's crest in a show of devotion, then finds him cavorting with another woman in his apartment. Vowing to never love again, she flees halfway around the world to the U.S., to stay with her cousin Sam Poore in a small midwestern town. Life there proves to be anything but relaxing as she becomes the subject of malicious gossip that attracts the attention of the town's self-righteous D.A., Richard Granger. Despite what he hears about her, he falls in love with the vivacious and cultured countess. Mistaking her kindness towards his youthful assistant as a betrayal of him, he calls her "licentious" ways a threat to the town's morality and angrily orders her out of town. The countess, furious at being impugned, horsewhips Richard. Feeling guilty over slandering her, he accepts the lashes to prove his own devotion to her. The countess realizes she's in love with him and they marry.

Reviews

Variety was horrified:

> Poor Pola! If [Famous] can't pick stories any better than this, they should get someone who can; if it is a case of Pola selecting her own, then they had better stop her. If something isn't done, then Pola Negri's value as a box office attraction in the spots where that does exist is going to be wiped out.... It doesn't look as though it was going to be worth a nickel at the box office.[178]

Most film critics were sympathetic to Pola's plight. The *Film Daily* said she suffered through the "worst material that an artist of her ability could be given." The *San Francisco Call and Post* called the picture "a total loss." The *Washington Star* opined, "[A]s a dramatic vehicle for the display of the real talent of the screen's best actress, it is hopeless."[179] "Will someone please find a story for Pola Negri?" *Motion Picture Magazine* pleaded. "Not since *Forbidden Paradise* came out nearly a year ago has she had any worthwhile study in celluloid. If something isn't done quickly, her pictures are doomed—and Pola, herself, will pass into an eclipse."[180]

A Woman of the World is billed as a dramatic comedy although the drama is inconsequential and its broad attempts at humor seem like they wandered in uninvited from another equally unfunny picture. The only thing it has to commend it is Negri, and that's not saying much in so poor a picture. As the countess, she laughs and cries, gets angry and looks lovelorn, although as a total her performance looks "phoned in," as if she didn't know what to do with such a horribly underwritten part.

This is a picture undeserving of her talent. The fish-out-of-water plot is painfully old-fashioned: a smart and cosmopolitan countess dealing with ignorant small town gossips who paint her as a fallen woman. It's so trite that it's hard to believe they would cast a sophisticated actress in such a hoary tale. Granted, the unexpected whipping scene near the conclusion is a nice and, by today's standards, kinky touch. The righteous D.A. accepts a literal whipping for his sins and the countess stops punishing him when she realizes that he loves her so much that he's willing to take the lashes. Who came up with that weird sadomasochistic idea? Kudos to you, whomever you were. The comic moments don't come off. The bits by former Sennett comedy star Chester Conklin are excruciatingly bad. As a romantic picture, *A Woman of the World* is undercooked. All of the wistful looks among the principals don't really amount to "acting" and Pola, sorry to say, looks even worse with her haircut here, dubbed "the orchid,"[181] than she did in the lamentable *Flower of Night*.

She was losing fans. In *Photoplay*, letter writer Mary Reid of Pittsburgh questioned Pola's inclusion in the article "Beauties of the Screen": "Pola Negri, without her striking personality, would be simply a typical Polish girl, maybe a beautiful one in Poland, but not here.... Her face is too wide and her upper lip too short and thin. And I think she shows her gums when she laughs."[182] Reader Constance Schank wondered why any further "foreign" film talent needed to be imported after Pola showed an ability to command headlines but had only "occasional flashes of brilliance."[183]

The "brilliance" that had carried Pola to stardom seemed to be gone. Journalist Adela Rogers St. Johns blamed Pola herself. "Negri's work is married by self-satisfaction. And it is lazy work. Mentally lazy. Tags from this and ends from that. She knows better. She can do better. And we should insist upon her doing it."[184]

Even her most loyal admirers wondered why she settled for such mediocrity. She had become too tame in her pictures. Why didn't she demand better stories? Her stock was falling and she didn't seem to care.

The Crown of Lies

Distributor: Paramount
Released March 27, 1926

STATUS: Lost.
CREDITS: *Director:* Dimitri Buchowetzki. *Scenario:* Hope Loring, Louis Duryea Lighton. *Story:* Ernest Vajda. *Photographer:* Bert Glennon.
CAST: Pola Negri (*Olga Kriga*), Noah Beery (*Count Mirko*), Robert Ames (*John Knight*), Charles A. Post (*Karl*), Arthur Hoyt (*Fritz*), Mikhael Vavitch (*Vorski*), Cissy Fitzgerald (*Leading Lady*), May Foster (*Landlord*), Frankie Bailey (*Actress*), Erwin Connelly (*Stage Manager*).

STORY

Olga Kriga, eager to become a great actress, loses a promising stage role due to the jealousy of the leading lady. Dejected, she agrees to accompany her clumsy admirer, John Knight, a young flivver salesman, to a small Balkan country on business. On their arrival, Olga meets Karl, who is convinced she is the lost queen of Sylvania and persuades her to return to his country to rally the oppressed population and restore the throne. Thinking it the acting role of a lifetime, she agrees despite John's misgivings. In Sylvania, Count Mirko and his ministers greet her as the true queen, but the scheming count arranges with the country's tyrant leader, Vorski, to eliminate her. Olga is shot and wounded by assassins, but recovers to win the army to her side. A revolt breaks out against the Count and Vorski. Olga is installed on the throne to the cheers of the people. In the end, she declines the crown and returns to New York with John.

REVIEWS

Critics took a dim view of this picture, although none of them was willing to blame Negri for its shortcomings. The *New York Post* called the picture "a tremendous fuss over nothing," and the *New York Sun* said, "[I]t is one of the weakest Negri films made in the U.S.A."[185] *Screenland* added, "I'm sure Pola was only fooling when she made *The Crown of Lies*, but she managed to keep a straight face and that was more than I could do."[186] *Photoplay* wrote: "Poor Pola, she has our sympathy. About two more pictures like this and as far as the movie public is concerned, she will be through."[187]

Negri only made two movies in 1926 and this first one, *The Crown of Lies*, was her worst reviewed picture since *The Cheat*. It is also marks the moment she fell from the first rank of relevant silent screen artists. This creaky Ruritanian fantasy, straight out of the *Prisoner of Zenda* playbook, was by-the-numbers. It doesn't seem to be much more than a dull fantasy with nothing at all to commend it. Unfortunately, Famous Players–Lasky could find no story to fit her talents and, instead, continued to cast her in poor vehicles that did nothing to save her sinking career.

This third time was not a charm for director Dimitri Buchowetzki. It was clear from the poor reviews of the film that the "experiment" of teaming Negri with former Ufa directors had failed. She needed a genius like Lubitsch. The studio's stubborn reluctance to sign him to direct her grew more egregious with every one of her pictures that died at the box office.

Commenting on Negri's still-short hair in this picture, Mrs. PWH from Pittsburgh, wrote "I would like Pola Negri ... and anyone else who has an abbreviated or 'freak' hair cut ... to be spirited away and kept in hiding until the mutilated locks have assumed a more normal appearance and the owners look once more like charming women, which was their original state."[188]

In a review of recent box office returns, *Photoplay* astutely observed that, "Pola Negri depends almost entirely upon her foreign following. Her popularity in Europe is great enough to make her of financial profit to her company, without consideration of her American clientele, which is small."[189] Just as *The Crown of Lies* was going into production, Famous Players announced that Negri would be heading back to Germany to make a new Ufa picture under an agreement between the two studios. Then, just as quickly, it was announced that she would *not* be going to Germany, but that Ufa director Erich Pommer would be brought over to supervise a future Hollywood picture for her. It seems as if Famous Players lacked faith in the success of anything they might try with her now.

Negri in a scene from *The Crown of Lies*, Paramount, 1926, Directed by Dimitri Buchowetzki.

Good and Naughty

Distributor: Paramount
Released June 7, 1926
Alternate Titles: *The Peacock Parade*;
The Pasteboard Queen; *Naughty Cinderella*.
(In some foreign markets, the picture was known as *Pola Negri in Florida*.)

STATUS: Lost.
CREDITS: *Director:* Malcolm St. Clair. *Scenario:* Pierre Collings. *Story:* Avery Hopwood.
CAST: Pola Negri (*Germaine Morris*), Tom Moore (*Gerald Gray*), Ford Sterling (*Bunny West*), Miss DuPont (*Claire Fenton*), Stuart Holmes (*Thomas Fenton*), Marie Mosquini (*Chouchou Rouselle*), Warner Richmond ("*Bad News*" *Smith*).

STORY

Homely secretary Germaine Morris is in love with her boss Gerald Gray, an interior decorator catering to a rich New York clientele. Gerald is having a secret affair with Claire Fenton, wife of a wealthy Wall Street broker. When Claire invites Gerald on a romantic boating trip to Florida, his concerned friend Bunny West invites showgirl Chouchou

Negri in a scene from *Good and Naughty*, Paramount, 1926. Directed by Malcolm St. Clair.

Rouselle to come along and end the affair by posing as Gerald's jealous fiancée. But quick-thinking Germaine goes glamorous and takes her place. While in Florida she attracts the attention of all the men, including her boss, and causes a quarrel between Claire and Gerald. Thomas Fenton arrives in Florida hoping to catch his wife with Gerald and sue him as co-respondent in a divorce action. Gerald, captivated by the now-beautiful Germaine, confesses his love to her. The Fentons put aside their differences and reconcile. Germaine and Gerald decide to return to New York, but are confronted by Chouchou's boyfriend "Bad News" Smith, who mistakenly believes that Gerald has taken up with her. The two men fight and Gerald wins, proving his love for Germaine, who accepts his marriage proposal.

REVIEWS

Variety noted that this picture gave her a chance to act rather than just look beautiful.[190] An indifferent *New York Times* reviewer said that she had given the same "natural" performance as she had in her other pictures.[191] The *New York Post* said the picture wasn't sensible enough to be continuously interesting, while The *New York Sun* called the film "a generally entertaining if not outstanding program picture."[192] The *San Francisco Bulletin* echoed the lament of many, declaring, "[O]ne longs for the Pola of old."[193] It's worth pointing out again that no one was calling her a bad actress. She did the best she could with the flat material given her.

Two comedies—two failures. The reviews here are an improvement over *The Crown of Lies*, but not by much. Malcolm St. Clair, who directed *A Woman of the World*, also helmed *Good and Naughty*. From the photos, Negri does manage to portray a rather unattractive version of herself through the aid of some clever makeup, but she was still completely miscast as someone's devoted secretary. That was more Clara Bow's turf. Was there any *good* reason for putting her in a weak picture like this?

The October 1926 issue of *Motion Picture Classic* offered a frank assessment of what had gone wrong with Negri's career, declaring that her biggest mistake was coming to America. In her German films she had been so natural and spontaneous, eschewing the usual posing that passed for acting, that she came off as remarkable. Upon her arrival in America, instead of relying on her talent, she decided to become a screen beauty and, in the magazine's opinion, could not compete with the locals. It's hard to believe that anyone would think that Pola was *not* an attractive woman in her own right! They then chided her for thinking more about camera angles and foregoing her natural spontaneity—completely absolving the studio of their responsibility for the poor quality of her pictures.

"What are they doing to Pola Negri?" a *Photoplay* reader asked. "Of course, the stories they give her are atrocious. I want to say that Pola, the wild and terrible, is far, far too tame.... Why doesn't she demand good pictures? Pola Negri is too fine an actress to lose to the machine."[194]

According to a studio press release, her next picture was to be a new version of *Camille*. Uncharacteristically, Famous Players' publicity implicitly acknowledged that her pictures hadn't matched her reputation:

> In *Camille* the public can hope to see the creature of *Passion* again on the screen, captivating, alluring, flaming, moodful, sparkling.
> Since Pola Negri came to America something greater has been expected of her than what she has accomplished. In *Camille*, she will get her chance."[195]

Unfortunately, she never got the chance. *Camille* was never produced. Famous Players gave up on her.

Hotel Imperial

Distributor: Paramount
Released January 1, 1927

STATUS: A public domain version is available on DVD.
CREDITS: *Director:* Mauritz Stiller. *Scenario:* Jules Furthman. *Story:* Lajos Biro.
CAST: Pola Negri (*Anna Sedlak*), James Hall (*Paul Amasy*), George Siegmann (*General Juschkiewitsch*), Max Davidson (*Elias Butterman*), Michael Vavitch (*Tabakowitsch*), Otto Fries (*Anton Klinak*), Nicholas Soussanin (*Baron Fredkison*), Golden Williams (*Major General Sultanov*).

STORY

During World War I, six Hungarian Hussars, weary from weeks of fighting, ride into a frontier town and discover it occupied by Russian troops. During a pitched battle, Lt. Paul Amasy rides off with Russians in hot pursuit. He eludes them by jumping off his horse. Seeking shelter, he breaks into the seemingly empty Hotel Imperial. He falls asleep and in the morning is discovered by servants Anna, Elias and Anton, who move him to a room upstairs. When Amasy awakens, they tell him that he will have to stay as there is no way for him to get back to his unit. Russians under the command of General Juschkiewitsch enter the town and establish their headquarters at the hotel. Anna convinces Amasy to pose as their waiter until he can find some way to escape. The general attempts to seduce Anna with perfume and expensive clothes and she intercedes with him to spare Amasy when he is arrested for not having official papers. The hotel is visited by a Russian spy, Tabakowitsch, who has stolen the Hungarian attack plans; Amasy is determined to stop him before he reveals them to the general. During a drunken party, Anna fends off the general's sexual advances while Amasy deals with the spy, shooting him in the bath. When the spy's death is uncovered, Amasy is questioned by the Russians. Anna saves him by lying that he spent the night in her room. The general, played for a fool, humiliates her. Amasy escapes during the night and the Hungarian Army stages its counterattack. The Russians are driven from the town and Amasy's unit enter as liberators. Amasy and Anna are briefly reunited, knowing they will only have a short time together before he goes off to battle again.

REVIEWS

The *New York Times* reviewer praised Negri's "effective eyebrows."[196] *Photoplay* thought her performance "corking" and called it her "best role since *Passion*."[197] Despite critical acclaim for the picture, exhibitors reported she was no longer a draw. One Soldier, Kansas, theater manager wrote *The Exhibitor Herald* to ask, "Why didn't Paramount give Miss Negri some real plays to screen, there are plenty of good stories for her and not a lot of morbid Russian stuff? This was really worthwhile, but they had killed her by previous trash."[198]

This is the best of all of Negri's surviving Paramount movies. She actually gets the chance to act in something other than just a facile story and she is excellent in it. Years of poor movies had done nothing to diminish her talent. Her character, Anna, is gracious and beautiful and she willingly takes risks to aide Amasy, although she is constantly threatened with rape from the moment the Russian general enters the picture. The role allows her to touch upon every emotion and she reacts to the plot with total naturalism in her gestures and, particularly, in her expressions. Watch her eyes whenever the leering general comes near. Her look of fear is chillingly real, although Anna is no mere frightened doe. In the scene where the general orders her out of the clothes he's purchased for her, she surprises him by ripping the clothes off in front of everyone. Her look of fury will make you glad you are not the target of her ire. While comedian Max Davidson appears as a hotel staff member, there is no needless comedy to mar the dramatic mood. Leading man James Hall looks and acts the part of a ramrod soldier for the Austrian army, although he and Negri have no chemistry together and they have just the one scene at the end that could be considered "romantic."

Negri was originally supposed to make this picture under the direction of Erich von Stroheim. Temperamental actress vs. tyrannical director—now *that* would have been a battle for the ages! The picture was helmed by Swedish director Mauritz Stiller instead. His meticulous von Sternberg–like direction and Negri's assured acting made this more like a European than an American production. The story's wartime setting was one Pola could obviously relate to, having experienced the German occupation of Warsaw during the Great War. Many of *Hotel Imperial*'s thematic elements were repeated in her next picture, *Barbed Wire*, but in a far more pacifist context.

Negri was filming this picture in Hollywood in August 1926 when she received word that Rudolph Valentino had fallen gravely ill in New York. When he unexpectedly died, a grieving Pola left immediately for his memorial service, halting production of the picture for a month.

Interlude: Rudolph Valentino

Even though the narrative of her life abounds in contradictions, Pola Negri always insisted that Rudolph Valentino was her one true love and that they had been engaged to wed prior to his untimely death in August 1926. Right to the end of her life in her San Antonio hospital room, she kept by her bedside a framed photograph of him signed with an intimate message to her in French. But the facts do not support her claim they were once engaged. Did she really love him or did she court Valentino solely for the publicity it brought her? Did Valentino even return her "feelings" for him?

Based on her romantic history, there is ample room for conjecture Take her string of engagements: In 1924, one newspaper piece dubbed her "The Artful Dodger of Matrimony," delineating her string of broken engagements to Chaplin, Bill Tilden, Rod La Rocque and William Haines.[199] Pola was quoted as saying: "Everybody is insisting that I marry someone."[200] She had said or hinted numerous times that she was to marry, yet her "fiancé" always vanished with the next day's headlines. Wouldn't her "engagement" to Valentino be more of the same? Pola, however, maintained to the end of her days that her deepest regret was that his death had kept her from marrying him.

Negri penned (although more likely it was ghost-written for her) an article, "Rudy Valentino and I: My Great True Love Story" for the April 1934 issue of *True Story Magazine*.

The "true" in the title is debatable. It's the kind of piece you would expect from a former silent movie queen: colorful, hyperbolic and tragic. It's more about *her* than her *and* Rudy. The most interesting thing in the article is her revelation that she received an admiring fan letter from Valentino in 1919—about the time that *Madame DuBarry* became a hit throughout Europe. She recalls being drawn to the photograph of himself that he included in a fan letter to her (Valentino was a classic narcissist). She found his name funny and had her secretary send him a reply and a photograph of her. Then she promptly forgot about the letter until years later. Yet, Pola being Pola, wrote about the letter as if it were a foreshadowing of their destiny—a sign that she and Valentino were always meant to meet.

In their book *Valentino, the Love God*, Noel Botham and Peter Donnelly contend that Negri "stalked" Valentino "with the "guile and dedication of a trained seductress."[201] They assert she had matrimony in mind from their very first meeting and everyone in Hollywood was aware she intended to take Valentino down the aisle.[202] "Once Rudy has experienced my love," they quote her as saying, "he will forget other women. I am ready when he is." That sounds like the writing of a tabloid reporter.

At the time of her introduction to Valentino, Pola was romantically linked in the newspapers with her *Forbidden Paradise* co-star Rod La Rocque. She called their relationship "merely friendly," although *Motion Picture Classic* reported them to be engaged[203] and another movie magazine related tales of soulful looks and love letters between them, with Negri asserting she was "truly in love for the very first time."[204] Silent film actress Miriam Cooper, however, claimed in her autobiography that Pola told her that La Rocque was "mean" to her and that many a time Negri cried on her shoulder over some hurt he had inflicted on her.[205]

According to Valentino biographer Emily Leider, Rudy and Pola were introduced by director Raoul Walsh in 1924. Gossip columnist Louella O. Parsons gave herself the credit for introducing them. She claimed that she and Valentino—they were good friends—were lounging around film star Marion Davies' swimming pool one afternoon when he requested she set up a meeting. "Introduce me to Pola Negri," he told her. "I saw her last picture and I think she is fascinating. Can't you arrange for her to come to one of Marion's parties?"[206]

Pola claimed it was Marion Davies who insisted that she and Valentino meet—for Rudy's sake. Valentino was depressed over his separation from his second wife Natacha Rambova, and lost without romance in his life. Davies set up several rendezvous for them, but for one reason or another Negri cancelled every time; "Attempting to get us together became an amusing game that all of our friends played with great gusto."[207] Parsons, always one of Negri's detractors, claimed she "played hard to get."[208]

Negri found the prospect of meeting Valentino, in her words, "frightening" and "foreboding." The fatalist in her rose to the surface whenever matters of the heart came into play. This was a woman every man had abandoned, a woman who repeatedly stated in interviews that she would never find happiness in love. Deep down, she suspected that meeting him would only lead to disaster.

But she agreed to attend a costume party being hosted by Davies, knowing Valentino would be there. Originally, her escort for the evening was to be La Rocque, but he backed out. Aware of the film colony gossip, he refused to play second fiddle to Valentino in any kind of romance with her. So Negri went alone to the party, dressed as the Empress Catherine from *Forbidden Paradise*.[209] Valentino soon arrived, escorted by his blonde co-star from *The Eagle*, Hungarian import Vilma Banky. They were rumored to be romantically involved with each other.

Parsons wrote that she took her time in introducing Rudy to Negri, even though she felt the "undercurrent of excitement in both of them."[210] According to journalist Adela Rogers St. Johns, Davies made the introductions. "Pola gave him a white ringed hand and he kissed it. They danced together and somehow the floor cleared so that they were dancing almost alone."[211]

Botham and Donnelly wrote, "Pola said she found [Valentino] handsome and artless and desperately sincere, although completely lacking the intense sexuality that dominated his screen personality. There was a look in his dark eyes, she said, that appealed more to the maternal than the amorous."[212] It is telling that Chaplin had the same initial appeal for her. As they danced, Negri was "captured" by his sexuality.[213] Both left the party alone at the end of that night, but for her the die had been cast. She wrote: "Call it fatalism, but from our very first meeting I knew that somehow this man had the power to either destroy my life or so irrevocably alter its course that it would never be the same again." The thing that drew them together, she concluded, was their unhappiness and she knew then that they were destined to be lovers.[214]

Emily Leider contends that their spontaneous love and passion too quickly erases Rudy's wife Natacha Rambova from his life.[215] Valentino, she maintains, depended a great deal on Natacha, and her decision to end their marriage wounded him greatly. In Irving Schulman's Valentino biography, he wrote, "[I]f Valentino came to regard Pola Negri as an act of God, sometimes amusing, often a nuisance, but always invaluable publicity for his own pictures, he solaced himself with the knowledge that while she had seized public possession of him ... his private life ... was still his own."[216] Another Valentino biographer, David Bret, insisted in *Valentino: A Dream of Desire* that Rudy was a closeted gay man so Negri's relationship with him wasn't really anything more than a publicity stunt to support his public persona as "The Great Lover."

In her *Memoirs*, Negri described Valentino as pathologically unhappy and brooding, haunted over failed loves, his unsatisfying film career and a ruinous financial situation. She played both mother and lover to him, soothing his bouts of insecurity and providing him with an escape from the pressures of Hollywood. They were similar people. Both were immigrants in a land suspicious of foreigners; both were sensitive artists who cared a great deal about their work; both had friends but preferred solitude; both loved luxury and spent a great deal on clothes and jewelry; and both, deep down, were fatalists.

Valentino's manager George Ullman wrote of their relationship in a book published after the star's death:

> At the conclusion of Valentino's work in *The Eagle* he began to deliberately seek the society of Pola Negri, who had previously given evidences of her interest in him.
>
> Well he knew the effect that this would have upon Natacha, as Pola Negri was the one woman whose fascination Natacha feared.
>
> The Polish beauty is the antithesis of the Rambova type. Natacha is cold, mysterious, Oriental, languorous and beguiling. Pola is passionate, hot-blooded, hot-tempered, tempestuous and volcanic. Both are equally fascinating. And both are so supremely beautiful in their different types that it just depends up one's individual taste which is preferred.
>
> Just as Rudolph was more in love than Natacha, so Pola, in my opinion, was more in love than Rudy. But Valentino was always gentle and yielding where a beautiful woman was concerned.
>
> Pola Negri knows very well what she wants. None better. And from this time on, Pola and Rudy were as continuously in each other's company as their arduous work would permit.[217]

Motion Picture Classic noted, "Pola Negri was looking at some of the stills showing Valentino making violent love to Vilma Banky in *The Son of the Sheik*. 'Ah!' exclaimed Pola. 'He make love to Vilma, but all the time he think of me!'"[218]

Their relationship was passionate and, by press accounts, fraught with insecurities, fights, petty jealousies, infidelity and wounded pride. *Photoplay* hinted at quarrels suggesting either a "flaming romance" or a "not-too-private war."[219] Harry Carr wrote about meeting Pola on the Lasky lot shortly before Valentino's death and remarked how everything must be going well with her. Pola glumly replied, "Business very good; love very bad."[220] Leider recounts that Negri would have her chauffeur wait outside Falcon's Lair, Valentino's home, during the evenings when she visited in case she felt the need to escape after an argument. They fought, followed by passionate lovemaking. Journalist Rogers-St. John wrote: "They lived at the top of their emotional natures ... a passion that swept Rudy along on its turbulent course."[221]

Motion Picture Classic observed that while Pola's feelings for Valentino were clear, there were questions about Rudy's reciprocity. "Rudy has many admirers among those he admires, but he is apparently heart-free, which does not at all please Pola, who proves it by slapping his face occasionally."[222] Ellenbarger wrote,

> Whatever it was that attracted Rudy to his "Polita," no one could say. Perhaps Pola brought some sort of mental stimulation and excitement to Rudy's life and made him forget the unhappiness he felt over his recent divorce. Rudy missed Natacha's companionship, which Pola provided in part. The difference being, not once did Rudy stray from his commitment to Natacha; never was there a rumor of a dalliance on his part. But with Pola it was different. During their separations it was as if Pola did not exist. Rudy openly dated other women and unashamedly took them out on the town, even though his romantic obligations were reportedly to Pola.[223]

According to legend, Pola slapped his face because she'd been told that Valentino, while in Europe obtaining his divorce, made the acquaintance of a Lady Longborough and apparently spent a few days—and nights—in her company. Upon hearing the gossip, Pola sent him telegrams demanding to know the truth and Rudy assured her that there was nothing to the rumors. Yet after his return to America, Lady Longborough turned up at Falcon's Lair, much to Pola's dismay, as the guest of honor at one of Rudy's parties. According to lore, during the party Pola snuck up to Rudy's bedroom and found framed portraits of two women there. Author Cal York wrote, "Only one of them was Pola." He continued, "Pola, who had of course, been invited to the party, took one look at this strange phenomenon, and turned the exclusive and delightful little evening into a Fourth of July celebration."[224]

Pola forgave him for the affair, but after that their relationship ran hot and cold. *Motion Picture Magazine* parodied their mercurial natures in "The Week's News in Hollywood"[225]:

> Monday: Pola says "Yes" and Rudy says "No."
> Tuesday: Rudy says "Yes" and Pola says "No."
> Wednesday: Pola says "I go to Europe."
> Thursday: Pola says "I do not go to Europe."
> Friday: Pola has dinner with Rudy.
> Saturday: Rudy has dinner with Pola.
> Sunday: A holiday.

Still, in the months preceding Valentino's untimely death, Pola was his preferred companion. There are photographs of them together at Norma Talmadge's beach party and at silent film star Mae Murray's wedding to David Mdivani.[226] The latter eerily foreshadows

Negri's own future involvement with the Mdivani family. They jointly hosted visitors, Valentino's brother and his family, and there is a photograph in *Memoirs* of them sitting poolside. Valentino is in a swimsuit while Negri, glass of champagne in hand, looks on in adoration. There are surviving home movies of them together. They were openly living together at Falcon's Lair—unmarried. No other film stars of the time could have pulled that one off. Then again, they were both *European*.

Was it all just for show? Actress Miriam Cooper said their relationship played "like a press agent's dream," although she asserts it was real.[227] Yet at the same time, their public courtship was a series of insinuations, declarations and refutations with the truth left entirely open to interpretation.

For example, there is the saga of Pola's train trip to Albuquerque, New Mexico, in February 1926. Pola was accompanied by her mother and her secretary. Rumors had her meeting up with Valentino. Negri emphatically refuted them, claiming she was in town on "oil business" and "to buy land."[228] Here is the exchange between Negri and the local press as reported in the *Salt Lake Telegram*:

> Pola indignantly denied she would see Rudy and declared that she was in Albuquerque on "oil business."
> "We don't have any oil around here," a reporter told her.
> "Well, then I'll buy a ticket back to Hollywood."
> She did, leaving Albuquerque at midnight.[229]

According to *Variety*, actress Eleanor Boardman claimed she left Los Angeles with Pola and knew the original plan was for Rudy and Pola to meet and marry in New Mexico, but the wedding was called off when word of the impending nuptials got out. Valentino called reports of a wedding "ridiculous."[230] The *Salt Lake Telegram* stated that Pola returned to Los Angeles on orders from her studio, which did not want her seeking "sensational publicity."[231]

A week later, the newspapers reported of Pola hosting a "Welcome Home" party for Rudy at her Beverly Hills residence. According to the press, Negri intended it as "an opportunity to announce an engagement to Rudy, but neither would make any statement to the press about it on the morning after."[232] Pola apparently talked a reluctant Valentino into taking a vacation with her in Delmar, the same place where she had announced her engagement to Chaplin. According to reports they visited writer Gouverneur Morris and went fishing, dining later on Rudy's catch of mackerel.[233]

It was Negri who "broke" the news of an "experimental" engagement between her and Valentino in March 1926, telling a reporter that she was planning a four-mouth stay in Europe to film a new picture there and visit the 18th-century Seraincourt chateau she had purchased the year before. She said that if she and Rudy both still felt the same way about each other on her return, she saw no reason why they could not wed.[234] When asked if they were already engaged, she laughed and refused to elaborate.

Valentino's friends reported that Pola's all-out pursuit was "the last straw" for Rudy.[235] According to Adela Rogers St. Johns in 1950—and St. Johns was a prominent exaggerator and fabricator in her own right—Rudy arrived at her house one evening, distraught, and told her that the engagement was nothing but a drama. While Pola believed in some great romance between them, he didn't—and he didn't want the drama. He said the relationship was wrong for him, but then asked her, "What can I do?"[236] In the April 1931 issue of *New Movie Magazine*, Warren Nolan wrote in "Things That I Know to Be True" that Valentino told him about Pola, "What else can I say.... If I say I don't love her, I'm a cad. If I say I love her she'll want to marry me and God knows I don't want to marry her."

Replying to Pola's announcement, Valentino told the press, "We have not even discussed marriage. Both of us have lots of work ahead of us. We are not engaged. I do not like the word 'engagement.' It sounds too much like a contract one has to perform by a certain date."[237] After that, *Motion Picture Magazine* reported things were "definitely off" between them.[238] Yet despite his denial, it was reported that Pola and Rudy would star together in a film adaptation of *Anna Karenina*.[239] In June, Negri's mother announced to the newspapers that her daughter and Valentino were indeed engaged and would marry in Paris in March 1927.[240] Valentino, preparing to leave on a publicity tour for his latest picture *The Son of the Sheik,* would neither confirm nor deny the story. The parallels to Pola's relationship with Chaplin are unmistakable.

So were they ever truly engaged? Valentino's repeated denials would seem to answer that question and Jane Ardmore writes in her Mae Murray biography that by this time Pola had left Valentino behind and grown close romantically to Serge Mdivani.[241] Yet after all of the negative coverage of Valentino's marriage to Natacha Rambova, it could also be concluded that he didn't want to deal with any more questions about his private life while trying to re-establish a film career that had recently lost momentum. Valentino, much like Pola, also understood that *any* publicity regarding possible nuptials, regardless of whether they were true or not, could only help his image and career.

Valentino left on a two-week tour to promote *The Son of the Sheik* in August 1926. He collapsed in New York near the end of the tour, suffering from a ruptured appendix. Surgery was performed, and it was believed that Rudy was strong enough to recover. Negri was then filming *Hotel Imperial* at the Famous Players studio in Los Angeles and the company would not allow her to go to him. That came as a relief to United Artists, who feared her appearance at his bedside would shift the attention of the press to her. In an age before antibiotics, Valentino developed peritonitis, lapsed into a coma and died on August 23, 1926. Negri learned of his passing when a reporter called her at the Ambassador Hotel and asked for her reaction to his death.

Pola collapsed upon hearing the news and was taken to the home of a friend to be tended to by physicians. According to sources, she tearfully insisted on visiting Falcon's Lair. She lay there in a drawing room which featured two large Beltran portraits of Rudy, one of him in costume for his role in *Blood and Sand* and one of him in a costume of a warrior. Witnesses said she continually sobbed, "Oh, why did he leave me? Why did he not come back as he promised?" and had to be sedated several times before she finally fell into a restful sleep.[242]

Louella Parsons, who seemed to have been *everywhere* in Hollywood whenever something of historical importance happened, claimed to have been present, along with Marion Davies, to witness Pola's grief. "She wept, she wailed, she clutched her long black hair.... She fell on her knees crying to high heaven to let her die, too. Never in her most scenery-chewing moments as an actress did Pola stage such a performance as she put on before Marion and me."[243]

It should be noted that Parsons used the word "stage," as if to suggest that none of Negri's emotionalism was genuine. Parsons was one of the gossipy "sob sisters," who suggested Pola "stole" Valentino's funeral for her own purposes.

Famous Players–Lasky released a statement stating that Negri would not attend Valentino's memorial service in New York as *Hotel Imperial* production could not be held up. They didn't seem to understand that the decision wasn't up to them. Pola insisted on going and when they clashed, the studio blinked. According to Ellenbarger, Famous Players president Adolph Zukor told studio manager Charles Eyeton: "Put a nurse and a publicity man on the train ... and ask Pola to guard her statements to the press."[244]

During Negri's slow-moving train trip to New York, the press bombarded her with questions such as whether Valentino would be buried in California or in Italy. She replied through written messages (being too distraught to take questions in person) that Valentino had loved America and that she would attempt to intercede with Rudy's brother and sister and have him buried in Hollywood.[245]

She then surprised everyone with the news they had been engaged to wed. "Mr. Valentino proposed to me after he returned from Paris a free man," she said. "There was only one thought in our minds. We looked forward to the time when we could be together for eternity."[246] Reporters snickered, gave each other dubious glances, and Valentino's grief-stricken fans, for the most part, reacted violently to her assertion. It could not be so! This was, after all, Pola Negri, famous for her "scene-stealing" antics and her string of broken engagements, making the claim. To complicate things further, Valentino had apparently never told anyone he was engaged to her. When asked, most of the actor's closest friends stated they had never heard Rudy mention an engagement. *Follies* showgirl Marian Benda, Valentino's companion on the town the night he had collapsed, said, "Valentino was not engaged to marry Miss Negri.... You'll notice that all the statements about the supposed engagement have come from her. He never denied any of them because he was too fine. He did think a great deal of her, but he had many friends."[247]

Upon Pola's arrival in New York, the press sensationalized her grief with a little more than just a touch of exaggeration. Typical of the coverage was this:

> Pola Negri alighted from the Twentieth Century Limited this morning in her 3000 dollar mourning costume and drove immediately to the undertaker's to lay a floral blanket, costing $2000, of unbelievable size, over Valentino's casket.[248]

Pola's blanket of roses was a romantic gesture, though viewed as wildly overdramatic and self-serving. In addition, her black crepe mourning dress, estimated to cost between three and twelve-thousand dollars, gave some the impression of a woman far more interested in making a fashion statement than mourning the death of her lover. Such accusations were baseless, yet seemed somehow perfectly reasonable.

The newspapers insinuated that Pola's demonstration of grief was *too* dramatic to be credible. According to press reports, when she arrived in New York and was met by George Ullman, she cried out, "Why did you not bring him back to me?" Apparently the last thing she had told Ullman before Valentino's departure from Los Angeles was, "Be sure and bring Rudy back to me."[249]

Pola collapsed at the foot of Valentino's bier at Campbell's Funeral Parlor. Kneeling at his casket, she prayed, according to Ullman, for about 15 minutes, and then fainted away. It took 20 minutes to revive her.[250] She again steadfastly insisted to reporters they had been engaged and lamented the fact that they hadn't married months ago. They had put their careers first and now it was too late. She sadly declared she would always remember him, and claimed that she hadn't come to him earlier because the seriousness of his condition had been kept from her at Rudy's insistence.[251]

Yet despite her passionate assertions, there were many who refused to believe her; a press that ridiculed her; and fans who jeered at her during the memorial service. A tearful Pola wondered how people could be so cruel in her time of grief. When Valentino's brother Alberto was asked if she and Rudy were really engaged, all he could offer this:

"Probably it was so. I know they were very fond of each other."²⁵² Ullman had a different idea altogether:

> Were Pola Negri and Valentino engaged? I repeat that, although I was entirely in his confidence, he never told me so, and I never asked him.
> He did tell me, however, that until he had completed his career he had no intention of marrying anybody.²⁵³

If there was one thing that Pola could take comfort from, it was Rudy's last words. According to a letter hand-delivered to her by Mary Pickford, Dr. Harold Meeker, who had attended Valentino at the end, wrote that the actor had said, "Pola—if she does not come in time, tell her I think of her." According to Ellenbarger, Pola read the letter out loud and then told the reporters packed into her hotel room, "There! If you knew, if you could only look into the bottom of my heart, you could not do the cruel things you have done."²⁵⁴ She then composed herself and asked to be allowed to get some rest.

Almost immediately, Dr. Sterling C. Wyman, Negri's attendant during her New York stay, told reporters that Ullman had confided in him that there was no engagement, but Valentino had not denied it because it "would help, Pola."²⁵⁵ As things turned out, Wyman was the one who was untrustworthy. He wasn't even a doctor. He was a professional impersonator who achieved fame by passing himself off as doctors, lawyers and even diplomats. He was just one of the characters who turned Valentino's memorial service into a colorful and chaotic carnival.

After the celebrity-packed service in New York, Pola accompanied Valentino's body back to California for burial per an agreement with his family. During the journey she told a reporter that although she'd had many love affairs in her life, Valentino was the man she had been waiting for all along. The reporter didn't buy it, musing that Pola "cannot know where the woman ends and the great emotionalist begins." When asked about all of the men in her life, Pola reportedly responded in great dramatic style, "I am a woman of peculiar temperament.... Without love, I am hungry and cold and lonely. Love is the flame that burns in my soul and makes me a great artist."²⁵⁶

To this day, Negri, in her "$3,000 mourning dress" and her "$2,000 blanket of roses" stands forever accused of hijacking the solemnity of Valentino's death for her own publicity—the greatest job of "scene-stealing" of all time. There is the oft-repeated tale that Negri fainted solely for the benefit of the photographers at the service and when a photographer complained he hadn't gotten a decent enough shot of her fainting, she obliged him by doing it again.²⁵⁷ Most Internet sources repeat the falsity that she "threw herself" at Valentino's coffin. One source even recounts how Negri threw herself at the coffin, kissed Rudy's corpse and declared, "I will love you always"—which is what actress Mary Miles Minter allegedly whispered to the corpse of her murdered love, William Desmond Taylor, in 1922. The story that she repeatedly fainted over and over or deliberately did it for the press, is untrue, and under the circumstances, cruel. Yet, because this was Pola Negri and because the public had become accustomed to her "antics," the notion that she would make a spectacle of herself at the funeral simply *had* to be true.

Apparently, her real crime, if there was one, was expressing her grief in a very public fashion. *Moving Picture Magazine* defended her, nothing that as a foreigner, it was natural for her to show emotion: "[S]he is very much as she appears on the screen, nearer her screen personality than almost anyone we have ever met." She had suffered "more poignantly and more intensely" than most people suffer and who was the magazine to say that her grief was any less?²⁵⁸

Years later, there were still those who suspected that Negri, ever the cunning opportunist, had pulled off a publicity coup. "Pola could turn any public event to her own use to get free publicity," wrote one writer. "She was a better publicity getter than she was an actress…. She went into the deepest mourning and give a better performance as a tragic, broken-hearted woman than she had even given on the screen."[259]

At Valentino's memorial service in Hollywood, there were no desperate histrionics or "antic" behavior that the carrion press could feast on. A few days after the service, Negri announced that she would see his body interred in a grand tomb of her own design, but nothing ever came of that. In fact, Valentino's remains occupied the tomb of his friend, writer June Mathis, for several years as he had never purchased his own burial space. When Mathis unexpectedly died, Valentino's body was moved to the crypt that Mathis had purchased for her mother and there he remains today.

Over the next few years, Negri periodically announced plans to buy Valentino's Falcon's Lair mansion and move in, but she never did. She did abandon her own Beverly Hills home, claiming she couldn't bear to live there alone after Rudy's death, and for the rest of her time in Hollywood resided in her bungalow suite at the Ambassador Hotel.

She raised a few eyebrows when she sued Valentino's estate for $15,000, seeking repayment for a loan that she had made to Rudy a few months before his death. It further fed suspicions that her proclamation of an engagement had been nothing but a sham. But sympathetic magazine editors rallied to her defense, calling the accusations against her exaggerated and shameful. One movie magazine wrote:

> Pola Negri has given us some of our best screen art. We know her to be temperamental—a hurricane of emotions. In her grief she was sincere, distraught, mad, racked, torn and inconsolable. Others mourned the actor or grieved for the friend, but she alone lost her lover. It is enough for us that Pola's name was whispered by Rudy as he closed his eyes and stepped out into the lonely way of Death. He cannot defend her now.

Barbed Wire

Distributor: Paramount
Released August 26, 1927

STATUS: A public domain copy is available on DVD.
CREDITS: *Director:* Rowland V. Lee. *Scenario:* Jules Furthman *Story:* "The Woman of Knockaloe" by Hall Caine.
CAST: Pola Negri (*Mona*), Clive Brook (*Oskar*), Einar Hanson (*The Brother*), Claude Gillingwater (*The Father*), Gustav von Seyfferitz (*The Neighbor*), Charles Lane (*The Commandant*), Clyde Cook (*Hans*), Ben Hendricks, Jr. (*The Sergeant*).

STORY

It's harvest season on Mona's family farm in pastoral Normandy when World War I begins and the call comes for men to take up arms. Mona's brother enlists, leaving her to cope with the farm and their ailing father. French authorities confiscate part of the farm to build a camp to house German prisoners. Mona detests the Germans, even more so after she learns her brother has died in action. Yet she is attracted to Oskar, a prisoner sent to help her with farm work. Kind and honorable, he gallantly saves Mona from being assaulted by a French sergeant. When she speaks up in his defense at trial, she becomes a traitor in her neighbors' eyes. She is also disowned by her father, who is so outraged that he suffers a fatal stroke. When the Armistice finally comes, the lovers find that they are not welcome anywhere. Mona is forced by her neighbors to choose between her farm and Oskar, and chooses Oskar. As she departs her farm for good, she is met by her returning brother—who has been blinded. Changed by his experiences in combat, he delivers a lecture to their neighbors about the need for peace and brotherhood in the hope that the dead will not all have died in the name of hatred.

Reviews

Screenland described *Barbed Wire* as "simple, direct and touching," and declared Negri's acting "superb."[260] *Motion Picture Magazine* called her performance her best to date.[261] *Variety* didn't find her performance convincing and thought her "camera conscious," rehashing the theory that she was lost in front of the camera unless she had the right director to guide her.[262] An exhibitor called the picture "a dramatic masterpiece" and said that Negri's acting "met all expectations"—but he also noted that while it was better than what he had seen from her recently, the picture "did not pay."[263]

She had lost none of her dramatic intensity. *Photoplay*'s William H. McClegg wrote of his visit to the *Barbed Wire* set in his December 1930 article "Is Acting Madness?" According to McClegg, during the filming of the military trial scene, a spark from an arc lamp dropped onto her bare shoulder. She grabbed his arm and shrieked expletives. "The rescue crew arrived. Even then, La Negri, shudderingly still, refused to loosen her hold on me. So I, too, had to go with her and her supporters to the star's throne. No frenzied person could have gripped an arm with more fury than Pola gripped mine. It was black and blue for weeks afterward. But such marks were dear to my heart, having been caused by the stranglehold of genius while in the throes."

After playing conventional modern heroines in most of her American movies, it is a little odd to find Pola playing servants and farm girls in *Hotel Imperial* and *Barbed Wire*. One take is that these roles were a deliberate return to the "earthy" character roles of her German pictures, and it was hoped that the change would meet with audience approval. Yet after all of the publicity portraying her as exotic and colorful, casting her as common woman fit neither her screen image nor her real-life persona.

Whereas *Hotel Imperial* is a love story set during wartime extolling the virtues of duty and sacrifice in the name of patriotism, *Barbed Wire* is a love story with a pacifist heart. None of the German prisoners are villainous. They simply long for the war to be over so that they can go home. It is the French who are the despicable characters. There is the prison camp sergeant who attempts to rape Mona, and the club-footed villager, a rejected suitor, who rallies the neighbors to force her off her land. It doesn't take actual fighting to bring out the worst in some people during wartime.

Negri always rose to the level of her material. In the case of *Barbed Wire*, it isn't much of a stretch. Her acting in this picture is composed of glances of longing and sadness and lots of tears. She is a *beautiful* crier—yet at the same time her character is curiously inert. At points she seems to sleepwalk through the proceedings as if the plot didn't concern her character at all. The picture's pacifist tone has a quasi-religious component that probably appealed to Negri's Catholicism, but it also produces some rather banal intertitles that would have sounded even less convincing as dialogue in a sound picture. The ending, where she and her lover are saved from ostracism by her peace-preaching brother,

Pola Negri in a scene from *Barbed Wire*, Paramount, 1927. Directed by Rowland V. Lee.

is a clumsy and highly improbable plot device and one melodramatic apple too many on something of an overloaded cart.

Barbed Wire is proof that she had lost her way. Gone was the unique actress who had once enthralled audiences in *Madame DuBarry*. That flame, that subtle naturalness and effortless acting of her German pictures had been extinguished. She was now just another actress in routine program pictures. *Photoplay* reader E. Islett Kelly of Princeton, New Jersey, asked in a letter, "What is it in American films that seems to stifle the genius of artists who come here from other countries?… The most glaring example is Pola Negri. No one will deny that her European pictures were masterpieces … yet, she has done nothing in this country that can rank with them."[264]

In her *Memoirs*, Negri notes that *Barbed Wire* opened in strong fashion, but attendance dropped quickly after the disclosure of her marriage to Prince Serge Mdivani. Valentino fans who had shown sympathy towards her were outraged that she should wed less than one year after his death. Her "antics" during Valentino's memorial service returned to the forefront of newspapers, heaping further helpings of scorn on the beleaguered star. Good pictures would have helped her, but none of the remaining films that she did under contract to Famous Players did anything to boost her standing.

Negri's increasing penchant for "forgetting" to pay her bills made headlines again when she was named as the defendant in a suit filed in Superior Court by the Margraf Company of Berlin to recover $16,000 in loans. According to the plaintiffs, Negri had closed her accounts with the Harrison National Bank of New York City when they had tried to garnish her account to collect on three loan notes she had taken out during her last trip to Europe.[265]

Interlude: Serge Mdivani

"What Do Women Seek in Marriage" by Doris Denbo quotes Pola:

The man I shall marry? Ah! He must be unselfishly considerate, immaculate in appearance, artistic in nature, have an intelligent mind and an affectionate disposition.

He would not necessarily have to be famous *but* he would have to be gifted above the average.

We would have to have a community of friendships and viewpoints on life. I would expect the utmost courtesy in little things from the man who becomes my husband.[266]

Negri married Serge Mdivani on May 14, 1927, in Paris. He had none of the qualities she said she wanted. It would be a disastrous union for her, both personally and professionally.

Serge Mdivani's family came from Inertia, one of the three kingdoms of Georgia, annexed by Russia in 1810. The patriarch of the family, Zakhary Mdivani, was a colonel in the Ervian cavalry regiment of the Imperial Russian Army. His wife Elizabeth Sobolevka, a Pole, bore him five children: Nina, Serge, David, Isabel Roussadana and Alexis. The family moved from Tifflis to St. Petersburg when Mdivani was promoted to an aide-de-camp to Tsar Nicholas II.

After the Russian revolution, Georgia Armenia, and the Tartar Republic broke away to form independent non-Bolshevik republics.[267] Zakhary Mdivani was named governor of Batumi, an oil port on the Black Sea that had been part of the Ottoman Empire until 1918. Georgia's independence, however, was short-lived. In February of 1921, the Bolsheviks, seeking to forcibly annex the republic into the Soviet Union, laid siege to the city.

Nina, Isabel and youngest son Alexis were evacuated to Paris. David and Serge were sent to America in the care of a family friend, Zenas Ward Crane—scion of the Crane Typewriter Company.

David and Serge were schooled stateside for one year at Crane's expense. They were nearly expelled several times for bad behavior before they quit and returned to Paris where the rest of the family had settled after the fall of Batumi. Since there were no jobs for them there, they traveled back to California, ostensibly to study American oil production methods as their family held concession rights on land in both Russia and the United States.

In America, the brothers billed themselves as exiled Georgian "princes." Nothing could be further from the truth. During the early 1920s, America was flooded with would-be princes and pretenders from all over Eastern Europe. With all the postwar turmoil and with ancient records missing, who could contradict their claims? But the Mdivanis were never royalty. They were, at best, "landed gentry" lacking any kind of royal lineage. As far as studying American oil production methods, that story was phony as well. They were after money—preferably someone else's money. Notoriously charming scoundrels, they were adept at persuading wealthy women to marry them. David Mdivani married Mae Murray in 1926. Alexis wed heiress Louise Van Arlen and, after divorcing her, moved on to the even wealthier Barbara Hutton. They gained the reputation for being professional "adventurers"—the male counterpart to the "gold digger."

Pola explains it all like this: "I adored Valentino.... But Serge means more than all to me." She says he is the perfect husband for an artist, willing to give up everything himself, and asking her to give up nothing.[268]

Negri met Serge through David Mdivani, who had befriended her mother Eleonora during her stay in Hollywood in 1925 and '26. *Photoplay,* however, reported that Negri and her future husband had been childhood friends.[269] The *New York Times* quoted Mdivani as stating he had known Negri since he was 14 and she was 16.[270] Bunk. Negri's autobiography makes no mention of this. During Eleonora's stay, Negri opened her Beverly Hills mansion to the influx of European actors and directors who had emigrated to Hollywood, thereby providing her mother with company. The Mdivanis were among the frequent visitors to her home and when David wed Mae Murray after a *three-week* courtship, Negri served as Mae's matron of honor as a favor to him. She and Murray actually detested each other.

Negri's *Memoirs of a Star* characterized Serge Mdivani as intent on marrying her almost as soon as they were introduced. She described him as dark and Latin-looking.[271] Still mourning Valentino's loss, she welcomed his weekly visits to her house and admired the friendship he and David extended to Rudy's brother, Alberto. As previously mentioned, the Mae Murray biography *The Self-Enchanted* describes Pola and Serge as "inseparable" even before Rudy's death. Like Valentino, Serge Mdivani was smooth and cosmopolitan and had a sense of fatalistic gaiety that she, another fatalist, found comforting. That was really the only quality they ever had in common.

After completing *Barbed Wire,* Negri went to France to research her upcoming film role as the celebrated French actress Rachel and to visit her mother at the Chateau de Seraincourt. She wrote in *Memoirs* that on the eve of her departure for New York, she received a call from gossip columnist Louella Parsons asking her if there was any truth to the rumor that she was involved romantically with Serge. Negri says she "laughed uproariously" and replied that they were friends, nothing more.[272] *Photoplay* reported,

Portrait of Serge Mdivani and Pola Negri.

"There is absolutely no truth to the story that Pola Negri is in love with Mae Murray's husband's brother. The younger of the Mdivani boys means nothing in Pola's life. So there!"[273]

Yet upon her arrival in New York, she was astounded to find Mdivani staying in the same hotel on the pretext that he had business in town. Negri didn't believe his story, but nevertheless agreed to have dinner with him. She was aware he was courting her, but had "no sexual curiosity" about him.[274] When she discovered that Mdivani had booked passage on the ship she was taking to Europe, he claimed it was a coincidence that he was aboard and headed to Paris as well.

Serge proved to be a suave and relentless suitor. During the voyage he freely admitted his intention to get her to marry him. She told him she did not return his affections. In France, Mdivani used his father's position as Georgian diplomatic consul to get her through customs without delay. Negri then greeted her mother and Casimir De Hulewicz who, much to her surprise, asked her about the telegram sent from the ship to a dozen or so newspapers announcing their engagement and wedding date.[275] Before a stunned Negri realized what Serge had done, she was besieged by Mdivani relatives offering congratulations and leading her to a quick press conference to confirm their engagement. Strangely enough, she said nothing at the time to dispute the announcement, although she had doubts about going through with it. *Photoplay* editor James Quirk offered his acid assessment of this sudden development:

> The wilted tiger lily of Hollywood has metamorphosed into a blushing rose. The funeral weeds of autumn bloom forth as the bridal gown of spring. Pola Negri, by this time, is probably the Princess Serge Mdivani of Georgia.... Ah, well. Ain't love wonderful?[276]

If Negri had no feelings for Mdivani, it begs the question of why she simply didn't say so when the engagement was announced. Why would such a strong and opinionated woman allow herself to be rushed into a marriage with a man she barely knew? Her most trusted confidantes, De Hulewicz in particular, warned her against marrying. It was too soon after Valentino's death, she was told, and the public would turn against her if she married so quickly. Famous Players–Lasky sent word by telegram forbidding her to either confirm or deny the engagement until they had a chance to see how the news of it would affect her career.

Negri remained ensconced in her chateau, pondering whether she should marry him. Mdivani insisted on a quick wedding, giving her little opportunity to object, and he and his family went on a charm offensive to ensure that she didn't change her mind. Friends in Paris feted them with parties in their honor and on one such occasion Negri received a true glimpse of his personality when Serge angrily accused her of humiliating him by flirting with another man in front of the guests. A furious Negri ordered him out of her chateau, telling him it was over between them. When he later tearfully apologized and begged her for forgiveness, she fell for his declarations of love and agreed to marry him before returning to America. (Brother David Mdivani pulled the exact same act in persuading Mae Murray to marry him.) They wed at the chateau with Negri telling reporters that her wedding bouquet represented her happiness. "Red roses for passion!" she said.[277]

Newspapers contradict Negri's "revisionist" recollections. According to a 1936 article by David Mdivani, Serge met Pola on a sea journey to Paris, probably in 1925 when Negri sailed to France on holiday from the studio. According to the account, Pola and Serge spent a good 30 minutes together aboard ship chatting. After the Mdivanis returned to

California, wrote David, "the friendship that had begun somewhere between the United States and Europe was renewed between my brother and Miss Negri. They took long drives along the sea coast, through the orange groves. Without saying, they saw life together."[278]

This would seem to confirm Jane Ardmore's assertion in *The Self-Enchanted* that Negri and Serge had been keeping company even while she was supposedly "engaged" to Valentino. Pola would only admit that Serge had been a comfort to her while she grieved over Valentino's death.[279] So the assertion that Negri had little interest in Mdivani prior to their ship voyage rings hollow.

David Mdivani wrote that Serge was headed back to Europe on business on the S.S. *Acquitania* when he again encountered Pola onboard. Neither of them had known the other was on the ship. Serge joked about having left her there a year earlier and Negri allegedly replied, "I was waiting for you to return."[280]

It probably didn't happen that way, either.

Consider this. It took all of three weeks for the foolish and impetuous Mae Murray to agree to marry David Mdivani. If you believe the newspaper's version of the story, it took less than one week for Pola to make the worst mistake of her life by agreeing to marry "Prince" Serge. By the time their ship reached Cherbourg, they were engaged and there is no evidence that Negri took time to think about it, as she related in her autobiography.

Happiest about the engagement announcement, according to reports, was Eleonora, who was quoted as saying she was thrilled to see her daughter marry "Serge, her childhood friend"—contrary to her objections noted in *Memoirs*. She called the prince "very cultured and more handsome than Valentino." Eleonora's words are further proof to the notion that Negri and Mdivani were in a relationship even before Valentino's death. Evidently at the time when Serge's brother married Mae Murray, she said "Serge and Pola saw a good deal of each other and the childhood flame rose again."[281] If this is all true, doesn't it mean that all of Pola's tears and mourning over the loss of Valentino really was the acting job of a lifetime and that she is guilty of scene-stealing as so many have suggested?

Though suffering from seasickness, Pola was said to be elated by the prospect of becoming a princess. She was quoted as saying, "We are so happy.... And we are very much in love with each other. Serge has been wonderful to me. My love for him came suddenly though I have known him for many years."

And what about Valentino, whom she had declared to be the love of her life? She replied, "I adored Valentino and it is not a lack of reverence for his memory that I am in love and am going to marry Serge."[282]

There was some initial drama when, contrary to Negri's account, none of Mdivani's family showed up to meet them upon their arrival in France. Mdivani's father had apparently made public his reservations about Serge marrying Pola on the grounds that "one movie star in the family is enough." Sergei, however, made it clear that parental approval was unnecessary. "My family is not altogether opposing the engagement, but it is rather surprised. If they oppose it I will renounce everything in order to become Pola's husband."[283] The same newspaper story then reported Pola's hiring of two press agents to spread the word that she wasn't marrying for the title, but for love. After Valentino, who would believe her otherwise?

The crisis was resolved. When Pola met with her future father-in-law, he was gracious and charming. He had failed to meet the ship because he was not feeling well. There were no other objections to the marriage nor, probably, to the size of her bank account.

A civil wedding was performed in the town hall of Seraincourt, located about 30 miles outside of Paris. The bride wore a medieval-style wedding gown of white satin with a narrow waist and a long spreading skirt adorned with silver fabric. A scarf of tulle was draped around her shoulders. She put on an ermine coat for the drive to the village and back.[284]

After the ceremony, the Prince and Princess Mdivani returned to her chateau for a reception attended by scores of their friends. Mae Murray, Pola's new sister-in-law was not present, nor was David Mdivani, Serge's brother. According to representatives of the bride, they had not been invited.[285] As Pola and her prince "promenaded" up a walkway, an orchestra played "Lohengrin" and the guests stood to applaud them. After the festive reception concluded, the Prince and Princess Mdivani drove to Deauville for a short honeymoon prior to departing for America.[286]

Negri's reason for marrying Serge Mdivani had everything to do with her loneliness, her heartbreak over Valentino's loss, and an urgent need for calm in her frantic life. He seemed strong and steady to her, the kind of man she could see herself being happy with—the same thing she had thought of Chaplin during their ill-fated romance. She needed someone who wouldn't abandon her as so many had done before and Mdivani acted so eager to be with her. So the fatalist gave love one more chance. In retrospect, her biggest blind spot was in her choice of men. *Memoirs* paints Serge Mdivani as interminably jealous, possessive, and keen on liberally spending his new wife's money as if he'd wed a cash register. (His brother David treated Mae Murray in the same fashion.) During their honeymoon on the Normandy Coast, he discovered a casino next to their hotel. He racked up quite a bill in gambling losses that Negri was forced to cover.[287] He purchased new clothes and a Rolls-Royce for himself without any consideration as to their cost. When Pola complained of his extravagances, he angrily reminded her that he was a prince and told her she should show respect for his standing and authority as her husband. On their voyage back to America, he repeatedly accused her of flirting with other passengers and told her to remain in their cabin until he summoned her. Unbelievably, she did as told, to avoid arguments.

During a stop in Chicago on her way home, a reporter addressed her as "princess." The *Ogden Standard Examiner* recounted:

> She interrupted, "Miss Negri, not princess."
> Rudolph Valentino was mentioned. Miss Negri clutched her throat.
> "Please!" she whispered. "That is a very sacred thing to me. I will not discuss it."

In the same interview she denied rumors she was retiring from the screen to concentrate on being the Princess Mdivani. She intended to work for two more years to complete her contract and would then "become a thoroughly domesticated wife, and perhaps raise a large family."[288] Upon returning to Hollywood, she discovered the fears regarding marrying Serge so quickly were well-founded. *Barbed Wire* had opened to strong box office returns, but ticket sales had quickly plummeted after the news of her wedding. Her fan mail, which had required a staff of secretaries, dwindled to mostly abusive letters from Valentino fans. She wrote in *Memoirs* that "the American Valentino cult was determined to ruin me for daring to live a life that was not completely dedicated to the memory of Rudy—as if I would ever really be able to forget him."[289]

The public felt cheated. Even her staunchest defenders, who had dismissed reports of her "antics" during Valentino's funeral, now felt as if it had been all entirely for show.

How could Pola Negri, in less than a year, marry someone else after having tearfully called Valentino "the love of her life"? Her display of grief at his death had touched hearts in the most romantic sense, yet now it seemed as if she'd never meant it. It wasn't just disappointment, it was a betrayal of the public's trust. She had *deceived* her fans. At the very minimum, she had proven to be a flake. One *Picture-Play* reader wrote:

> I want to throw the biggest brickbat I can at one of screendom's greatest stars—Pola Negri! When the world was plunged into grief by the death of our idol, Rudy Valentino, Miss Negri announced that she had been engaged to him. And we were grieved. We could imagine her sorrow. I had always liked Pola. She is a lovely woman and a fine actress. But ask me if I like Pola now, and my answer will be a big "no!" And why? Because, only nine months after the death of Rudy, she announced her engagement and approaching marriage to Prince Serge Mdivani! Of course, Miss Negri deserves her happiness, but my goodness, why did she say to the newspapers that this was the first time she had ever really loved? Could she have loved our Rudy if that's what she says now? Applesauce![290]

Another reader wrote:

> I lose all patience when I read passionate defenses of Miss Negri. There is not an actress on the stage or screen who has taken more pains to air her frequent love affairs than has Pola Negri. We are constantly confronted with her latest amours, we are continually hearing her impassioned protest, "Ah love! It is not for me!" And now we are expected to sympathize with this "frail, broken flower" because death has robbed her of one man and forced her to get herself another. It is a slap at the public's intellect. Pola Negri is, in one respect, right. Real love is not for her.[291]

Photoplay sounded an ominous warning: "Pola has made what is probably a fatal error.... There is one thing that is insurmountable if it creeps into the gossip about anybody. And that one thing is ridicule ... but now she has made people laugh and that, in America, is worse than first degree murder."[292]

Photoplay took the extraordinary step of chastising her in print. Editor James R. Quirk asked whether someone should counsel her to stop living her emotional life in public. He wrote, "[W]e make no charge of insincerity, nor have we any right to criticize Pola's personal temperament, but it is no wonder that the public, judging all screen stars by the emotional outburst of a few, are quite ready to believe they are all temperamental freaks."[293]

Quirk also revealed that *Photoplay* had made a cursory check into the royal claims of the Mdivani family and a genealogist had found no record of their princely status in Georgia. The undeniable inference of the piece is that the Mdivanis were frauds. Serge and Negri threatened to sue for libel over the allegations, but nothing ever came of it.

The Woman on Trial

Distributor: Paramount
Released September 25, 1927

STATUS: Lost.
CREDITS: *Director:* Mauritz Stiller. *Scenario:* Elsie von Koczain. *Adaptation:* Hope Loring. *Photographer:* Bert Glennon.
CAST: Pola Negri (*Julie Morland*), Einar Hanson (*Pierre Boulon*), Arnold Kent (*Gaston Napier*), Andre Sarti (*John Morland*), Baby Dorothy Brock (*Paul*), Valentina Ziminia (*Henrietta*), Sidney Bracey (*Brideaux*), Bertram Marbrugh (*Moreland's Lawyer*), Gaye Whitman (*Julie's Lawyer*).

6. Pola Negri in Paramount Pictures

Negri plays "Julie" in *The Woman on Trial*, Paramount, 1927. Directed by Mauritz Stiller.

STORY

Julie Morland, standing trial for the murder of Paris art dealer Gaston Napier, testifies in court. She fell in love with Pierre Bouton, a poverty-stricken artist with a serious illness, and during a party at Gaston's studio she stopped him from committing suicide. Julie later met John Morland, a wealthy suitor who proposed marriage. She accepted, because his money would allow her to care for the stricken Pierre. They wed and she had a child by Morland, but she continued to see her true love through his illness. Her husband discovered her infidelity, forced her out onto the street, and refused to let her see her child. Desperate, Julie kidnapped her son and then gained custody of him in her ensuing divorce. Her embittered ex-husband forced the hapless Gaston to blackmail Julie into returning the boy. Gaston did as told and threatened her. When he and Julie tussled over a revolver, she shot him by accident. In the end, she is acquitted by the jury and returns to her son and a now-cured Pierre.

Reviews

Variety called the picture "thoroughly theatrical and strangely alien in tone and locale…. Coming to life only for a few minutes in the end when the vitality is rather the flamboyant emotional acting of the star, than anything stirring in the play itself."[294] The *New York Times* said, "Miss Negri serves the film well as she can, but even she is asked to express herself awkwardly."[295] The *Film Daily* concluded, "Pola's acting makes the mechanical effort worthwhile."[296]

From the synopsis and surviving photographs, *The Woman on Trial* looks to have been one of Negri's blandest efforts of her American tenure. She looks positively radiant, clad mostly in white dresses that emphasize Julie's purity and sacrifice for love. The plot, however, is very thin and undemanding and, once again, any actress could have been plugged into the role—this sounds like something Norma Shearer might tackle—making Pola Negri's presence in the picture inconsequential. She didn't need to be in a film like this. She needed a story as unique as herself, but she wasn't going to get that from Famous Players.

The public now ignored her pictures. With plenty of empty seats to be had when her name appeared on a theater's marquee, she continued to decline in value to exhibitors. The Rivoli Theater in Baltimore reported: "Pola simply lacks punch here; all recent Negri's under par, and this one no exception."[297] The manager of Tombstone, Arizona's, Crystal Theatre said, "Pola Negri is slipping with us, she does not draw as of yore. We sometimes wonder if the people do not tire quicker of some players than others."[298]

In November 1927, it was announced that Negri had been hospitalized for an allergic reaction to a heart tonic. The problem was actually a nervous breakdown.[299] It should not have come as a surprise, considering all the recent upheaval in her life. She had tragically lost a fiancé, seen her popularity plummet, and married a fortune-seeking adventurer who turned out to be a burden. Serge Mdivani made a nuisance of himself on the *Woman on Trial* set, jealously railing against her love scenes and throwing a fit any time someone at the studio addressed him as "Mr. Negri." To give him something to do, she set him up in the real estate business, but Serge had no business sense and showed a propensity for backing outlandish schemes with his wife's money. Pola was ultimately forced to close down the venture to keep him from freely spending her fortune.[300]

She was no longer the only European actress in Hollywood. Vilma Banky (Hungary), Lya De Putti (Hungary), Garbo (Sweden) and Olga Baclanova (Russia) were the movies' new "foreign legion." *Variety* sarcastically reported:

> Pola claims … she had to encounter and beat down much antagonism because of her nationality. The present cordial reception accorded English, Swedish, German, Austrian and other alien filmmakers and actors is attributed by Pola to the missionary work performed by herself. She made Hollywood safe for foreigners, claims Pola.[301]

Famous Players said she would next work with acclaimed director Josef von Sternberg, but what might have been a sensational pairing never happened. The studio that had signed her with such fanfare no longer wanted her.

The Secret Hour

Distributor: Paramount
Released February 4, 1928
Alternate Titles: Sun Kissed; Beggars of Love

STATUS: Lost
CREDITS: *Screenwriter-Director:* Rowland V. Lee. *Story* "They Knew What They Wanted" by Sidney Howard.
CAST: Pola Negri (*Amy*), Jean Hersholt (*Tony*), Kenneth Thompson (*Joe*), Christian J. Frank (*Sam*), George Kuwa (*Ah Gee*), George Periolat (*Doctor*).

STORY

Tired of lifelong bachelorhood, Tony, an elderly fruit grower, sends a photograph of Joe, his foreman, in place of one of his own photos to capture the heart of Amy, an attractive waitress. She falls for the man in the photograph and makes plans to marry him, unaware that a switch has been made. Tony's plan backfires when an automobile accident prevents him from meeting her train and he is forced to send Joe to collect her. Joe and Amy are immediately attracted to each other and secretly marry. They later regret their betrayal of the well-meaning older man. Amy dutifully tends to Tony, nursing him back to health as he romances her, but all the while she wishes to be with her husband. When Tony discovered that Joe and Amy are married, he furiously orders them to leave, but after a change of heart forgives them and wills them the fruit farm after his death.

REVIEWS

Critics were wildly divided on this movie. *Variety* called it "dull and bordering on stupidity" and warned that it spelled "bad business for any downtown house showing it and will be a chaser for the neighborhoods."[302] But the *New York Times* commended Negri on her acting and thought the picture was a dignified interpretation of Sidney Howard's play.[303] *Photoplay* called it "rather wishy-washy. Pola Negri ... does not impress. Jean Hersholt as Tony is great."[304]

The stage version had been adult and frank in tone in its depiction of a love triangle, but the film was devoid of anything that might be controversial or censorable. Even after five futile years, Famous Players–Lasky was still trying to make Negri's pictures safe for American moviegoers. Even so, one indignant exhibitor wrote:

> Brother Exhibitor, if you have any moral people in your town who you are depending on for your business, don't play *The Secret Hour*. Absolutely the poorest picture we have ever played in my many years of experience in the picture business. I can't understand how the stars could have made this picture without showing a red face. Let's have morality in our picture business for humanity's sake.[305]

This is one of Negri's least-known pictures—apparently hardly seen in its day and now lost altogether. Even photographs from this picture are hard to come by and it's

Negri and Kenneth Thompson in *The Secret Hour*, Paramount, 1928. Directed by Rowland V. Lee.

telling that the photos this author has seen don't convey even a hint of the story. In most of them, Pola looks older and a little worn, as if she knew her acting wouldn't make a difference to the picture's success or failure. She wasn't being asked to do anything special. She was simply going through the motions.

Her marquee value continued to plummet. The Paramount Theatre in New York reported a box office take of $61,200 for *The Secret Hour* with *Variety* declaring that this "again demonstrates that Negri doesn't mean much in New York."[306] A Minnesota movie house told the *Film Spectator*, "Pola Negri no magnet here. Around $1000. Bad."[307]

Her entire 1928 output of pictures fell into the category of "programmers"—"B-movies" as they would come to be known. Previously she had released a film every quarter, but her pictures were now dumped on the market in rapid succession without much build-up or fanfare. Famous Players no longer considered her a top actress and the mediocre reviews made her release at the expiration of her contract inevitable. Just as well, seeing how she had lost patience with the American methods of production. She would be gone from Hollywood by June 1928.

As the box office declined, the press turned on her. For the January 1928 *Picture Play*, Malcolm Oettinger wrote an infamous portrait of Pola that was etched in the most venomous vitriol:

Pola Negri ... belongs to those old days, those days that held the stars up as immortals, that protected them from prying eyes, that veiled them in elaborate secrecy, that enshrined them as super people in a superior world all their own. Pola lets you feel, though graciously to be sure, that you are lucky to be standing, hat in hand in the Presence.

The ballyhoo that attended Pola's entry into American pictures some years ago was so prolonged, so deafening, and so thoroughly overdone in every way that Pola still hears it echoing in her ears.... She is living in a haze of old press clippings, clippings that announced her as the Bernhardt of the silver sheet, the Modjeska of the movies, the star of stars. Pola, unaccustomed to such supreme publicity, took it seriously instead of laughing it off. Her grand manner of today is the result.

She is dark and cold, and pictorially effective in an artificial way. Her hair is black, her face a mask of white enamel, her lips a glowing gash of scarlet. Purple about her eyes lends an interesting touch. While the cameras, lights, and so forth, were being made ready for the scene in hand, she sat on the set contemplating the table in front of her. She seemed indifferent to everyone about her—a trifle contemptuous, infinitely bored.

Some say she is beautiful. There is a magnificent vitality about her, a certain magnetism, but it can hardly be called beauty. She is short and slender and dynamic. She is artificial and affected and theatrical. Pola is another name for pose.

In the course of my hour's conversation with her, Pola was not herself for an instant. Her speeches were stilted, measured, sonorous. They sounded memorized. Her opinions were cameos of tact, her reasoning stereotyped.[308]

Picture-Play readers were outraged, calling Oettinger "mean-spirited" and "prejudiced." Negri, however, had too few American fans left to show their support. She seemed to be slipping everywhere. *Variety* reported, "Although Pola Negri has been Par's best on the foreign market, it is said that with pictures released by Jannings, that picture for picture, he is outselling her. The American following of Miss Negri seems to be getting away from her bit by bit."[309]

Miss Negri's hands and footprints in the cement at Grauman's Chinese Theatre, Hollywood, California (photograph by author).

New legal troubles made the newspapers. The March 28, 1928, *Perth Daily News* revealed that Pola had settled her suit against jewelers who sold her $28,000 worth of jewelry and advised her there would be no duty owed on the gems. Negri, obviously not having learned much since the last time she tried to bring jewelry into the country without declaring it, wound up paying a duty of $20,000 on the gems. To make it worse, Pola claimed to have returned the gems, but had gotten a bill for the same jewelry for more than $75,000.

In a happier moment, Pola became the tenth person to leave her hands and footprints in concrete in the forecourt at Grauman's Chinese Theatre on April 5, 1928. Her message to Sid Grauman says, "Dear Sid: I love your theatre." Both prints and message are still there today.

With her career as a viable American film star winding down, it had become apparent that her only remaining value was as filler in newspaper gossip columns. *Picture-Play Magazine* labeled her a "tragedy queen" and concluded, "It really does not matter what she says, so long as what she does is intriguing."[310]

Three Sinners

Distributor: Paramount
Released April 14, 1928
Alternate Title: Her Second Life

STATUS: Lost

CREDITS: *Director:* Rowland V. Lee. *Scenario:* Doris Anderson, Jean De Limur, from the play *Das Zwete Leben* by Rudolph Osterreicher.

CAST: Pola Negri (*Baroness Gerda Wallentin*), Warner Baxter (*James Harris*), Paul Lukas (*Count Dietrich Wallentin*), Anders Randolph (*Count Hellemuth Wallentin*), Tullio Carminati (*Raoul Stanislav*), Anton Vaverka (*Valet to Dietrich*), Ivy Harris (*Countess Lilli*), William von Hardenburg (*Prince von Scherson*), Olga Baclanova (*Baroness Hilda Brings*).

STORY

Escaping what she believes to be a failed marriage, Gerda, the Countess Wallentin, travels by train to Vienna to visit relatives. En route, the lonely woman is seduced by Raoul Stanislav, a famous musician. Later, after she disembarks from the train during a brief stop, the train departs without her. The train crashes, killing everyone on board. She goes to Vienna, dyes her hair blonde and starts a new life as the hostess of an exclusive gambling den. She keeps various lovers until the day her husband visits the den and finds himself attracted to her because of her resemblance to his "late" wife. Overwhelmed to hear his admission of love for her, Gerda confesses her secret, but learns he never really loved her. She leaves for America with a wealthy gambler.

REVIEWS

Variety called the picture "another story which offers Pola Negri a pale role for her vivid type of acting. It's a programmer of moderate worth, dependent upon the star's name.... The play is so old-fashioned in its artificial motivation and there isn't a spark of humor in the whole business."³¹¹ The *Film Daily* thought it was the best thing she had done in some time.³¹² "This is heavy drama, adroitly handled and exceptionally well acted." *Photoplay* wrote. "Pola Negri should satisfy her European following and intrigue American audiences."³¹³ One exhibitor told the *Film Spectator*: "I believe this picture is going to be the most popular with American audiences that Pola has made in this country.... [T]hose exhibitors who had the idea that American audiences do not want Negri's pictures should try this one on their patrons. I think they'll like it."³¹⁴

No one liked it. The picture bombed. *Variety* reported, "Negri continued her habit of dropping the Paramount, this time $4000 below the previous week, although *Three Sinners* is considered better than some of her other late ones."³¹⁵

Negri in *Three Sinners*, Paramount, 1928. Directed by Roland V. Lee.

From all of the European-sounding names in the credits, you might think this was a German movie out of Negri's early days with Ufa. Photographs from this lost picture suggest that it was a ponderous affair. But Negri looks good in a blonde wig and when she gives you those eyes while holding a cigarette, she absolutely smolders. Her acting in the picture was considered acceptable, but by now audiences were more interested in talkies and newcomers with voices than the dying breed of silent film stars.

Negri's contract called for an increase to $15,000 per week if Famous Players elected to renew its option. It shocked no one when the studio declined to do so. She no longer had a viable domestic appeal and with the foreign demand for her pictures waning, a larger salary was an extravagance in a time when studios were spending a fortune on the transition from silent to sound pictures. The decision to let her go made perfect business sense—and Negri, tired of it all, was ready to go anyway.

"Paramount has become the 'killer of stars'—and their worst crime has been the killing of Pola Negri as a star," wrote a *Picture-Play* reader in 1928. The letter continued:

> She is a wonderful actress with her emotional powers ever growing. Paramount, in its quest for new and cheaper talent, has ignored the talent of their established stars. Pola Negri suffered not so much from poor stories as she did from neglect. Paramount was too busy bringing trivial players to public notice, so, naturally, we saw a great deal of such players and their reliable talent had to take a back seat. This is dangerous and most unfortunate for any star, but to think that the star of *Passion* and *Gypsy Blood* should meet with such a fate is outrageous. Perhaps it is best that Pola does separate from this company. Pola can be independent now, and she can show Paramount her real worth and what they have missed—that is, if she chooses to join another company.³¹⁶

Rumor had it that upon leaving Famous Players, Negri would sign for $10,000 per week with Universal. There were also indications that she would star in a version of Emile

Zola's *Zaza*. The press hinted she had signed a contract with United Artists. They said she thought she could produce new pictures in Europe for $60,000 per film and have Paramount distribute them stateside. Then there was talk of her making a film in Germany and returning to America with a new contract with Fox. Then it was said she would make four new pictures in Europe or she would make a picture with British International or that she was contracting with an independent French producer to make pictures there.

None of these things ever panned out. Despite frequent hints in the trade magazine as to what Pola Negri would do next, she was out of a job and had no takers for her services.

Loves of an Actress

Distributor: Paramount
Released August 18, 1928
Alternate Title: Rachel

STATUS: Lost
CREDITS: *Screenwriter-Director:* Rowland V. Lee. *Story:* Ernest Vajda.
CAST: Pola Negri (*Rachel*), Nils Asther (*Raoul Duval*), Mary McAllister (*Lisette*), Richard Tucker (*Baron Hartman*), Philip Strange (*Count Vareski*), Paul Lukas (*Dr. Durande*), Nigel De Brulier (*Samson*), Robert Fischer (*Count Morency*), Helene Giere (*Marie*).

STORY

Born into a family of poor peasants, Rachel becomes a famous stage actress in the *Comedie Francaise* through her relationships with Baron Hartman, the wealthiest man in France; Count Vareski, a relative of Napoleon; and Dr. Durande, a leading newspaper publisher. They all swear their love for her, but her heart lies with handsome Raoul Duval, who is in line to become the next French ambassador to Tsarist Russia. A vengeful Durande threatens to publish Rachel's private love letters to Duval if she does not agree to become his mistress. To save Raoul from scandal, Rachel tells him that she was only toying with his emotions and never truly loved him. Raoul goes to Russia and his diplomatic post. They are separated for decades until he comes once more to see her on her deathbed.

REVIEWS

The *New York Times* reviewer thought certain scenes showed Negri's acting ability in a good light and that her character's relationships with others were well-done, but that the total effect was just another picture.[317] *Variety* claimed the role of Rachel was better suited to a Gloria Swanson instead of the "brunette star's severe personality" and declared that the role required "a certain degree of exoticism which Miss Negri does not quite attain."[318]

The *New York American* called her performance "maudlin" and the *New York Evening World* said she was "tame and unconvincing." *The New York World* sarcastically opined: "It did seem to me that the entire play might very well have been run off while the leading woman reclines on a divan, so recurrent and so often did this particularly property come into use."[319]

Negri in a scene from *Loves of an Actress*, Paramount, 1928. Directed by Rowland V. Lee.

The displeasure of exhibitors mounted. The Star Theater in Villa Grove, Illinois, called it "not much of a picture." "One of those ancient settings they just won't come out to see," said the manager of the Legion Theater in Hollyrood, Kansas. "As for the picture it is very good. Personally I like the acting of Pola Negri, but her stories have been such that she is not a drawing card with the majority of picturegoers."[320] According to *Variety*, at least one St. Louis theater wanted nothing to do with any Pola Negri picture: "The screen advance ballyhoo made no mention of Pola as the star player.... It described in glowing adjectives the story of the plot, with naive interferences that the tale is that of the great Bernhardt, but not once was Negri's name visible."[321]

The manager of the Selma Theater succinctly summed up the picture's appeal as "zero at the box office."[322]

Negri had high hopes for this production. She fought with the studio over the script and their constant attempts to cut costs. She went to Europe—at the studio's expense—to research the real-life Rachel and even received carte blanche to purchase costumes and props for the picture. When asked about Rachel, she said:

> And what a woman was Rachel!... What a life she had. What an exciting, devastating creature! And what tragedy! A woman of many loves, of course, whom men courted, admired, coveted. Yet how she suffered! I feel that I myself am Rachel's living counterpart. I have always known her, loved her, understood her. I have always wanted to portray her.
>
> When I first came to America I begged to be allowed to bring the life of Rachel to the screen, but it could

not be. Convention has us bound. But now I can enter into her very soul, because she is and always has been very close to me. Rachel was a real human being. Her faults were the faults of all flesh and blood and it was not the irony of fate that, although all men loved her, the only one she really loved turned on her, left her, lest she ruin his career.

And how she carried off that situation! How she kept her colors flying, while all Paris watched, until she was finally received at court by the stiffest of all sovereigns, Queen Victoria, is a story of a brave woman's triumph! Do you wonder that I admire her and want to make her live on the screen? Do you wonder that I go to Paris to search for every possible clue to her innermost self, that I may portray her as she really was—that I may wear the jewels she wore, wave the fan she carried, and surround myself with the gewgaws that she loved?

My days in Paris will be busy ones, for I must leave no stone unturned to reconstruct the life of that courageous creature in all faithfulness.[323]

All of her hopes and wishes were for naught. It's easy to understand the appeal to Pola of playing the real-life Rachel, a famous French actress of the mid–1800s, yet this author wonders why anyone at Famous Players believed that American audiences might be interested in the story of a foreign actress that they had never heard of. It would appear that *Loves of an Actress* was more along the lines of a "vanity production" and even with great dramatic potential, it just wasn't all that interesting. The mention of Negri's "severe personality" is a puzzling throwback to some of the criticism leveled at her as early as *Bella Donna* and *The Cheat*, but the notion she lacks the "exoticism" to play the role is a very strange thing to say of someone whose "exoticism" had been one of her original selling points. Had she finally become so conventional?

There was news that Pola might make two new pictures for a British company or two pictures for Ufa. There were also hints that she was considering divorcing Serge Mdivani.[324] *Variety* called the rumors a "publicity stunt" to attract headlines. Who could blame anyone for believing them?

The Woman from Moscow

Distributor: Paramount
Released November 2, 1928

Status: Lost.
Credits: *Director*: Ludwig Berger. *Screenplay*: John Farrow, from the play *Fedora* by Victorien Sardou.
Cast: Pola Negri (*Princess Fedora*), Norman Kerry (*Loris Ipanoff*), Paul Lukas (*Vladimir*), Otto Matiesen (*Gretch Milner*), Lawrence Grant (*The General*), Maude George (*Olga Andreavitshka*), Bodil Rosing (*Nadia*), Jack Luden (*Ipanoff's Brother*), Martha Franklin (*Ipanoff's Mother*), Mirra Rayo (*Ipanoff's Sister*), Tetsu Komai (*Groom*).

Story

During Tsarist times, Princess Fedora's fiancé Vladimir is found murdered in a deserted summer house on his father's estate. Vowing to avenge his death, Fedora seeks out Loris Ipanoff, the man she suspects of the crime. She meets Loris and without knowing his name falls in love with him. Upon learning his true identity, she refuses to believe him guilty, yet to her astonishment, he confesses to the killing. Fedora betrays him to her fiancé's vengeful father. She later learns that Loris killed Vladimir (who had violated his sister) in self-defense and she saves him from assassins hired by the father. Yet as punishment for Vladimir's death, Loris' family is sentenced to exile in Siberia and his brother is slain while resisting arrest. Loris turns against Fedora. Guilt-ridden, she commits suicide by taking poison. A contrite Loris returns to her just in time to hold her in his arms as she dies.

REVIEWS

This sounds like a rotten picture. *Variety* pulled no punches: "Pola Negri in more than an hour of an old-fashioned melodrama ... with an unhappy ending at that, is not stimulating. Pictorially, it's a marvelously artistic production; on its entertainment side for modern screen purposes it just won't do."[325] *Liberty Magazine* called the picture "horrendous" and advised readers to "stay away from the box office." "Pola Negri's last picture for Paramount *should* be her swan song," said *Photoplay*.[326] The *Motion Picture News Daily* said her role didn't feel genuine and was out of date.[327]

The Exhibitor's Daily Review sounded the sole note of optimism: "Pola Negri never looked quite so good as she does in *The Woman from Moscow*. She looks gorgeous. We rather liked the picture.... [O]n the strength of what we saw at the Paramount last night, that very talented actress is due to return to our shores. She is too great a bet to lose.[328]

The manager of the Strand Theater in Minneapolis reported to *Variety* that *The Woman from Moscow* had resulted in the "worst week of the season," and added, "[T]hey just stay away when [Negri] is in the picture."[329]

This was the last picture produced under Negri's contract with Famous Players–Lasky. The story goes that she walked out of the studio for good as soon as shooting wrapped. She had already cleared out her dressing room which was to go to Clara Bow, now the reigning actress on the studio lot. No longer employed, Pola announced to the press that she would take a three-month auto tour of Europe with her husband.[330] After that? No one had any idea what she would do next. She never made another movie for Famous Players and in studio histories of the Paramount Pictures company, the once-celebrated Pola Negri is scarcely, if ever, mentioned.

Portrait of Negri for *The Woman from Moscow*, Paramount, 1928. Directed by Ludwig Berger.

7

The Anatomy of Failure

Most discussions of Pola Negri's film career list three main reasons for her loss of popularity: her voice, unsuitable for talking pictures; the establishment of the Hays Code; and her behavior at Valentino's funeral which turned audiences against her.[1] These reasons, cited over and over, have nothing to do with what happened.

Her voice was not a factor in Famous Players' decision to let her contract expire in 1928. Negri never took a voice test for the studio nor spoke in any of her Paramount pictures. Her last two Paramounts, *Loves of an Actress* and *The Woman from Moscow*, contained recorded music and sound effects, but no spoken dialogue. Negri did not speak in an English-language picture until *A Woman Commands* in 1932.

Anger's *Hollywood Babylon* and the movie musical *Singin' in the Rain* (1952) are the main culprits behind the assertion that many actors of the silent era didn't make it into talkies because of their voices. John Gilbert and Marie Prevost are offered up as prime examples in Anger's tome. Their thin voices, it is suggested, didn't match their romantic screen images—Gilbert's voice, it is said, got him laughed off the screen. Unable to make the transition to sound, they became destitute, alcoholic and dead at an early age. It's an enjoyably ghoulish story in a way, but *it's not true*.

The technology of early sound pictures (circa 1928–1929) was primitive. The competing sound processes, Warner Brothers' Vitaphone, Fox's Movietone and RCA's Phototone, varied widely in quality of sound reproduction. The big bulky microphones of the times were stationary, so actors had to stand in close proximity to them; hence the need to hide the recording equipment in the shot by use of a lot of plants and flowers and a lot of standing around talking. Most actors' voices, no matter how good they were, recorded poorly in the beginning. There was no way to precisely adjust the volume, so crumpling up a piece of paper sounded like a raging forest fire on the soundtrack. Recording quality eventually improved, but only after a long period of trial and error revealed what did and didn't work when it came to spoken dialogue.

Despite what has been written, Negri's voice was fine. Remember that she had been a star of the stage in Warsaw and Berlin before getting into pictures, so she understood tenor and voice modulation. Her accent, although a bit heavy, was still as understandable as Garbo's turned out to be. There really was no problem with how she spoke. She could and eventually did make the transition to sound.

Second, the assertion that the Hays Code stopped her from "essaying her vamp roles" is another oft-repeated "fact" that has no bearing on what happened. *Bella Donna* and, to a lesser degree, *The Cheat* were the only two American pictures in which she played a role that approached the "vamp" characterization established by Theda Bara. The vogue for that kind of role had already long-passed by 1928, although it still appeared from time to time, particularly as played by actresses Nita Naldi and Olga Baclanova, both never true leading ladies in pictures. This "vamp theory" is wrong because, on the whole, Negri didn't really play that kind of part.

In addition, what is generally thought of as "the Hays Code" is actually the "Breen Code," named after Joseph Breen, who took over administration of the Production Code starting in 1934. The Breen Code codified what had been mere suggestions to that point, instituting a stricter code of censorship prohibiting glorification of crime and depictions of sexuality. *A Woman Commands*, released in 1932, was Negri's first and last American film of that decade. She was away from Hollywood when the Code came into being. It never really affected her.

The most difficult of the three reasons to dispel is the one concerning her drop in popularity, blamed on her so-called "antics" at Valentino's funeral. True, her popularity dipped sharply after that event, but her standing was already in decline from a long string of mediocre film vehicles and a public tired of the publicity that had engulfed her. A change in the kind of roles she played might have helped her, but a change to *what* exactly? Pola was not the "All-American girl" or "the sweetheart-next-door." She was too worldly and sophisticated for audiences in small towns who shunned pictures with European actors as "too continental." She was a particular type with a limited appeal. So it's no surprise that Paramount declined to renew her contract when the returns from her pictures dried up.

Negri, of course, wasn't blameless in what happened. Her second contract with Lasky gave her the right of approval over scripts and directors. She chose to make *Loves of an Actress* and *The Woman from Moscow* with their trite and old-fashioned plots even as silent pictures reached their peak of perfection in 1928. Marrying Serge Mdivani so soon after Valentino's death was terrible timing, making her seem hypocritical. She overvalued her value to the studio and they decided she wasn't worth it. She was perceived as a walking temper tantrum making pictures that exhibitors didn't want. What the press wrote about her was unfair and mostly untrue, but what the public read, they believed, and Pola Negri was finished in America because she *became* her publicity.

An article in *Photoplay*, "The Passing of Pola," offered a requiem of her American tenure.[2] Writer Leonard Hall concluded that Negri was oversold by the studio's publicity machine and fed poor material by the script department. Yet, according to Hall, the true reason for her fall was "a failure of the mind and spirit."

The Pola Negri who made her mark in *Passion*, he wrote, was a "fiery woman who had set ablaze with her genius the screens of the world." Famous Players snuffed out that fire, by taming her look and convincing her that she was a movie star, filling her with arrogance and delusions of self-importance. She never again regained her flame, repeatedly looking hunted and haunted by failure. She became self-conscious and measured her acting for effect instead of throwing herself instinctively and recklessly into her work. So instead of the greatest actress in the world, instead of the fearlessness that made her one-of-a-kind, American moviegoers got, Hall concludes, "a queenly clotheshorse, the like of which roams wild and wholesale in Hollywood." Once she was the same as everyone else, she really had nothing to offer.

According to *Picture-Play*, Pola was misunderstood by the American public. "It was difficult to penetrate the shell of mystery that encased her. She was berated as temperamental, moody, cold. Her dark eyes gleamed unreally from the pallor of her sullen face. Artists are never understood. They are too high-strung, too finely tempered, too uncanny to be understood by the throng."[3] "Pola was natural," wrote one of the magazine's readers. "But America proved so intolerant that she was forced to veil her feelings with indifference—an unnatural pose."[4] Yet another letter to *Picture-Play* lamented that her kind of acting had gone out of style:

> What is Pola Negri's tragedy as an actress?... It is in the following things: too much love fire, too much passion, blood and flesh in the primitive thing called love. Such a feeling has outlived itself in life and could not stay long on the screen.... Look at life, at modern literature, the contemporary state—does the primitive Pola Negri love have a place there?
>
> The primitive love fire, the emotional way of portraying it, makes us put Pola Negri in the first rank of all great actresses of past screen traditions.[5]

Without a new contract or prospects for work in America, Negri and her husband left for France. They insisted they "were done with movies"—meaning they were done with the studio. Pola then announced she would dedicate her life to making pictures for "art's sake"—in Europe. Hollywood had proven to be a very bitter experience for her. In America, she said, "I felt like a bird in a gilded cage; here in Europe art is surrounded and protected by traditions and can spread its wings and fly. I will make two pictures a year; if you make more, you sacrifice art."[6]

According to Negri's *Memoirs,* she chose not to review her contract and left America because she was expecting a child.

8

Pola in Purgatory

According to her *Memoirs,* Negri settled in at her renovated eighteenth-century Seraincourt chateau with its 42 rooms, 22 servants, a private chapel, vast gardens of flowers and produce of all kinds, streams full of trout, and a network of secret underground labyrinths that connected her estate to the nearby town.[1] It was her palace and she was, after all, a princess. Even without a studio contract, she was set. She had several million dollars in banks in Paris and in New York and a steady income from rental properties she owned throughout Los Angeles.

During her pregnancy, she took care of herself: eating better food, getting more exercise and abstaining from alcohol.[2] Her marriage was more tranquil now that she was away from Hollywood. Film offers still came her way. England's Gaumont Films reportedly expressed interest in starring her in a number of pictures and there was talk in the trade papers of her returning to America to make a picture called *Loves of Sappho.*[3] Negri publicly maintained she was not interested in returning to the grind she had just left and refused all offers, claiming she was fully retired from pictures. That was just fine with Serge, who didn't want a movie star wife, but had no qualms about freely spending the fortune she had earned as a star.

Rumors as early as July 1928, two months after she left America, had her already contemplating a divorce from her prince.[4] *The Exhibitor's Daily Review* noted she would divorce Mdivani on grounds of incompatibility and her "lingering love for Valentino."[5] Negri called the reports nonsense. The prince, she said, was "the love of her life," and Mdivani chimed in that all of the rumors about them were making it harder for him to land his wife a contract for new pictures.[6]

There is no mention of her pregnancy in any of the press of the time. Perhaps she chose to keep such a matter private and it would certainly be understandable, given what she had learned about demonstrating emotion after the Valentino fiasco. *Memoirs,* her very self-serving autobiography, is the only source of this information. It is unlikely that 40 years down the road Pola would *invent* a pregnancy that never happened, yet there is nothing in the historical record to corroborate her story.

Her pregnancy ended in tragedy. According to *Memoirs,* she was caught outside her chateau one afternoon in a violent thunderstorm. She was standing under a tree that was struck by lighting and the current passed through her, causing a miscarriage. Once again, however, this narrative is at odds with what appeared in the press. A September, 9, 1928, dispatch from Paris reported she had been hospitalized with critical internal injuries after a fall from a horse.[7] A passing motorcycle frightened her mount, which reared back and threw her. Mdivani, who had been riding with her, flagged down a passing car and she was taken to the American Hospital in Paris.[8] She suffered no broken bones or head injuries,[9] yet the words *internal injuries* could refer to a miscarriage. Euphemisms have always been used by film stars to mask the truth. Mdivani later told the press that her injuries were severe enough that it was feared she would not recover. Not surprisingly, there were also those who wondered if the report was just another one of her publicity stunts, seeing as how her name had been out of the headlines for a while.[10] Whichever story it was, however, Negri never had a child.

Negri wrote in *Memoirs* that after the tragedy, she retreated from the world, refusing to leave her bedroom for months. In her grief she took to drinking heavily. Her husband busied himself with social events and hosted dinner parties at the chateau. At that point she realized that the only thing that had kept her and Mdivani together was their child. Without a child, there was no marriage. She decided then to resume her screen career.

The newspapers of the time tell a different story. Instead of spending months shut in her room and sliding into alcoholism, a rather clichéd turn to a tragic story, there were reports of her working on her movie comeback just *three months* after her "near-death" accident. She went to England to see playwright George Bernard Shaw about purchasing the film rights to his play *Caesar and Cleopatra*. She claimed to have charmed the notoriously grumpy Shaw and succeeded in convincing him to let her do the picture, something other film producers had sought and failed to do. The playwright, she proudly told reporters, would assist with the production and approve the casting. She, naturally, would play Cleopatra. Negri said: "With his cooperation, I shall give my very life, and very blood, to make the picture a success."[11]

In December 1928, the *Film Daily* noted the formation of the film company Pola Negri, Inc., that would acquire and produce movies for her financed by European investors.[12] No American money would be involved. The first two pictures on her slate would be *Caesar and Cleopatra* and a film version of Alexander Dumas' *La Courier de la Reine* (*The Queen's Courier*). The pictures would have sound effects but no dialogue. My guess is that the decision to go with only sound effects had less to do with her accent and more with budgetary considerations.

Variety claimed her meeting with Shaw was nothing more than a publicity stunt. There was no agreement with Shaw for the play rights and if Negri was expecting a wealth of headlines from her announcement, she didn't get them.[13] The film never materialized and Pola Negri, Inc., never made a picture.

With her American real estate holdings floundering due to a lack of management, Pola persuaded Mdivani to return to Los Angeles to look after them. One presumes that she didn't want the jealous Serge around with all of the talk of a movie comeback. Distance, however, didn't improve relations between her and her husband.

According to Pola, she went to Paris to play Marie Antoinette in a picture titled *The Queen's Necklace* for Pathé Films. Serge returned from America at the start of production and was very unhappy to see her in front of a camera again. She claims that her husband refused to let her do the picture, citing a scene in the script in which she was to be flogged with a whip while appearing partially nude. His opposition to the scene was so strident, she says, that she dropped out of the production rather than fight with him over it.

Negri's recollection of events, again, leaves something to be desired. According to

Motion Picture Daily News, The Queen's Necklace began on March 1, 1929. She abruptly walked off the picture on March 23, citing her dissatisfaction with the screenplay; with the working conditions at the French studio (particularly a lack of a bath); and her disagreement over the continuity of the picture.[14] Pola later revealed she paid the producers $120,000 to buy her release from her contract after objecting to a scene in the script requiring her to bare her breasts.[15] "For once," she told a reporter, who insisted on quoting her phonetically, "I showed zee temperament. I would not conseeder zee peecture…. I dislike especially zee undressing scene. I pay half meelion marks to be released from zee contract…. I deed not even start to act in zee peecture…. I theenk eet is lewd."[16]

Like Eugene Dombski before him, Mdivani enjoyed the prestige of being married to a movie star, but he did not want her making movies as he was jealous of any attention afforded her. He preferred the life of the idle rich, while she craved the mental stimulation and challenges that acting demanded of her. Film opportunities still came her way and there was some interest in having her appear as a vaudeville attraction in London, although her price for appearing on stage was a *bit* steep: $60,000 for six weeks of work.[17] Nothing seemed to pan out and Mdivani became upset with her whenever the idea of a new picture came up. Yet doing nothing and simply being the Princess Mdivani bored her to tears.

She left Dombski when he stood in her way, so it really didn't surprise anyone that she filed for legal separation from Mdivani in April 1929. "Incompatibility of temperament is the sole cause of the divorce," she told a reporter. "The prince loves to go out in society to dance or to gamble at Monte Carlo … while I am quiet by nature and prefer to stay at home and devote myself to my art."[18] Serge, strangely enough, confirmed her explanation. "Pola is a sweet and wonderful girl, but there are times when two people do not agree. Recently I went to Monte Carlo alone. Pola objected. I went nevertheless. Our characters are so different that we cannot agree."[19]

It wasn't as cut-and-dried as the quotes indicate. During his sea voyage home from tending to his wife's American properties, Serge met Mary McCormick, a beautiful American opera singer, and persuaded her to join him in a weekend trip to the casinos of Monte Carlo. When Pola found out about her husband's unscheduled side trip with another woman, she called her lawyer. According to those ever-quotable "friends" of the couple, another source of conflict in the marriage was her continued mourning for Valentino. According to one story, her chateau was heavily decorated with photographs of Rudy, and there were rumors of Negri driving around Paris, looking for any cinema showing an old Valentino picture.[20]

Legally separated from Mdivani, she signed a contract for $75,000 to appear in a picture called *The Golden Moth*, to be produced by *A Woman Commands* screenwriter Charles Whittaker and directed by former Ufa director Paul Czinner.[21] She then made a brief return visit to America, she said, to inspect her real estate holdings. She declared she had no interest in returning to American pictures. Sure. More likely she was looking for work and found no interest from the film studios. There was talk of her returning to Ufa for a film version of *The Shanghai Gesture,* but nothing came of that. So she returned to England, telling reporters on her arrival that she had come to make a great film, the one that would end her career. She added, "[A]fter that is made I shall devote myself to charities. In Poland, my homeland, I support two orphanages. After I leave the films, my life will go to those children. It will be farewell to Pola Negri so far as the public is concerned."[22]

The picture she made, her last silent picture, was the story of a French prostitute in Cornwall, known on release as *The Woman He Scorned.*

The Woman He Scorned

Released May 1929
Alternate Title: The Way of Lost Souls

Status: A public domain print is available on DVD.
Credits: *Director*-Story: Paul Czinner. *Screenwriter-Producer*: Charles E. Whittaker.
Cast: Pola Negri (*Louise*), Warwick Ward (*Maxim*), Hans Rehmann (*John*), Cameron Carr (*Magistrate*), Margaret Rawlings (*Woman*).

Story

A lighthouse keeper meets a flirtatious French prostitute and her pimp. He tries to ignore the girl, but when the pimp attempts to beat her up, he knocks the pimp out with a punch. The woman, to whom no one has ever been kind, begs him to take her with him. He refuses, but on the way back to the lighthouse, his tiny skiff sinks in a raging storm, and he promises God that if he is saved, he will do something for the lowliest of His creatures. Spared from death, he keeps his oath and marries the prostitute to make her an honest woman. At first their relationship is uneasy, but they soon warm to each other. Her former pimp, now on the run for murder, finds her and convinces her to let him hide out in her house. When her husband finds out about it, he threatens to throw her out if she helps him again. The pimp returns needing money to leave the country and she gives him what's she saved. Now her husband shuns her. Distraught, she takes a rowboat and deliberately crashes it into the rocks, drowning herself and ending her life.

Review

Variety wondered if *Woman He Scorned* producer Charles E. Whittaker had been hired by Paramount to ensure that Pola Negri was kept out of pictures. They thought the story was terrible and the acting worse: "Negri looks like everything but a screen actress. She mumbles and flutters, there is no sign of any characterization nor of any comprehension of her part, though lord knows the part is bad enough to begin with."[23]

The picture, shot at England's Elstree Studio with location work in both Cornwall and Marseilles, has all the hallmarks of a German production, from the expressionistic shadows to the downbeat ending. It isn't a very good picture, but this author takes issue with the comment about Negri's acting. In her role she foregoes every mannerism and camera-conscious movie star trapping of her Paramount years, resulting in a very natural performance that would have been right at home in a sound picture. In one standout scene she stares into a vanity mirror and removes her thick makeup, uncovering a face of simple beauty. Her expressive eyes and forced smile transform her into a vision of loveliness that is quite touching. She is remarkably low-key, creating a memorable character that invites the audience's sympathy. You can tell from her spot-on acting that this was a project she believed in, a redefining moment to show that she had lost nothing during her "retirement from pictures."

The Woman He Scorned was a terrible flop. Imperial Films went bankrupt and Whittaker sold the picture's American distribution rights to Warner Brothers for a measly $20,000. It had a total of three bookings in America before it was yanked from distribution. It might have fared better had it been a sound picture.

It had to be a shock to Negri that the film fared so poorly. What was it like to have once been so famous and acclaimed, and suddenly be consigned to the trash heap—unpopular and unwanted? Her name had absolutely no value as a screen attraction and in America she was regarded more as a running tabloid item than as a serious actress. A similar fate befell most of the great stars of the silent screen, but for a proud woman like Negri, the taste had to be very bitter indeed. She had counted on a film career in Europe to boost her reputation and return her to glory in the States, only to find she was no longer a draw anywhere.

During his separation from Negri, Serge Mdivani took up again with Mary McCormick.[24] McCormick told the press how much Mdivani loved her and how his divorce from Pola couldn't happen soon enough. Pola, however, hadn't suffered the slings and arrows of her broken marriage alone. During the filming of *The Woman He Scorned,* she was introduced to dapper, wealthy Englishman Glen Kidston, who served as her local guide in Cornwall. He was a director of the Bentley Automobile Corporation as well as an aviator who enjoyed racing planes and had set a few air speed records. He sent her orchids every day and routinely flew his plane out to the location where she was shooting the picture. Although Kidston was also mired in a troubled marriage, they fell in love.

With no offers of movie work forthcoming, she entertained another offer to make a few vaudeville appearances in London. She had put on a considerable amount of weight in the last year and a half and planned to go to the spas at Baden-Baden, Germany, in an attempt to slim down. Her plans were scuttled by the calamitous October 1929 Wall Street Crash that all but wiped out her personal fortune of five million dollars.

Deep in debt due to indulgent over-spending and an 18th-century chateau requiring thousands of dollars in upkeep every month, she needed to focus on finding work and that meant shedding a useless distraction like Serge Mdivani. She filed for divorce in Paris in November 1929. "Being a princess isn't as much fun as I once thought," she said. She insisted she still loved Mdivani, but her career came first—it always had—and she needed to be free to return to America. She said, recognizing that making "art" as she'd wanted was no longer practical for her, "[A]fter all, there is nothing like liberty, even though one is forced to be a film slave."[25]

Yet on the eve of their final divorce hearing in a Paris courtroom in December 1929, the wily Mdivani—still tied to her purse strings—persuaded her to reconcile with him. Surprised by his declaration of love, she agreed to give their marriage one more try, telling reporters, "We were separated eight months, but never separated in our hearts."[26] She then declared, "We are going to St. Moritz for our second honeymoon. We will return here in January and will probably sail for America towards the end of January or the beginning of February." She added: "I am a fatalist, but I never dreamed of a reconciliation."[27]

On hearing the news of their reunion, Glen Kidston telegrammed his congratulations. Ever the gallant Englishman, he ceded her back to her husband without raising a fuss. But Mary McCormick fumed publicly, complaining she would now have to return the Rolls-Royce that Serge had bought for her—with Pola's money.

Curiously enough, Negri didn't entirely withdraw her divorce action. Was she hedging her bets? Instead, she asked the French court to extend the "period for renunciation" in order to "obtain" better grounds for divorce.[28]

Her Wall Street losses were severe. Reluctantly she put her chateau, her dream palace, up for sale. According to *Variety*, which seemed to take a great delight in reporting her misfortunes, she built a new house outside of Paris, but spent only one night there before moving out and putting it on the market because the trash men made too much noise during their early morning labors.[29] The story is nonsense. Money problems landed her back in the newspaper headlines when the prominent Spanish painter Beltran Masses sued her for $5000, claiming she hadn't paid him for a portrait he had done of her posing with a ghostly image of Valentino hovering in the background. Pola countered that she didn't pay him because she didn't like the portrait. Then, during a holiday trip to Berlin with Mdivani, a former theatrical agent obtained a writ of execution to seize a valuable pearl necklace to satisfy a judgment for commissions due him on a deal allegedly arranged for her with Ufa before she left for America in 1922. Negri angrily denied she owed him any money and told reporters that she would ask her attorneys to file slander charges against the agent. Whether the suit was ever filed is unknown.

Her money problems were consternating—and fatal to her reconciliation. For Serge, anything less than a life of luxury was unacceptable; it was why he had married her in the first place; and ironically, several of the California oil wells his family held leases on had recently yielded black gold. The wells promised to make him wealthy and he wanted to be with Mary McCormick. When it became clear to Negri that he wanted out of their union, she restarted her divorce action in September 1930.

From the *Perth Western Mail*, September 18, 1930: "I filed my divorce petition today.... I do not wish to speak of Serge. We were so happy once together, but when two people cannot live together affectionately the divorce court is the only way out."

As her divorce wound its way through the French legal system, she yet again announced that she was working on her memoirs, tentatively titled *My Confession*. She promised her public the truth: "People do not know me, they know only the Pola Negri that the Hollywood press agents have manufactured. I assure you I have suffered from their machinations. I am writing my own story of myself, so that I can correct a lot of false impressions."[30] "The truth" wouldn't emerge for another 40 years—and not even then.

At about the same time, *Variety* reported that she was going "legit": She had an offer to appear in a play called *Cocktail* in Berlin and was said to be considering appearing in a Broadway stage adaptation of a novel called *La Gondole aux Chimères*.[31] She signed up instead for a headline appearance at the Colosseum Theatre London in a playlet called "Farewell to Love," for which she was paid $2,500 per week. The show opened to a sell-out crowd. *Photoplay* printed a photograph of her arrival in London in its April 1931 issue. Negri looks about 20 pounds overweight and the caption asks the snarky question, "Doesn't our girl friend look—er—plump?" She lost the extra weight and then took to the London stage, appearing in a short drama entitled *The Last Tango*. She was well-paid for what was basically a 20-minute sketch in what England called *variety* and America called *vaudeville*. As a recognizable "name," she drew big audiences.

While in London she resumed her romantic relationship with Glen Kidston, who was now in the middle of his own divorce. Although she did not refer to him by name, she told a reporter that she considered an Englishman "to be the ideal husband."[32] Make of that what you will. It is possible that she was merely "playing to the locals" by calling Englishmen superior marriage material.

Although vaudeville paid the bills in the short term, she still hoped to return to pictures. There were reports in the trades that she had been signed by Pathé–RKO Radio Pictures to make six features. The first, *Likes O'er*, was to be filmed in London with a British cast and crew.[33] It turned out that there was no picture for her there, but RKO offered her a chance to come to Hollywood for a voice test. If the results were satisfactory, they were prepared to put her under contract for one picture.

Perfect timing. The French court granted her divorce from "Prince" Mdivani on April 2, 1931, on the grounds of abandonment. Pola received news of the decision aboard a ship bound for America. There were no tears shed for her failed marriage. She declared she had learned her lesson. She told a reporter "an artist should never marry" and said that the main difficulty in her marriage was Serge's inability to "understand her artistic temperament."[34]

Negri was, unfortunately, far from done with "Prince" Serge. Years of litigation followed their divorce. In 1931, she sued him for repayment of an $80,000 loan. He countersued, claiming he had loaned $119,000 to her. Both suits were dropped. In 1935, she sued her former husband in a French civil court, charging him with embezzling money from a Mdivani-owned oil company that she had invested in during their reconciliation. Serge did not contest the case and she obtained a judgment against him. Whether she ever collected on that judgment is unknown.

Serge and Mary McCormick married in secret the day after his divorce from Pola was final. A child was born and shortly thereafter they divorced. McCormick repeatedly had to sue him to collect back child support. Serge's third wife was his late brother Alexis' first ex-wife, Louise Van Arlen.[35] A month after that marriage, on March 15, 1936, Serge Mdivani died after being kicked in the head by his polo pony at a Florida country club.

Despite what she had said about learning her lesson, Negri and Glen Kidston planned to meet up in Hollywood after his divorce was finalized and then get married. Yet two weeks after her return to America, a telegram arrived informing her that Kidston had crashed his plane in a sandstorm near Cape Town, South Africa, during an attempt to set a new air speed record and been killed.

There was no public display of grief on Pola's part and one would think there would be. Based on her record of alleged marital announcements, her account in her *Memoirs* of their plans to marry leaves room for doubt. The sole public mention of their relationship outside of her autobiography appears in a *Silver Screen Magazine* interview in 1931. She does not mention Kidston by name, telling her interviewer, "You probably know who he is" and mentioning his plane crash.[36] She then added her by-now-familiar lament:

> I am fated to be unhappy in love. I know it. Each time that I meet someone whom I truly love, something happens.... I shall not love again, for it brings me only pain and loneliness in the end.[37]

Yet in a newspaper item from May 5, 1931, on the same day that news of Kidston's death made front pages around the world, there was Pola's proclamation of a new man in her life. "Yes, there's going to be a new husband. He's an American, too. Very wealthy and prominent, but I will not tell his name until I see how my first picture turns out."[38] She might have said this to curry public favor, much as she had while in England. The other conclusion to be reached is that there never really a serious relationship between her and Kidston. Either that or her insensitivity defies description.

In *Memoirs* she repeats her assertion that after Kidston's death she vowed to never fall in love again, to never experience the pain that she associated with emotional involvement.[39] She would put work first and that would be her salvation. She would do her RKO voice test and then embark on a comeback that would put her name back up in lights where she knew it was supposed to be.

9

The Wandering Star

Reports persist that Pola Negri is coming back to American to make talkies. She's said to have a one-picture contract with Radio Pictures, with options. It would be her first audible screen effort.
Well, doggone it, come on, Pola. Hollywood's been getting a bit dullish.[1]—*Photoplay*, May 1931

The July 1931 *Picture Play* reported that Pola "has rather dropped out of sight now that she is living in France.... It is most improbable that she will make any more American pictures; a star who is once 'finished' over here seldom makes a comeback." In a similar vein, *Motion Picture Magazine* noted that with the troubles Pola had fitting into screen roles and the challenges her accent presented, she was most likely the one star who "has surely severed relations with the American screen."[2] They were both wrong.

She had been away from Hollywood for three years, nearly a lifetime in the picture business. Time had rendered her a memory, an afterthought. *Picture Play*, looking back a decade after *Passion* and *Gypsy Blood* had caused a sensation, called them "odd" and "now forgotten" and declared her "long-gone" from the public mind."[3]

Yet why couldn't she make a comeback? There were more foreign stars in Hollywood than ever before and few of them could match her talent or her charisma. Those who had interviewed her knew that her voice would not present a problem for the sound engineer. *Picture Play* called her voice "fascinating" and lamented that she never had a chance to try it out in pictures before Paramount dropped her contract. They asked, "Why doesn't some producer give her another chance? Now that she has lost her prince, can't someone induce Negri to return?"[4]

Her faithful fans were eager for her to make a reappearance. They thought she had been dismissed unfairly from American pictures. "Seeing what an unhappy life Pola has had," a reader wrote to *Picture Play* magazine, "I think the least one can do is to refrain from unkind criticism such as I have read in American magazines, and try to help instead of hinder her, even though she is foreign and different."[5] "Foreign and different"—Negri couldn't escape her old publicity. "Pola has not lost popularity here, because we don't believe all we read. We know that she feels every emotion she portrays and has a greater soul than any of her critics."[6] Another fan asked, "Why is it that most of the fans are exclaiming about Greta Garbo being such a wonderful actress?... In my estimation there is only one real actress in the world today. That is Pola Negri."[7]

Ernst Lubitsch weighed in on the Pola vs. Garbo debate: "Ya. Pola is greatest but she came at the wrong time. She came in the sugar period. They didn't want truth. Greta came at the right time. If Pola had come now it would be different."[8] The right time had come. She no longer needed to compromise her dramatic prowess for the sake of profit and popularity. All she needed was a hit picture and she would rise to the top again.

She returned to America in May 1931, having traveled 6,000 miles to take on the biggest risk of her professional career: talking pictures. She also had a little something extra now to offer movie producers: a serviceable singing voice to go along with her dramatic ability. Her entire future hinged on how she sounded. At least if she didn't pass her voice test, Pathé-RKO would pay her passage back to Paris.

She told reporters that she was interested in doing a film version of a story titled *East River* or one of the several plays she had purchased while abroad.[9] Hollywood had changed in her absence and as *Photoplay* noted: "Pola's going to a new Hollywood—where queens are out of fashion. Now it's a place where a lot of hard-working men and women live. She'll work hard, because she's very ambitious. But she probably won't find a loose throne around the place."[10] She was said to be so anxious to make a successful return that, in order to concentrate on her test, she refused lucrative offers to appear on the radio and on the vaudeville stage.[11]

Putting the lie to what was written about her "unsuitable accent," the RKO voice tests showed she recorded as a pleasant contralto, husky and heavily accented, but still perfectly understandable. As a result, Pathé-RKO signed her to a three-year contract at $3,000 per week, less than half of what had earned per week at the height of her Paramount years. While looking forward to a new picture, she was adamant about not playing the Continental seductress again. She would not emulate the Garbo-style seductive siren so popular at that time. She said she had a different idea.[12] She didn't say what that different idea might be. The *New York Times* reported, "Miss Negri will confine her characterizations to the exotic and foreign types, not because she feels limited by an accent, but because her temperament calls for it and she thinks audiences like the foreign twist."[13]

Letters to *Modern Screen Magazine* heralded her second coming. "Are we glad Pola Negri is back?" asked one letter. "Foolish question. There's only one Pola!" Another fan chimed in: "I'll be glad that Pola Negri is back…. Her comeback is a risky thing, but having seen Pola at her best in the past, I think she'll come through."[14]

Despite her disdain for her old publicity, Negri was again hailed as exotic and mysterious, once again a queen of flame and desire—just like in the old days. *New Movie Magazine* called her a "fiery gypsy actress" and "a devastating charmer" and said that, with a picture tailored to her talent, she would "be today at the top of the world with Marlene and Garbo."[15] Mary Sharon wrote in *Silver Screen Magazine*:

> Like most persons of genius, Pola dramatizes herself. She is always the actress…. She bears up under blows that would crush an ordinary person, because she views her tragic moments and her climaxes as glorious parts to be played. And how she plays them![16]

While waiting for a suitable script, Negri moved into a Santa Monica beach house rented from former silent star Bebe Daniels. *Photoplay* complimented her on her serene new persona: "Pola Negri, 1931 model—no temperament, no swank, no carrying on. Some change from the Warsaw Rose of five years ago, who clawed and snarled at life. Today, in Hollywood, she's leading a quiet life."[17] She seemed primed for a glorious comeback. It just had to be the *right* picture.

Pola was keenly aware that sound limited the type of character roles she could do for a film. Her accent was too pronounced for her to credibly play an American or Englishwoman. Being reminded all of the artificial roles she had played during her Paramount years pained her. She called those movies "terrible" and said, "I suffer from them, yes. I am not a Talmadge, a Pickford, even a Garbo. I cannot fit into their patterns. I am Negri—I have my own place." She was glad to be back and thrilled to be wanted again. "People have not forgotten me.... All along the way how the people received me. Every place they said, 'We are glad Pola is back!'"[18]

Few silent stars crossed successfully into talking pictures. Most fell by the wayside while some lingered on in second- and third-rate pictures, a mere shadow of themselves, and their names barely noticeable in the credits. The former idols of silents went unmourned by a fickle public. They were reminders of a dizzying decade that no one was really keen to remember in the depths of the Depression. Members of the old guard were unemployable in the new world of sound. Even if their voices were suitable for talkies, the public was no longer interested in seeing them.

But RKO believed that Negri still had commercial appeal—she could be their Garbo—so they hired Spanish writer Mercedes De Acosta to devise a suitably "literary" vehicle for her. That was their first mistake. De Acosta's most promising idea was for Pola to star in the life story of Mata Hari, a role that would have suited her perfectly. Yet when MGM announced its own version of the story with Garbo in the leading role—not so coincidentally, De Acosta and Garbo were lovers—RKO scrapped the project. The studio then announced that Negri would appear in an adaptation of the story of Maria Draga, a chanteuse who rose in fortune to briefly become queen of Serbia. Terrible idea. Paul Stein, who directed Pola in Ufa's *Arme Violetta*, would helm the new picture in Hollywood and, according to *Film Daily*, her leading man was to be a British newcomer, Laurence Olivier.[19] Olivier, however, would drop out of the cast to be replaced by Basil Rathbone in his first starring role. Negri would also have the chance to showcase her singing talent in the film.

It had to work. She was in desperate need of a hit. If the new picture, *A Woman Commands*, failed, she was finished as a bankable Hollywood star.

Just before filming started, she cut recordings of two "gypsy songs" on the Brunswick record label: "Farewell My Gypsy Camp" and "Black Eyes." Both were sung in Russian and her voice was described in one review as "a mezzo soprano with that husky vibrato of intonation we feel we should associate with film stars and novel heroines."[20]

As her comeback picture neared completion, she said she would next like to do a film version of Dostoevsky's *The Idiot*, and hoped to alternate between stage and screen and do no more than two pictures a year.[21] Pathé-RKO gave her as much publicity as it could. A profile of Pola from the *Perth Western Mail* from this time reads:

> She always wears sandals, even for evening wear, and has a hundred pairs[;] likes to build bonfires on the beach; is a grand whistler; plays the harp grandly; was most in love with Rudolph Valentino[;] loves a good joke; prefers eggs Florentine for lunch; never stands up when she can recline; has an amazing knowledge of trees and speaks six languages.[22]

With her picture in the can and favorable comments from advance screenings, there was a possibility that her three-year contract would be extended to seven. Yet Pathé suddenly split from RKO in a financial dispute. Pola's contract with Pathé was verbal only and in the midst of the "divorce," they declined to pick up her option for a second picture. Fortunately for her, RKO stepped in and took up her option, announcing that they were already seeking a suitable story for her second film.

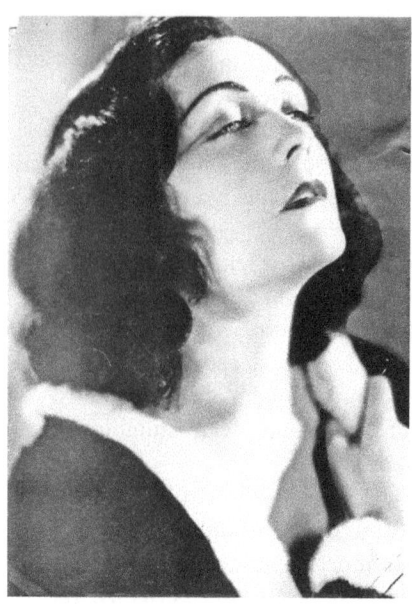

Publicity portrait for RKO Pictures, Hollywood, 1931.

When RKO offered *A Woman Commands* to the Roxy Theatre for its world premiere and an exclusive New York run, the Roxy declined as they did not believe Negri to be a big enough attraction to fill their 6000-plus seats. The film was booked instead into the smaller Mayfair Theatre in Times Square. It was also announced by the studio's publicity department that Negri would do four weeks of guest work on NBC radio programs to promote the picture.

On December 16, 1931, Negri was stricken with what appeared to be appendicitis and rushed to a Santa Monica hospital for emergency surgery. Her appendicitis turned out to be an acute intestinal blockage. She was listed in severely critical condition and there were reports in some newspapers that she was not expected to live. Her condition was daily news fodder over the next week.

Pola recovered, although her weight dangerously plummeted to 90 pounds. According to one story, she told her secretary that if she should die, it was her wish for her coffin to be borne back to Europe on a ship flying the Polish flag. When told that finding such a ship was unlikely, she defiantly told her secretary, "Then my dying will have to wait."[23] After a hospital stay of nearly three months, she left for Palm Springs, looking weak and fragile. She convalesced there for four weeks before returning to New York to make a few personal vaudeville appearances and attend the premiere of her comeback picture.

In hindsight, she needn't have rushed back.

A Woman Commands

RKO Radio. Released January 1, 1932

STATUS: A public domain DVD is available.
CREDITS: Director: Paul L. Stein. *Scenario:* Horace Jackson. *Story:* Thilde Foster.
CAST: Pola Negri (*Madame Maria Draga*), Roland Young (*King Alexander*), Basil Rathbone (*Capt. Alex Pastitich*), H.B. Warner (*Colonel Stradmirovitsch*), Anthony Bushell (*Lt. Ivan Petrovich*), Reginald Owen (*The Prime Minister*), May Boley (*Mascha*), Frank Reicher (*The General*), George Baxter (*Chedo*), David Newall (*Adjutant*), Cleo Louise Borden (*Crown Prince Milan*), Frank Beek (*Major Domo*), Frank Dunn (*Royal Servant*), Carl Stockdale (*Priest*), Lorimer Johnson (*Minister*), Paul Porcasi (*Nightclub Proprietor*).

STORY

Maria Draga, a cabaret singer, is romantically involved with Capt. Alex Pastitich of the Serbian Army. His gifts and financial support to her have put him in debt, jeopardizing his promising military career. His commanding officer pleads with her to save her lover's career by abandoning their affair. She agrees, selling off the jewelry he bought her to pay his debts. She leaves to pursue her singing career and becomes an international star. One night while performing, she catches the eye of King Alexander I, who invites her to visit him at the palace. Maria resists the king's shameless attempt at seduction there. After pleading to be allowed to leave, one of the king's aides—Alex—is assigned to escort her back to her hotel. Her ex-lover is unhappy with the duty foisted on him and tells her he'd hoped never to see her again. To escape the king's attention, Maria boards a train to Vienna but is forcibly taken back to the palace on the king's orders. He proposes marriage and she reluctantly accepts, hoping that as queen she can advance Pastitich's military career. The wedding occurs despite the disapproval of the king's ministers.

At a parade honoring the royal couple, Pastitich refuses to salute her and is sent to prison for insubordination. Maria uses her influence with her husband to get him pardoned. The king's devotion to his wife and disinterest in affairs of state riles the military. They launch a *coup d'état* to force him to step down, and Alexander is unexpectedly shot dead by a revolutionary. The army's ruling committee then tries to force Maria to abdicate the crown and annul her marriage, but on learning that they would also make her son illegitimate, she refuses. The military committee orders her shot by firing squad, but Pastitich, still in love with her, refuses to carry out the execution. His commanding officer shows mercy and allows Pastitich to free her from prison. The lovers escape the country and head into exile.

Roland Young and Miss Negri in a scene from *A Woman Commands*, **RKO Pictures, 1932. Directed by Paul Stein.**

Reviews

The *New York Times* covered *A Woman Commands*' January 1932 premiere at the Mayfair Theatre in New York City. Negri, still looking ill, was introduced to the crowd by a late-arriving Mayor James E. Walker. The *Times* reviewer noted, "[I]n most of the sequences, Miss Negri is attractive. Her accent is strongly foreign and her voice is a contralto. She sings and hums a song which drew applause from the crowded house."[24] The *Film Daily* said, "Miss Negri appearing in her first talker made in this country is glamorous and expert in a part which does not afford her the best opportunities."[25] "What a pity that Pola Negri should return in such a trite, impossible and worn-out theme," *Photoplay* wrote.[26] *Motion Picture Magazine* piled on: "What a shame that Pola Negri couldn't have commanded or commandeered a story worthy of her debut in the talkies, or at least a role that would have made sense!"[27]

Despite all of the hopes pinned on it, *A Woman Commands* bombed. According to *Motion Picture Magazine*, its star-studded opening night was the only spectacular thing about it. Its run at the Mayfair lasted only a few days; there were too many empty seats.[28]

A Woman Commands is a terrible picture, embarrassing and painful to watch. Negri's voice is no problem: Speaking or singing, she does fine, even with the cringe-worthy dialogue. The plot, however, is a total disaster. It seems the screenwriters couldn't quite decide whether they were making a romantic musical drama or a tragedy and didn't succeed at either. Maria Draga lacks any kind of real personality. She acts with a certain silent picture majesty ill-suited for a talkie, but even a great performance wouldn't have salvaged such an old-fashioned story. The original ending called for her to die by firing squad, the real-life fate of Maria Draga, but her climactic death scene did not test well with advance audiences so a happy ending was shot and tacked on. It seemed to have been an unhappy affair for the actors as well. Poor Basil Rathbone looks uncomfortable and awkward throughout. It is clear that he was entirely unsuitable as a romantic lead. Pola was ill with stomach problems during production, leading to her hospitalization and near-fatal surgery. She blamed the producers for the picture's failure. It was now clear that she would never again be a marketable movie star in America.

A Woman Commands cost $400,000; Negri was paid $60,000. Delays during production and retakes doubled her original salary. There were rumors—weren't there always?—that she had been difficult to work with on the set, and had bickered with former silent actress Dorothy Mckaill, who called her "condescending" after Negri had "lectured" her on her acting.

Negri made no more pictures for RKO. The studio kept her on its roster for another two years and then let her contract expire. Without any film work for her, they were not obliged to pay her. There was some talk of MGM borrowing her to replace a reluctant Garbo in *Grand Hotel* (1932) with RKO getting Clark Gable for one picture in return.[29] It didn't happen. According to one source, the Halperin brothers were interested in casting her in *Supernatural* (1933) to be released by her old studio, Paramount, but nothing came of that either and no additional offers were forthcoming.[30] In her autobiography, Pola surmises that her near-death illness gave the picture business the impression that her health was too precarious to withstand the rigors of filming. She was unemployable. The reality is that the moviegoing public was no longer interested in her.

Yet, just as if it were still 1923, she hinted at *another* engagement. The man was supposed to be from Chicago but, as always, she would not mention his name.[31] Newspapers identified him as Philip Chancellor, a manufacturer.[32] Chancellor neither admitted nor denied being engaged to her and the story quickly faded, replaced by tabloid gossip regarding a romance with bandleader Russ Colombo, who had turned the *Woman Commands* song "Paradise" into a big band standard. It was the old publicity all over again. Neither of these gentlemen are mentioned anywhere in Negri's memoirs.

Hospital bills ate up much of her savings and with no film work forthcoming, she accepted an offer to make a vaudeville tour by bus. The master of ceremonies was a young comic named Milton Berle. He is cited as one of her lovers, but in his autobiography he claims that the woman he was involved with was a former silent star whom was as big in her day as Negri—but was not her.[33] He describes a dressing room seduction scene with the anonymous actress, and from her manner and her accent it is hard to believe that it *wasn't* Negri. In one of his columns, Walter Winchell mentions Negri ardently waiting at the stage door for Berle to emerge.[34] In her autobiography Negri doesn't mention any relationship with him at all.

Her vaudeville act consisted of a sketch called "So This Is Love"; in it, she played opposite a man who has loved her has grown tired of her. This allowed Negri a few dramatic moments to showcase her acting chops. The act also incorporated her rendition of "Paradise." She appeared on stage at Shea's Buffalo Theatre in Buffalo and the Paramount Theater in Manhattan's Times Square.

Variety categorized her week-long stint at the Paramount (March 1932) as less than entertainment and more in the way of a personal appearance:

> Miss Negri's facial expressions were hardly discernible. Any emotional power she might have injected in the drab lines was lost, for her face was not seen and her voice not heard. Miss Negri and the man were just two figures carrying on a vague conversation.[35]

The strain of traveling from city to city took its toll on her. She was still not in good health and wound up hospitalized for exhaustion at the end of her Times Square appearance. To be fair, it was not the last time that she would become ill *after* she received a bad review. Her hospital stay forced a cancellation of her scheduled appearance at the Brooklyn Paramount. Upon recovery, she was booked for personal appearances in support of *A Woman Commands* at the Hippodrome in Baltimore, the Stanley Theater in Pittsburgh and the E.F. Albee Theater in Brooklyn. With no film work to be had, Negri settled into her new career as a vaudeville attraction, hardly the star she had once been, but (according to *Variety*) still earning $6,000 a week for three shows a day. She returned to New York in May 1932 but again used illness as an excuse for canceling her appearance at the Loew's Valencia Theater in Jamaica, Queens.

Now whenever she was mentioned in the press, it had nothing to do with movies. There were reports of a new romance to an Englishman named John Loder,[36] whom she quickly dropped, and then an "engagement" to an unnamed Chicago millionaire. "I think Americans are adorable," she told reporters. "I wouldn't ever marry another European after my last experience."[37] Her Chicago millionaire was identified as Harold F. McCormick. He denied the rumors, of course.

The novelty of her personal appearances quickly waned. She appeared at the Orpheum Theater in Minneapolis, Minnesota, in October 1932, performing her usual act. *Variety* noted that she wasn't a big attraction there, adding that "her name doesn't mean much locally anymore."[38] She went on to the State-Lake Theater in Chicago, where she apparently caused fireworks backstage with her temper. She also appeared on a local radio

Above: Portrait, New York, 1932 (photograph by Ben Pinchot). *Right:* Portrait, France, 1933 (photograph by Piaz Studios).

show with Polish-born Mayor Anton Cermak. Pola told the press she would start a new picture in January 1933. Rumor had it she would sign a contract with Universal, but, as always, the rumors came and went with no new picture for her.

There was also mention in the trades of her graduating to the legitimate stage and appearing in a Broadway show. *Variety* had her appearing in something called *Nons* and then said she was supposed to be in a play called *The Empress.* Nothing happened.

In January 1933 she hit the road for five weeks, appearing in RKO theaters in Kansas City, Omaha, Louisville, Paterson, New Jersey and Newark. While in Kansas City, she was quoted—although it was more likely her press agent doing the talking—as saying: "Pola has been battling the depression and she's got it licked. I've been a big success at every movie theater I've played during the last 18 months. I've pulled theaters out of the red everywhere I've gone."[39] In truth, people stayed home. The crowds who came out to see her were small, and although she struggled gamely to retain what was left of her former stardom, it was clear that she had little appeal either as a vaudeville star or even as a "has-been" celebrity attraction.

She turned back to Europe. In February 1933, she announced she was off to Paris to negotiate for stage work abroad. On the eve of her departure, she was twice refused exit by the U.S. government on the grounds that she owed about $8,000 in back taxes and had defaulted on an agreement to pay $700 per month on the income she had earned during her previous time in America. *Variety* wrote:

> Miss Negri was booked for two weeks at $4000 each at the Rex, Paris, a picture house, commencing April 3.... If the Paris dates are to be played at all, a final settlement with Uncle Sam will have to be made by Miss Negri before she can sail.[40]

Her tax situation wasn't straightened out until April so she lost out on her foreign stage bookings. She then set sail for Paris to visit her mother Eleonora and look for work.

She signed with Paris-based Tobis films to make a new picture, *La Glu* ("The Glue"). Subsequently, however, she starred in an Alexander Dumas–like costume drama called *Fanatisme* ("Fanatic") for Via Films. The picture was allegedly shot in both French and English with distribution in Europe by Pathé. Negri plays an Italian street singer in France during the reign of Napoleon III. She sang three songs in the picture and *Variety* had a story that she took voice lessons to be able to speak French with an Italian accent! The film sank at the box office on its release in 1934 and has been rarely seen since. Via Films went bankrupt. It doesn't appear that the English-language version of *Fanatisme* was ever released.

She was set to return to New York in August of that year to appear in the Schubert brothers' stage production *A Trip to Pressburg*, apparently based on an old Viennese opera she had managed to acquire the rights to during her time in Europe. The need to shoot additional scenes for *Fanatisme* caused her to be delayed another two months and she not return to New York until October 1933.

Upon her return, Negri joined the *Pressburg* company at the Nixon Theatre in Pittsburgh where the play was having out-of-town tryouts. Her American stage debut didn't last very long. She fell ill with a gall bladder ailment after the first week and permanently left the show after generally unfavorable reviews of the production appeared in the trade papers. She then sued the Schuberts for $4,000, claiming compensation due for the part of the contract she had performed before her illness. The Schuberts countersued for $25,000, claiming she had willingly delayed her return from Europe to shoot extra scenes for *Fanatisme* and contending that her withdrawal from the play had caused it to close at a loss. Both suits went into mediation, but all claims were eventually dropped and the play cancelled by mutual agreement.

Now professionally adrift, she told the press that she had a picture in mind called *Tavaritch* that she wanted to make with Ernst Lubitsch. "I want to create the role of the ultramodern woman—ah, very ultra-modern, sophisticated, of the world, in the grand manner," she said. "You have not seen any such woman on your screen—not one—I know it." She desperately wanted to work with Lubitsch, the man with whom she had made motion picture history in the old days. "Together," she said, "we can do it again."[41]

Nothing went her way. She didn't work with Lubitsch again. She took on radio and more vaudeville work to keep from sinking into obscurity. She appeared as a guest star on the CBS radio network's *Underwood-Elliot Show* singing, of course, "Paradise." She then headlined at the Palace Theatre in Chicago, an appearance which *Variety* panned. It was clear that her options were dwindling. According to *The Hollywood Reporter*, she was supposed to appear in the Broadway comedy-musical *Yokel Boy Makes Good*, but the plan fell through.[42] *Variety* mentioned that she was trying to sell the American rights to a French film she had made—perhaps *Fanatisme*? There was also talk of her appearing in a film biography of Frederick Chopin that didn't materialize.

With no prospects in America, she received an offer from Universal Pictures founder Carl Laemmle to star in a new picture, *Mazurka*, to be filmed in Berlin by an affiliated film studio. He assured her that she would be perfect in the lead role. At first Negri was against the idea of returning to the place where she had begun her film career. Why should she have to start all over again?[43] She had also heard bad things about Chancellor Adolf Hitler and wasn't sure she wanted to work in Nazi Germany. Did she have any idea her pictures had been prohibited from being exhibited there because she was on a list of banned "Jewish" artists?[44] Laemmle told her not to worry about the Nazis as she was an

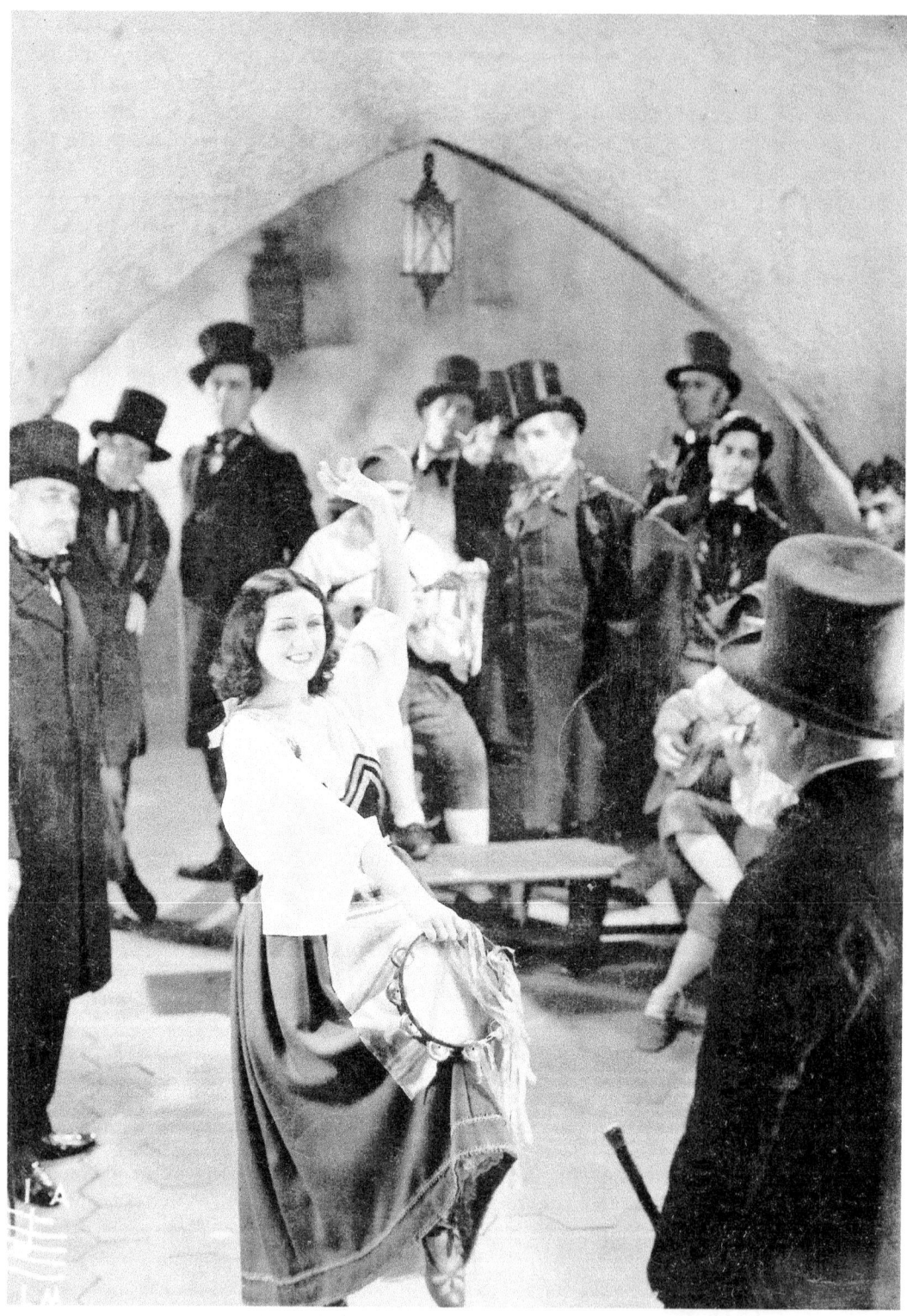

Negri dancing in a Paris cafe in a scene from *Fanatisme*, Via Films, 1934.

Pola Negri in *Mazurka*, Cine-Allianz/Tobis-Klangfilem, Germany, 1935. Directed by Willi Forst.

Aryan. Negri didn't know what "Aryan" meant. She would have preferred to make the picture in America, but financing dictated that it be shot in Germany. In the end, the script won her over and she was really in no position to refuse a $25,000 payday. She traveled back to New York, toasting New Year's Day on a cattle train—the only transport she could find. She sailed for Berlin on January 6, 1935.

A year later, on January 8, 1936, the Ambassador Hotel in New York was awarded a judgment of $5,350 against her for "unpaid rent" and "food services." Negri allegedly ran out on her hotel bill when she left the country.

10

Der Führer's Favorite

In her essay "The Opportunist," film historian Eve Golden questioned Pola Negri's motives for making movies in Nazi Germany, arguing that she would have seen what was happening to her Jewish colleagues, most of whom fled the country to avoid persecution. Why didn't she make a stand or show solidarity with her fellow artists by leaving as well? Golden wrote, "[W]hile not a sympathizer or even a collaborator, Pola must take blame for shutting her eyes and taking an easy paycheck."[1]

With all due respect to Golden, she is judging in hindsight. In 1935, the West viewed Hitler's Nazi regime with blinders in place. The United States, still recovering from the Depression and isolationist in sentiment, showed very little interest in what was happening inside Germany, while the other traditional European powers, France and England, were more concerned in preventing another ruinous war than in the plight of German Jews.

In her own naive way, Negri didn't think the situation inside Germany mattered at all when she arrived to film *Mazurka* in 1935. She was an actress being paid to act in pictures. Politics meant nothing to her. Perhaps she did turn a blind eye to Hitler, but so did everyone else until it was too late. To criticize her long after the fact is unfair. She never kowtowed to the Nazis or made movies to glorify their regime—the fate that ultimately befell the great Emil Jannings, her *Madame DuBarry* co-star.

Upon her return to Germany in January 1935, she found "unrest in the air and a rigidly enforced display of militarism everywhere."[2] She was back filming at Ufa's Templehof studio where she'd made *Madame DuBarry* with Lubitsch. Tensions ran high at the studio. New anti–Semitic laws had passed in the Reichstag, prohibiting non–Aryans from working in Germany. The edict severely affected Ufa, which had just come under the administration of Joseph Goebbels and the Ministry of Propaganda. *Mazurka* producers Arnold Pressburger and Gregory Rabinowitz were Jews making their last picture in Germany. They would exit the country as soon as filming was complete.

Carl Laemmle, who persuaded Negri to take the leading role, had assured her an "Aryan" such as herself would have no troubles with the Nazi government. Yet two days before filming was to commence, the producers received word that Goebbels had banned her from starring in the picture on the grounds that she was "non–Aryan." The Ministry of Propaganda claimed to have letters in its possession detailing her participation in anti–German activities during the Great War. Furious, Negri went to the Polish ambassador and asked him to inform Dr. Goebbels that if she could not work in the picture, she would be leaving Germany immediately.[3]

"I am not a Jewess," she was quoted as saying. "The whole world knows that I'm a Catholic ... and I have never been engaged in political activities against Germany."[4]

As she packed to leave, the studio received word that Chancellor Hitler himself had signed an order contravening Goebbels' ban. The press reported that an investigation had been made of her background, confirming her birth as a Pole, thereby making her "Aryan," and racially competent to work in German films. A "grateful" Negri was quoted as saying, "I am flattered that the Führer intervened personally on my behalf. He must be a brilliant man. I haven't met him before, but I would like to before I leave next April. You know I have a lot of big men in my memories."[5] This sounds more like the work of a press agent than anything she herself would say.

One newspaper columnist mocked Hitler's "official decision," claiming that Hitler had invented the "whitewashed blonde" by declaring the Polish-born brunette Negri to be Aryan. Then he added in a poem:

> Heil Hitler Hause dekorator
> New Germany's controller;
> Berlin you may have painted red.
> But you have whitewashed Pola.[6]

Hitler's order allowed her to work, but this wasn't the end of her problems. Although the chancellor had countermanded the decision of his Minister of Propaganda, crossing Goebbels meant incurring his wrath and Ufa was caught in the middle. Filming on *Mazurka* was delayed several months while delicate negotiations ensued. Goebbels was no fan of Negri—he detested Poles as an "inferior" race—or of the queenly salary she was earning.

As negotiations dragged on, a fed-up Pola decided that she didn't want to deal with Nazi meddling any longer and made plans to leave for her mother's villa on the Riviera. When the studio discovered her intention to leave, they put enormous pressure on her to stay, reminding her she had a contract and communicating thinly veiled threats that she would not be allowed to leave Germany unless she fulfilled her obligation.[7] On hearing that she had been finally cleared by Goebbels' office to appear in the picture, she changed her mind about leaving. Damn the politics. She believed the film's theme of heroic motherly love was universal and there was nothing whatsoever in the story that had anything to do with the ongoing events in Germany.

She also felt she had something to prove to her detractors. In *Memoirs* she wrote, "I was determined to show Hollywood that they had underestimated my value as a talking picture star by judging me on the dubious merits of one badly made film.... I was personally putting everything I had ever learned about acting into my performance."[8]

Most of her German pictures are available on DVD. They are not subtitled in English.

Mazurka

Cine-Allianz/Tobis-Klangfilm
Released in 1935

CREDITS: *Director*: Willi Forst. *Story*: Willi Forst, Hans Rameau
CAST: Pola Negri (*Vera*), Albrecht Schoenhals (*Grigorij Michailow*), Ingeborg Theek (*Lisa*), Franziska Kinz (*Mother*), Paul Hartmann (*Boris Kierow*).

Story

Negri portrays a famous opera star who betrays her military officer husband with an affair. When she becomes pregnant, her marriage and career are ruined. Fifteen years after giving up her child for adoption, she comes face to face with her grown-up daughter and, without revealing her true identity, tries to prevent her from becoming romantically involved with her father. When her ex-lover refuses her demands to leave the girl alone, she shoots him dead. At the conclusion of the trial, the judge shows mercy and gives her the minimum punishment with hopes for a full pardon at some later date.

Reviews

German critics praised Pola's performance. One reviewer wrote, "[H]er gestures are composed, poignant; one quiver of the corner of her mouth reveals an inner world, one glance runs the entire gamut from skepticism to understanding." *Variety*'s Berlin correspondent called the picture "her victorious re-entry into films."[9] When it premiered in London a year later, critics said she had matured as an actress and thought acting in the German language made her more natural.[10]

Mazurka was Negri's favorite talkie and her biggest success in Germany. It gave her the opportunity to sing, although the voice heard on the soundtrack belonged to someone else. This was also said to be Hitler's favorite movie. Whenever he suffered from insomnia he would have the picture screened and weep uncontrollably over her character's heroic sacrifice for her daughter.

There came a rumor that because of *Mazurka*'s success, Warner Brothers might import it to America and offer Negri a contract to return stateside. Then the studio bought up all the prints and locked them away from sight in order to prevent any comparison to their own 1937 version of the story, *Confession,* starring Kay Francis. They needn't have bothered. The American version died at the box office.

According to *Memoirs,* Negri returned to Cap Ferrat after completing *Mazurka* to see her mother. She was shocked by the news that Casimir De Hulewicz, her long time supporter and patron, was ill with cancer. Negri paid for his medical treatments—he had done the same for her in the past—but little could be done for him. After his death, she paid for his funeral and burial. These expenses drained her savings, so she signed a long-term contract with Ufa that would pay her 175,000 marks per picture and gave her script approval. Goebbels was again displeased with her large salary, but newspapers reported that she was under the "personal protection" of Der Führer and was to be given whatever she wanted. The Chancellery and the Ministry of Propaganda squabbled over her. She wrote in her autobiography, "[M]y reaction to all this kept swinging between the opposites poles of horror and hilarity."[11]

As always, Negri's memory is selective. Newspaper reports of the time find her back in Cap Ferrat in May 1935. Of course, as was her custom, she hinted to a reporter there that she was engaged to wed a man she would not name. She described him as a "middle-aged British statesman, a former member of Parliament, enormously wealthy—you'll be amazed whom you find out it is, in about two weeks."[12] A newspaper called the announcement an example of her living up to the "tradition of mystery as a film exotic."[13] Two weeks passed—she still did not name him—and then said she wouldn't marry him for another year.

As an intriguing personality she still continued to make headlines. A Paris judge ordered her to pay $2,310 to a furrier for a fur coat she had ordered. According to the *New York Times,* she refused to pay for the coat because she didn't like the way it looked on her.[14] In October 1935 she was hospitalized for two weeks at the American Hospital in Paris for a reoccurrence of intestinal pain, but no further surgery was needed. There were rumors of her making a new picture in Paris and then a second picture in London with Noah Beery. Despite the announcement of upcoming movies, the only country where she still had any worth as a film star was Germany.

In December 1935 she was back in London with *red* hair, her natural hair color, according to one news item. Other reports stated that she would marry her "prominent Englishman" on her birthday, December 31st. The day came and went without a wedding. Wasn't everyone tired of this by now? Another newspaper quoted her in January 1936 saying, "I am going to marry an Englishman, who is older in years than myself, but the same age as myself in spirit and outlook…. And I am going to settle down in England and live the quiet life for which my soul has always yearned."[15]

A quiet life? Maybe that's what she was looking for, but she certainly had an odd way of going about it because then she was suddenly back in Berlin in March, booked into the cavernous Scala Theater in a variety sketch entitled "Hollywood" which had been written for her. She was thinner and looked more Germanic with her pulled-back hairline and penciled-in eyebrows. She resembled a brunette Marlene Dietrich in publicity fliers for the Scala appearance.

Eerily enough, the sketch involved a film star trying to find work while her fiancé is dying. *Variety* wrote: "Miss Negri goes 100 percent emotional and puts it over in a dramatic song, trying hard to forget the impossible Scala stage. Audience is spellbound and baffled by the inspired Hollywood atmosphere on the stage, with all the studio paraphernalia."

The Scala *should* have known better. Negri's engagement there copied the disaster that befell *A Trip to Pressburg.* The production opened three days later due to her illness. After just two shows, she announced that doing both a matinee and evening performance was too heavy a strain, so she would forego any more matinees. Then she fell ill again and was out for six days. Business plummeted after that and the Scala's management pulled the plug on her.[16]

The Scala Theater reported a $12,000 loss on the aborted engagement and sued her in a Berlin court, alleging she was recording gramophone records while claiming to be too sick to appear in the show. Characteristically, Negri denied the allegations and countersued for what she was owed under her contract. In July, *Variety* reported that she had returned a portion of her advance salary for the 12 days she had missed in a gesture of good faith. Ultimately the matter was dropped by both parties. It was also announced that she had signed with Ufa for two films, *Moscow Shanghai* and *Countess Volescu.*

Her German films from the 1930s are a strange lot, a curious pastiche of musical numbers and heavy-handed drama. In most of the pictures, Negri plays a woman disgraced after indulging in an extramarital affair that leads to a separation from her child. She finds redemption in a noble sacrifice to protect her child from her past sins. Recall what American movie magazines said in the 1920s about Germans having a taste for the morbid and the unusual? Pola's Ufa movies from 1935 to '38 have the threat of incest as a dramatic element, which speaks to the fixation of Nazi ideology on maintaining racial and blood purity.

Moscow Shanghai
Ufa
Released 1936

CREDITS: *Director:* Paul Wegener. *Story:* Kurt Heynecke, M.W. Kimmrich.
CAST: Pola Negri (*Olga Petrowna*), Wolfgang Keppler (*Alexander Repin*), Gustav Diessl (*Serge Smrirnow*), Susi Lanner (*Maria*), Erich Ziegel (*Gen. Martow*).

STORY

A widowed Russian noblewoman meets a handsome young Imperial Army officer at a ball. Afterwards, she leaves her seven-year-old daughter with her personal maid to accompany her lover and one of her friends on a train trip to Moscow. The train is attacked by the Bolsheviks; her lover and friend are captured. The friend joins the Communists and prevents the lover from being executed. The noblewoman assumes a new identity and goes in search of her vanished daughter. The picture then jumps ahead to 1930. The noblewoman, now a nightclub singer in Shanghai, learns to her horror that her ex-lover is engaged to her daughter.

REVIEWS

Variety wrote in its review: "La Negri is very impressive.... It's another first-rate effort to exploit Pola Negri's acting ability as a great tragedienne in pre-war Russia and the revolutionary period.... Miss Negri wins 'em on the soul-stirring accentuations."[17] Photos reveal that she is also noticeably heavier. Despite the favorable reviews, the picture's plot sounds like a retread of the motifs from *Mazurka* and might easily be confused with one of her late Paramount period duds. While the picture was successful, the box office returns were less than its predecessor. It would find a second life via a re-release in 1958.

According to *Variety*, Negri showed a few flashes of the old "temperament" during the picture's production. She was displeased that her personal secretary, Louis Adlon, Jr., was barred from the studio lot and upset about being paid in lesser-value German marks rather than the foreign currency demanded by her contract. To show her discontent, she walked out in the middle of filming, loaded Adlon into a private plane and flew to Bern, Switzerland. She then sent back word she would not return to Berlin unless the studio met her *demands*. Ufa *swiftly* capitulated, agreed to allow Adlon on the set and promised to pay at least half her salary in foreign currency and half of the advance on her next picture. Satisfied with the terms, Negri coyly advised the press that her "slight touch of flu" was all better now and she was headed back to work.[18]

Negri, ca. 1936, Foto Sandau, Berlin.

Publicity noted that the picture's director Paul Wegener played the part of the sheik in Pola's *Sumurun. Moscow Shanghai* gave Negri another opportunity to sing and this time her real voice is heard. Recordings of her songs from this picture appeared in Germany on the Odeon label and in England on the Parlourphone label.

Then out of Germany came the surprising story that Negri just might marry Adolf Hitler. According to a report, two Polish newspapers were banned from sale in Germany for publishing a story alleging that Hitler had become infatuated with the Polish actress. Hitler, who had supposedly been frequently seen in Negri's company, reputedly yelled, "Slanderers!" when told about the rumor.[19]

As far-fetched as it all sounds, the improbable story spread around the globe like wildfire. Was Hitler really marrying Negri? "It is quite possible I shall marry an important German personality." Pola reputedly told a Berlin newspaper. "That's all I can say."[20] Her quote could mean anything, yet there were those in Germany who truly believed that she was Der Führer's favorite and his pick to be his wife.

In America, the story was met with rolling eyes of disbelief. Pola's former dresser at Famous Players–Laksy, Edna Grundstrom, scoffed, calling Negri a dictator who would never stand for taking orders from Hitler. She added that Pola got along with Serge Mdivani only because he usually gave in to her whims.[21]

The Hitler rumor had enough credibility in Germany that when Negri was briefly hospitalized in 1936 for a bad case of food poisoning due to tainted milk, there were insinuations she had been poisoned by one of Hitler's jealous girlfriends. A year later, American gossip columnist Louella O. Parsons printed a rumor that Pola was being held prisoner at the Dachau concentration camp for her failure to be discreet about her relationship with the German leader.[22] The gossip turned out to be untrue.

In her autobiography, Negri claims that during her entire time in Nazi Germany, she never met Adolf Hitler.

Madame Bovary
Ufa
Released in 1937

CREDITS: *Director:* Gerhard Lamprecht. *Story:* Erich Ebermayer, Hans Neumann, based on the novel by Gustave Flaubert.
CAST: Pola Negri (*Emma Bovary*), Aribert Wäscher (*Charles Bovary*), Ferdinand Marian (*Rodolphe Boulanger*), Werner Scharf (*Léon Dupuis*), Alexander Engel.

STORY

Emma Bovary, the wife of a small-town physician, longs to leave the tiny village of Yonville for the broader pastures of Rouen or Paris. Her husband bores her. She finds excitement first in a romantic fling with a young lawyer and, after his departure, falls in love with another man. Unbeknownst to her husband, her weakness for expensive clothing and jewelry incurs large debts that puts him at the mercy of his enemy, the town druggist. Her death by suicide brings the picture to an end.[23]

REVIEWS

Variety said of her acting: "Miss Negri as the ambitious and pleasure-loving wife is as effective as scripting and direction allows her to be…. Incidentally, she's getting better-looking all the time. Some of the closeups are great."[24]

Madame Bovary did not fare well in Germany. It was, ironically, her only German movie from this period to be released in the U.S. The *New York Post* wrote, "Pola Negri ... does not seem to have changed much from the days when her dark eyes grew large with sorrow on silent screens. She is a little more mature in figure, slightly heavier. Her features are as formerly. Her performance is good enough, but nothing to excite you beyond control."[25] The *New York Times* declared: "Pola Negri still has plenty of charm and acting ability and she seems to be staging a 'comeback' in Europe ever since her 'Aryanism' was established to the satisfaction of Adolf Hitler in January 1935."[26] Negri believed her *Madame Bovary* to be the best filmed version of Flaubert's novel. A French picture by the same name, directed by Jean Renoir, had been released in 1933.

Postcard image of Negri, ca. 1937, "Ross" Verlag A1197/1, Berlin.

Tango Notturno

Ufa
Released in 1937

CREDITS: *Director:* Fritz Kirchoff. *Screenplay:* Rolf E. Vanloo, Lothar Mayring
CAST: Pola Negri (*Mado Doucet*), Albrecht Schoenhals (*Jac Gerard*), Waldemar Leitgeb (*Lincoln*), Elisabeth Flickenschildt (*Bessie Godfrey*), Lina Carstens (*Frau Wattson*).

STORY

A man is on trial for the murder of his ex-wife Mado. A former cabaret singer, she had an affair with another man and has been reduced to prostituting herself to support her drug habit. Years pass, Mado and her husband encounter each other again and she threatens to blackmail him. When that doesn't succeed, she goads him into shooting her. After telling his story, the husband wins acquittal from the jury.

It is interesting to find Pola for once playing a remorseless fallen woman, foregoing the usual self-sacrificing character she tended to play in most of her German pictures of this era. When *Tango Notturno* turned out to be a money-loser, Joseph Goebbels blamed her salary. She was being paid more than any other actress on the Ufa roster, yet her pictures did not earn close to the box office returns that the Nazi-controlled studio sought. Despite the Ministry's animosity towards her, Ufa continued to employ her as she was at least still an internationally established name that gave legitimacy to the German film industry. *Tango Notturno* also allowed her to sing again.

After completion of *Tango*, she returned to Paris and discovered that the French magazine *Pour Vous* had published a libelous article about how she was "living the lap of luxury at Bertchesgarden," and claiming she could "twist the Führer around her little finger."²⁷ This article was partly responsible for the often-mentioned myth that she was Hitler's "favorite actress." Negri filed suit against the magazine in a Paris court for one million francs, claiming defamation of character. During the trial, she stated through her attorney that she had never met Hitler and the closest she ever got was seeing him from her hotel room balcony as he passed by below in a parade. She ultimately won a retraction of the story from the magazine along with 10,000 francs.

During production of her next Ufa picture, her clashes with Goebbels and the Ministry of Propaganda escalated. Before any picture could begin filming, its script had to be approved by the Ministry. Negri's contract, however, gave *her* script approval. According to *Memoirs*, the Ministry turned down every idea she submitted on the grounds they were "unsuitable" and insisted there be more "subtlety"—i.e., politics—in her pictures.²⁸ She steadfastly refused to be exploited for propaganda purposes, declaring that she would have nothing to do with political films. The Ministry finally relented and allowed her to make her next picture.

Illustrierter Film-Kurier, Nr. 1885 with Miss Negri on the cover for *Tango Notturno*, Ufa, 1937 (Germany). Directed by Fritz Kirchoff.

Die fromme Lüge

Ufa
Released in 1937

CREDITS: *Director:* Nunzio Malasomma. *Scenario:* Philip Lothar Mayring, Harald G. Petersson.
CAST: Pola Negri (Carmen Casini), Hermann Braun (Cecil Lasko), Herbert Hübner (Bartell), Harald Paulsen (Smith), Josefine Dora (Theres).

STORY

Famous opera star Carmen Casini has an adult son who is a race-car driver. After an accident at the track, she loses her singing voice. Her son takes up with the daughter of a wealthy man, not realizing that her father is his mother's ex-lover and that he is "the secret lie" of the title. His girlfriend's father is actually his own father, making the girlfriend his half-sister. The son attempts suicide when he finds out the sordid truth, bringing his mother and biological father together again in an absurd happy ending.

In Pola's next film, *Die Nacht der Entscheidung* (The Night of Decision), a singer tries to protect her child from the stigma of illegitimacy. It was filmed during the Sudetenland crisis in 1938 and, according to Kotowski, there was a work stoppage during filming when most of the technicians were pressed into military service.²⁹ They were replaced with a less capable crew. Wary of Nazi politics and nervous about the gathering war clouds, Negri dared not publicly voice her desire to leave the country out of fear she would be detained. She plotted a way out while continuing to resist all studio efforts to make her into a cinematic mouthpiece for the National Socialist cause.

The Sudetenland crisis was solved at the cost of Czechoslovakia's freedom. War was temporarily averted. Aware that she was under close surveillance at the studio by a Gestapo agent, Negri departed for her usual post-picture holiday in France, leaving all of her clothes and bank accounts behind to give the appearance that she would soon return to work. She had no intention of doing so. After a few months in France, she was visited at Cap Ferrat by a studio representative with a new script for a political picture they insisted she make. Negri presented him with falsified medical evidence to prove that she was too sick to leave France. The Ufa representative returned to Berlin without her. She never heard from them again.

In January 1939 she was back in a French court over a bill to a Paris furrier for 2,000 pounds. She had taken her luxurious mink coat to the furrier for repairs to the hem and was told that she could not have the coat back until the outstanding balance due on the original sale of the coat was paid. Negri complained to the judge that she would freeze to death without the coat. Unsympathetic, the judge ordered her to pay for the coat or lose it entirely.[30]

Negri settled in London. She had just turned 40 and, though she looked heavy, she was said "to have retained her good looks and acting ability."[31] It was reported that she had a deal to make two pictures in England with the first to begin filming in September.

Germany invaded Poland on September 1, 1939. The poorly equipped Polish Army was routed by the Wehrmacht's blitzkrieg and its remnants scattered to France. Negri dutifully joined the Polish Red Cross in Nice, France, to help tend to the wounded.[32] War engulfed the continent and the German army appeared to be unstoppable. In June 1940 Paris fell to the Nazis, Italian planes attacked Cap Ferrat, and for a few weeks aerial bombings became a daily occurrence on the Riviera, forcing Negri and her mother to seek shelter. After the French surrender, there was an uneasy peace as the collaborationist Vichy government took over administration of the Riviera. Living conditions were grim. Fresh food was scarce, so Pola and Eleonora planted vegetable gardens to supplement their meager diet.

After a year of wartime hardship, Negri decided to return to America to seek work. She still had some movie industry connections and needed to earn some money. Eleonora, citing old age and an unwillingness to relocate again, declined to accompany her across the ocean. Negri was allowed to leave as she was still a legal American resident with a re-entry visa and she heard that flights were leaving for New York from Lisbon.

Leaving her mother in Cap Ferrat with a sizable amount of money from her Swiss bank accounts, Negri traveled by train from Paris to Lisbon. On her arrival, she was informed that the last flight for America had already left. Now the only way out was by cargo ship, the S.S. *Excalibur*. While waiting to see if she could book passage, she told a *New York Sun* reporter that "the French people are becoming vindictive towards the Nazis" and that the populace was beginning to show signs of malnutrition due to food rationing.[33] She claimed she herself had lost 40 pounds due to the scarcity of food.

Fortunately for Negri, she was able to board the *Excalibur*. When she finally sailed for America, it was in a cramped second-class cabin, a far cry from the luxury suite she had once enjoyed as a film star. She had no money, a faded name, and no guarantee that she would find work. She had freedom, however, and that was enough.

11

All Too Soon Forgotten

Pola Negri returned to America on July 28, 1941, a refugee from the war. She disembarked at Ellis Island, was separated from her fellow passengers, and herded briefly into a detention area. Her re-entry visa had expired and she reportedly wept upon being told she would not be allowed to enter the country. It took several desperate phone calls to the Polish Embassy in Washington and help from her New York attorney to straighten out the immigration paperwork before she was granted re-entry into the country along with permanent residence upon her sworn affirmation that she intended to file again for U.S. citizenship.

While in Europe, she'd had no idea what the American newspapers and movie magazines had been saying about her. A New York friend provided her with a collection of clippings. A few tabloid publications insinuated she was a Nazi sympathizer and repeated the malicious gossip that she had been Hitler's lover.[1] With the help of cooperative journalists, she refuted the "Hitler romance" rumors in several national magazines.[2] She also proved her patriotic mettle. As a former film star she still had a certain name recognition and, eager to do her part for the war effort, toured a number of movie theaters in the east and made personal appearances at shows and dances to help promote the sale of war bonds.

Shortly after her return to New York, an offer came from her old studio, Paramount, to test for the role of Pilar in the much-anticipated film version of Ernest Hemingway's *For Whom the Bell Tolls*. Negri declined, telling Louella Parsons she didn't want to play a middle aged-woman (in other words, her real age): "I don't want to stamp myself as a character actress in my American comeback movie."[3] It didn't matter anyway. The picture was widely panned.

She still had her sights set on returning to the screen as a leading lady. "Fortunately, I can afford to wait until the right role comes along—something with character and emotional intensity," she told a reporter in 1941. "Which will give my talents as a dramatic actress full play."[4]

She would always be waiting. There were occasional reports of film offers: the starring role in a picture called *Claudia* to be filmed at Paramount[5] and leads in film versions of *Nana* and Sudermann's *Magda* to be filmed in Mexico City—with Pola playing the roles in Spanish.[6] Yet it was always mere talk. Negri was not in demand for anyone's picture.

One can imagine this being a desperate time for her. Unemployed, no money and no prospects—all this for a woman who had once been world-famous and wealthy. She was only 44, still young and quite beautiful, but by this time silent films had been relegated to the trash heaps and Charlie Chaplin seemed to be the only actor universally remembered from the era. Pola Negri was a relic and, worse, forgotten.

Her name was mentioned mostly in connection with lawsuits. The Ambassador Hotel, whose bill she had run out on in 1935, sued her and sought to attach a $2,500 fee she earned for writing a magazine article about her romance with Valentino.[7] The court ruled that she was entitled to the money, although legal fees ate up most of it. She was also sued by the estate of the late Col. Howard Thayer Kingsbury for repayment of a loan he had supposedly given her in 1930. His estate obtained a judgment against her in the sum of $7,277 after she failed to answer the suit.[8] Shades of the old days when no one knew anything about her—she was named in the suit as "Paula Schwartz a.k.a. Pola Negri."[9] Negri tartly remarked, "I owe no one any $5,000."[10] During a proceeding to collect on the judgment, she was summoned into court by Kingsbury's attorneys to answer allegations she had a "secret source" of income and was living the high life in exclusive hotels. According to the plaintiff's attorney she had owned "an apartment in Zurich, Switzerland, a villa at Capri, Italy, a castle at Cap Ferrat, France, which cost more than a million dollars, a villa near Berlin, and large amounts of jewelry when the war started." Where had it all gone? Negri replied that she had arrived in America with less than $100 in her purse and was living off of small loans from old friends.[11] Although the settlement of the court case required her to make modest monthly payments of $25 towards the judgment, she failed to pay even that small amount and was found in contempt of court on penalty of possible imprisonment. Payments began after that.

She was also sued by the Internal Revenue Service, which claimed she owed taxes on all of her German movie earnings. Without any work or real income to speak of, Negri was forced to sell off pieces of her fabled jewelry collection to settle some of her debts. She moved into a lower Park Avenue residential hotel and barely made the rent. In her *Memoirs* she recalled this as a period of black despair and hinted at suicidal thoughts when she struggled to find a reason for going on.[12]

Eight months after her return to America, she was offered a small supporting role in the United Artists screwball comedy *Hi Diddle Diddle*. The picture's male lead Adolphe Menjou had supported Negri in many of her Famous Players features during the 1920s. Other prominent cast members were Martha Scott, Billie Burke and June Havoc. Negri plays up to her old silent movie image in her role as a Wagnerian opera singer of volcanic temperament and eccentric habits. In her few scenes she's quite funny and memorable, even if most of the picture isn't.

The *New York Times* didn't think much of her broad comic performance, saying that the movie reintroduces Negri "and proves time has neither dimmed her beauty or improved her acting."[13] Although the money she earned wasn't much by earlier standards, it resolved her tax situation, lifting that burden from her shoulders.

Negri wrote in *Memoirs* that *Hi Diddle Diddle* typecast her as a low comedienne and that she was discouraged by the paltry film offers she subsequently received to do "the same thing over and over." There is no record in news clippings of any such offers. Rumors at the time had her in vocal training to fulfill her "lifelong" ambition to sing in the opera *Carmen* at the Metropolitan Opera.[14] Baloney.

News about her during this period reeks of desperation. Talk of another comeback went nowhere. At least one gossip columnist labeled her attempts to be relevant in

Portrait for *Hi Diddle Diddle*, United Artists, 1943. Directed by Andrew Stone.

Hollywood as "pathetic." Negri was a "has-been" with a long record of box office failures and in Hollywood that is unforgivable. Publicly, she continued to hope for redemption, claiming she was waiting for the right part.[15] Her enthusiasm for acting, however, waned. As she aged she found it harder to "make the journey into self," that allowed her to give a good performance.[16] Yet what else was an ex-movie star to do? Financially strapped, she earned $7500 from *American Magazine* to write episodes from her life for publication.

She accepted a two-week engagement to perform at a Boston supper club, singing "Paradise" and relating anecdotes about her Hollywood years. The engagement was successful and she was offered work by other night clubs, but she declined as she found it exhausting.[17]

If anything, her name now merely evoked feelings of nostalgia for a long-gone era. Newspapers columns rehashed her "fits of temperament," the "feud" with Gloria Swanson and her doomed romance with Valentino. Then there was the story of her walking a pet leopard on a leash down Hollywood Boulevard. According to one journalist, she once threw the animal at a reporter.[18]

Many historians and biographers of the silent movie era have repeated the leopard-on-a-leash story as gospel, but it never happened. Pola claimed that she did it for publicity—but then where are the photographs showing it? There are none. It's a colorful myth and makes Negri out to be at best, an eccentric, and at worst, a crazy Norma Desmond type.

Broke again and ensconced in another small residential apartment house in New York City, she continued to live off the financial support of friends. But there was a ray of hope on the horizon. The war appeared to be nearing its end and one day in 1945, Negri was overjoyed to receive a telegram from her mother after almost four years without any contact. Eleonora had survived the war at Cap Ferrat, none the worse for wear despite food shortages on the Riviera. Pola made immediate plans to visit her and to check on the jewelry, securities and Swiss bank accounts that she had left behind. It was a long wait as the U.S. government didn't approve travel to Europe until 1948. In the meantime, she ran out of money and jewelry and teetered on the verge of bankruptcy. Happily, Negri found someone she could financially rely on: Margaret West.

According to *Memoirs*, Margaret West was a NBC radio host and the "toast of New York" in the early 1930s.[19] She was the first radio personality to introduce country and western music to New York audiences. At the height of her popularity, she made personal appearances decked out in colorful cowgirl gear. She retired from the airwaves in 1935, but maintained a luxury apartment with her husband at Manhattan's Hotel Pierre.

Margaret had an ability to put people at ease. Negri wrote of their first encounter, "I felt as if I had just met a very close old friend."[20] Margaret was married to an art dealer, but the marriage was shaky. She dabbled in music composition. She was also, according to rumor, either bisexual or a lesbian.

Pola was not a woman with many friends and her own personal history reveals a very solitary individual for

Publicity portrait, 1943.

most of her life. Margaret turned out to be a lifeline at the time when Pola was in dire need of one. Pola wrote in her autobiography: "We had so many things in common—we were both lonely, unhappy and possessed of a deep and sensitive receptiveness to the arts.... It wasn't long before we were not only close, but best friends—the love that we felt for each other was that of deep friendship and mutual respect."[21]

At Margaret's insistence, Pola returned to Europe in 1948 to recover her personal possessions, dispose of her property holdings and bring Eleonora back to America. On her way home with her mother, she denied, for a change, any intention of ever getting married again, insisting that her thoughts were only on her comeback. "When I try for a comeback I do not intend to let any man interfere with my work. Marriage and art don't work together.... I've tried it twice. I don't intend to get married again."[22] She said she had decided to try to revive her career after witnessing Joan Crawford's success in 1945's *Mildred Pierce*. A comeback would never materialize.

On their return, mother and daughter moved in with Margaret in a leased beach house in Santa Monica, a palatial residence with five servants. There they entertained old friends from Negri's picture days and she was often photographed on the town, squired by the likes of actors Gary Cooper and Dennis O'Keefe. Eleonora, ever the faithful practicing Catholic, went to work raising funds for the expansion of the Church of the Holy Mother of Czestochowa, now known as Our Lady of the Bright Mount Catholic Church on West Adams in Los Angeles. Negri's own renewed adherence to her faith came as a welcome comfort when Margaret suffered a mild heart attack. Margaret recovered after several months of rest, but she would never again be 100 percent. Upon expiration of the beach house lease, they moved to a roomy house in tony Bel Air. Eleonora, now 88, and wanting a residence of her own, rented a house a few blocks away.

Negri called this her happiest period. She and Margaret led an active social life, invested in real estate and raised funds for Catholic Charities. She had finally achieved a peace, a domestic bliss that she had sought for so long. She didn't need film stardom. Having friends and her mother close by—that's all that mattered to her now.

In 1949, according to legend, she was approached by director Billy Wilder to play the role of Norma Desmond in *Sunset Blvd*. Either Wilder decided against giving her the role because of her heavy Polish accent or, more likely, Negri declined (threw him out of her house, so the story goes) because she didn't think it right to parody her silent movie persona. Her old rival Gloria Swanson wound up with the part and an Academy Award nomination for a picture now considered a classic. Pola never expressed regrets about turning Wilder down.

Her name pops up in a few newspaper gossip columns during the 1940s and '50s, although it was by now doubtful whether younger movie fans even knew her. She was an occasional guest on radio shows such as *Hedda Hopper's Hollywood*. In 1950, it was said she would play in a new picture titled *Fire Island, N.Y.*, to be shot on location.[23] Of course, any mention of Pola in a newspaper column inevitably included the well-worn story about her and Valentino or mentioned her infamous temperament. Howard Greer's *Town & County Magazine* article "My Perils for Pola" reads like her old publicity:

> La Negri was one of the queenliest movie queens.... Once she held up the cameras because her slipper did not exactly match the ruffle on her dress.... Maybe there's been greater beauties, but Hollywood never had a more colorful or more temperamental star than the great Pola Negri.[24]

Her name also continued to appear in court documents. In 1951, she was sued by a Gus Fragus on grounds of fraud. He claimed to have lent Pola about $3,000 on her assertion that she knew where in France a German Army officer had hidden some valuable jewelry and had promised to split the proceeds from their sale once she had retrieved them. The ridiculous allegation sounds like a plot right out of a movie. Pola denied the charge. The case settled out of court.

Pola finally completed the process begun in 1941 when she had taken U.S. legal resident status. Where she had once been a world-famous peripatetic traveler, she was now entirely content to permanently remain on American soil and on January 12, 1951, she proudly became a naturalized U.S. citizen.

In 1954, when she was 56, there were rumors about her about returning to Germany to again restart her film career. A newspaper article labeled the attempt as "brave, yet pathetic" and described her as "plump and matronly."[25] In middle age she scarcely resembled the screen beauty of old. She was practically unrecognizable and seemed to prefer it that way.

Eleonora was diagnosed with terminal pancreatic cancer in 1954. Pola dedicated her time to caring for mother, who died in 1955 at the age of 93, and was interred at the old Calvary Cemetery in Los Angeles. Negri suffered an emotional breakdown after her mother's death. Margaret had to make the funeral arrangements for her. It was a devastating blow. The one person in her life that she had loved the most was gone and she had no family left in the world.

In 1957, she moved with Margaret to San Antonio, Texas, Margaret's hometown. They lived quietly in the Olmos Park neighborhood, two middle-aged ladies dabbling in real estate and reputedly making a fortune. She visited L.A. now and again, often photographed making the round of nightclubs. In the photographs of the period she looks tired and bored by it all—as if life itself was too heavy a burden. She briefly returned to the Hollywood limelight in 1960 when she received a star on Hollywood Boulevard's Walk of Fame.

Film beckoned one last time. Negri received an offer from the Walt Disney company in 1963 to appear in *The Moonspinners,* a "Hitchcockian" picture being filmed in England. She was initially reluctant to make the trip for such a small cameo, but Margaret insisted she accept the role. Why not make one last movie and then formally retire from the screen as a star? Then, just before Negri was to head abroad, Margaret West suddenly died of heart failure in a San Antonio hospital.

Pola's relationship with Margaret West has caused considerable debate regarding her sexuality. Negri insisted in her autobiography that their affection was entirely platonic even if some believe otherwise:

> It was difficult for some of the so-called sophisticates to understand that there had not been until then, nor would there ever be in the future, the slightest tinge of the sexual as to what we shared together. It was so ironic that it was almost laughable that these worldly wise cynics doubted equally the intense sexuality of what existed between Valentino and me and the innocent purity of my feeling for Margaret.[26]

The relationship described in her autobiography, however, reads very much like a marriage and, thus, the insinuation that Pola Negri was bisexual.

Is there evidence anywhere of her sexual preference? No, but Negri has been allegedly "unmasked" by others as a lesbian in a number of books. According to several authors, bisexual actress Tallulah Bankhead called Negri a "lying lesbo" but never offered any proof. There are rumors that Negri had an affair with Hollywood's most notorious lesbian, Mercedes De Acosta, during her time at RKO. In his book *Silent Players*, film historian Anthony Slide said that silent film actress Alice Terry laughed at a section of Negri's

Memoirs describing Pola and Valentino making love on a bed strewn with rose petals, implying that neither was capable of the sexual act with "someone of the opposite sex."[27] Some writers attribute to Negri the quote, "Women are for loving, men are for business," as *clear* evidence of her sexual preference. Yet this quote is always cited entirely out of context. What Negri actually meant was that women love with their hearts, they are romantic, while men are usually all business. The quote has nothing to do with her sexual preference.

We can momentarily take into consideration another famous silent star who has also been scrutinized regarding his sexuality, Rudolph Valentino. In her biography of "the Great Lover," Emily Leider addressed allegations of Valentino's homosexuality raised by David Bret in his book *Valentino: Dream of Desire*, calling Bret's thesis factually weak.[28] She observed that most of the evidence for Bret's conclusion was based on second-hand recollections of sexual conquests that cannot be proven. Yet Leider, in her own book on Valentino, stated that Negri was bisexual with only her living arrangements with Margaret West to justify *her* assertion. It seems that Leider fell into the same trap that ensnared Bret.

The weight of anecdotal evidence does seem to favor the suggestion that Negri *was* bisexual. Apart from her engagement to Chaplin, she never actually came close to marrying anyone. Her supposed engagement with Valentino was denied by Rudy. Her engagement to Glen Kidston was never mentioned anywhere except in her *Memoirs*. There are also many instances of Negri *reportedly* being engaged to rich and wealthy businessmen who also denied the reports. All of her heterosexual relationships ended badly and it appears that only her relationship with West brought her happiness. Make of that what you will.

According to Anthony Slide, George Schoenbrunn, a friend to both Margaret and Negri, said that Pola had been exclusively heterosexual during her Hollywood career, but *thought* that Negri had become West's lover—after all, Margaret was taking care of her—but had done so without much enthusiasm for sex; "Maybe she tried it and liked it." Margaret West, Schoenbrunn claimed, complained to him that Negri was not very forthcoming with affection.[29] It should be noted that press photos taken in the '40s and '50s mostly show Pola in male company. She only appeared with Margaret in candid photographs taken by friends at their home. If this was done to "keep up appearances," it's understandable. Sexual relationships between women were not for display in those closeted days.

The one clear truth is that Negri *was* a kept woman late in life. Margaret supported her financially. A sexual relationship may have been the price of comfort for a faded actress with no other means of support. Negri may have simply done what she had to do to survive. In her will, West bequeathed Pola her condominium at the Chateau Dijon on Broadway Street in San Antonio and nearly $2,000 a week for her to comfortably live on for the rest of her life.

There is a notorious story—presented as gospel on several blogs and Internet websites—that at one point Margaret West became engaged to a man and Negri sued to stop the wedding from taking place, citing "alienation of affections." The story is a lie. There is no such lawsuit, just as there is no proof that she routinely slept with other women. There is no memoir or first-hand account by any woman claiming to be Negri's female lover. All of the rumors are a case of "someone saying that someone said so" or that someone *believed so*. Also remember that Negri and her mother were devout Catholics. Eleonora lived with the two women for years and she would have no doubt strongly disapproved of a lesbian relationship between her daughter and West. Pola strongly embraced Catholicism again later in life and it is questionable whether she would have gone into a relationship anathema to her faith.

The debate over her sexuality is, actually, moot. If she was straight, good for her. If she was bisexual, good for her, too. One more thing about sex and Pola: She was good at it. Lita Grey, Chaplin's second wife, recalled his telling her that she should learn to please him. He wanted her to be like just Negri, who was the most satisfying sexual partner he had ever had.[30]

After Margaret's death, Pola turned to acting, the same thing she had always done when confronted with intense grief. She flew to London to appear in *The Moonspinners*, her first movie in 20 years, to play the role of the colorful jewel fence, Madame Habib. Noting that her on-screen character had a pet leopard, she thought it might make for good press for her to appear with a leopard and in character at the press conference promoting the picture. She was right. Photos of her and a leopard on its leash appeared in newspapers all over the world. The publicity game might have changed a bit over the years, but Pola Negri had learned from the best.

Her ten-minute scene at the climax of *The Moonspinners* is a gentle ode to her movie star persona. Negri, 67 when the picture was made, is nearly unrecognizable in her costume and hairdo. With her self-assured, imperial bearing and outré mannerisms, however, she was the flamboyant figure old-time movie fans expected her to be. Even in such a small role she about steals the show from Hayley Mills. Her soliloquy at the picture's climax, where she speaks of her failed marriages and the wars she had survived, sounds like a summation of Pola's entire life.

After completing *The Moonspinners* Pola declared she had no interest in further movie work and went into semi-seclusion in San Antonio, making only the occasional public appearance. In 1964 she received an award for her work in the German film industry; in 1968 she got a Hemis-Film Award. In 1970 she released her long-delayed *Memoirs of a Star*—she had been talking about publishing her autobiography since 1928! She gave interviews to newspaper columnists to promote the book, rehashing her love affairs and her feuds, and contending with the same old questions about cats and her temperament. Briefly back in the spotlight, she was hailed as one of the movies' most colorful and original stars, although her autobiography was labeled a "work of fiction" by her own ghostwriter and was no best seller. In 1973, she was honored for her silent movie career at New York's Metropolitan Museum of Art with a screening of 1925's *A Woman of the World*. It would be her last major public outing. She occasionally traveled to California to visit old friends, but seemed content with her solitary existence in her San Antonio apartment. Alone. Maybe it was the way it was always meant to be.

In 1975, director Vincente Minnelli offered her a small part in his film *A Matter of Time,* but Negri declined due to poor health. Ingrid Bergman played the role instead. After nearly a decade out of the public eye, she reappeared in the February 1980 issue of *Life* magazine in an article entitled "Where Are They Now?" Then 83, she was photographed sporting an obvious black wig and sitting on a sofa under one of the famous oil portraits done of her back in the 1920s by Tadeusz Styka.

Her health declined during the 1980s. She grew fragile. She became a financial donor to a Catholic university, Trinity College, in San Antonio and occasionally ventured out to school functions, usually in the company of one of the school's priests. It's doubtful that many of the students knew who she was or had been. Of her former movie stardom there was an echo in the requests from fans to have her sign all manner of photographs and postcards—requests that she graciously honored. This author has several of her signed photos in his collection. In 1984, she was interviewed for a chapter in the book *Return Engagement,* which revealed her to be nearly blind. She blamed her failing eyesight on years of acting in front of klieg lights and said she had undergone several operations to save her vision to no avail.[31] She was diagnosed with a brain tumor a year later—more likely the real cause for her loss of sight—but refused any kind of medical treatment. In the last year of her life, blind and feeble, she contracted viral pneumonia which weakened her severely; she was hospitalized. She briefly rallied, only to succumb to brain cancer on August 1, 1987. She is entombed at the Calvary Cemetery in East Los Angeles next to her mother. Her private scrapbooks and prints of a few of her old films, most notably *Sappho*, were bequeathed to Trinity College.

The story goes that near the end of her life she was treated at a San Antonio hospital by a young physician who, according to her *Los Angeles Times* obituary, "obviously did not know who she was." Her reaction was just what you might expect from a fierce original like Pola Negri: "I was the greatest actress in the world," she told him, about rising out of her hospital bed, playing the imperious movie star to the last.

The young physician believed her.[32]

Chapter Notes

Preface

1. Carr, Harry, "The Mystery of Pola Negri," *Motion Picture*, February 1925.

Chapter 1

1. Kozarski, Richard, *An Evening's Entertainment: The Age of The Silent Feature Picture, 1915–1928* (University of California Press, 1990), 296–298.
2. Ibid.
3. Long, Christopher, "Barbara Apolonia Chalupec," *Handbook of Texas Online*, http://www.tshaonline.org/handbook/online/articles/fchtm.
4. Schickel, Richard, *The Stars* (Bonanza Books, 1962), 15.
5. Ibid.
6. www.stanford.edu/~gdegroat/negri.htm.
7. Golden, Eve, "The Opportunist: Pola Negri On Her (More or Less) Centenary," *Classic Images*, December 1997.
8. "Pola Negri, 'Vamp' of Silent Films, Dies," *Los Angeles Times*, August 3, 1987.
9. Bruno, Michael, *Venus in Hollywood* (New York: Lyle Stuart, Inc., 1970), 35.
10. Ibid.
11. *Salt Lake Telegram*, October 21, 1921, 12.
12. *Wyoming State Tribune*, April 29, 1921, 5.
13. "What Kind of Woman Attracts Men Most," *Photoplay*, February 1924.
14. Mallinson, Russell P., "Wielding Woman's Weapons," *Pictures and the Picture-Goer*, May 1923, 15.
15. *Picture Play*, October 1923, 110.
16. Negri, Pola, *Memoirs of a Star* (New York: Doubleday, 1970).
17. Bruno, 29.
18. Eisner, Lotte, *The Haunted Screen* (University of California, reprint, 1977), 82–83.
19. Bruno, 29.
20. Griffith, Richard, *The Movie Stars* (New York: Doubleday & Co., 1970), 70.

Chapter 2

1. *Charleville Times* (Australia), June 24, 1954.
2. Howe, Herbert, "Pola Speaks" *New Movie Magazine*, November 1930, 59.
3. Ibid.
4. Negri had first mentioned writing her autobiography in 1928. In the late 1940s it bore the tentative title of "As Much As I Dare," but did not finally see publication until 1970 as "Memoirs of a Star." It was not a best-seller.
5. "The Autobiography of Pola Negri," *Photoplay*, February 1924, 50.
6. *The Milwaukee Sentinel*, February 1, 1935.
7. "Pola Negri, 'Vamp' of Silent Films, Dies," *Los Angeles Times*, August 3, 1987.
8. Quoted in *Los Angeles Times* obituary.
9. Kotowski, Mariusz, *Pola Negri: Hollywood's First Film Fatale* (Lexington: University of Kentucky Press, 2014).
10. After she attained fame in the movies, she preferred for strangers and new acquaintances to address her "Madame" in the French style—and preferably with a French accent. *Perth Western Mail*, February 18, 1932.
11. *Photoplay*, February 1922, 85.
12. "The Autobiography of Pola Negri."
13. Negri, Pola, *Memoirs of a Star* (New York: Doubleday, 1970), 16.
14. *Sydney Morning Herald*, November 4, 1954.
15. "The Autobiography of Pola Negri."
16. *Memoirs of a Star*, 16.
17. "The Autobiography of Pola Negri."
18. Allvine, Glendon, "Meet Miss Chalupez ... and Learn the Real Truth About Pola Negri," *Motion Picture*, September 1922, 21.
19. *Memoirs of a Star*, 16.
20. Negri had a life-long aversion to cats.
21. "The Autobiography of Pola Negri."
22. "Meet Miss Chalupez." If this was true, it would make 1899 her actual year of birth.
23. *Memoirs of a Star*, 21.
24. "The Autobiography of Pola Negri."
25. Kotowski, 7.
26. *Memoirs of a Star*, 23.
27. *Memoirs of a Star*, 25.
28. *Memoirs of a Star*, 26.
29. "Pity The Poor Dancer," *Albury Banner and Wodonga Express*, September 25, 1925, 14.
30. "The Autobiography of Pola Negri."
31. *Sheridan (WY) Enterprise*, July 8, 1921, 3.
32. *Memoirs of a Star*, 58.
33. *Perth Times*, 1928.
34. *Sydney Times*, April 8, 1923, 17.

35. Glendon Allvine's 1922 *Motion Picture* interview with "Appollonia Chalupez" omits any mention of her ballet career or early Polish films and moves her name change to "Pola Negri" to 1918 after she had become a German film star. This is clearly in error, as her German films bill her as Pola Negri.
36. *Memoirs of a Star*, 79.
37. "The Autobiography of Pola Negri."
38. *Ibid.*
39. *Memoirs of a Star*, 89.
40. *Memoirs of a Star*, 93.
41. *Memoirs of a Star*, 101.
42. *Sydney Times*, April 23, 1922, 17.
43. *Ibid.*
44. "The Autobiography of Pola Negri."
45. *Memoirs of a Star*, 114.
46. *Memoirs of a Star*, 116.
47. Although "Pola" is not named "Pola Negri" in the picture, there is a shot of a publicity banner in her boudoir in this picture that seems to tout a "Pola Negri".
48. Shipman, David, *The Great Movie Stars: The Golden Years* (New York: Da Capo Press, 1979), 409.

Chapter 3

1. *Photoplay*, "The Autobiography of Pola Negri, Part 2," March 1924, 56.
2. *Ibid.*
3. *Ibid.*
4. *Ibid.*
5. Negri, Pola, "Secrets in Pola Negri's Life," *Sydney Times*, April 22, 1923, 17.
6. Shipman, David, *The Great Movie Stars: The Golden Years* (New York: Da Capo Press, 1979), 409.
7. Storyline quoted in *Variety*, December 23, 1921, 35.
8. http://www.silentsaregolden.com.
9. Negri, Pola, *Memoirs of a Star* (New York: Doubleday, 1970), 140. When this picture, retitled *Eyes of the Mummy*, was released in America a few years later, they gave the picture a "happy" ending by having Mara survive her fall. The original ending was perhaps thought too morbid.
10. *Motion Picture*, August 1926.
11. *Memoirs of a Star*, 142–143.
12. Muller, Jurgen, ed., *Movies of the 20s* (Munich: Taschen Books, 2007).
13. Howe, Herbert, "A Trip Through Europe's Filmland," *Picture Play*, March 1921, 17.
14. *Horsham* (Australia) *Times*, April 13, 1923.
15. Howe, Herbert, "The Loves of Pola Negri," *Photoplay*, November 1923, 37.
16. *Memoirs of a Star*, 141.
17. *Memoirs of a Star*, 147.
18. *Memoirs of a Star*, 149.
19. *Memoirs of a Star*, 150.
20. "The Loves of Pola Negri," *Photoplay*, November 1923.
21. *Memoirs of a Star*, 156.
22. *Perth Mirror*, April 8, 1923.
23. Kotowski, Mariusz, *Pola Negri: Hollywood's First Film Fatale* (Lexington: University of Kentucky Press, 2014), 39.
24. On October 6, 1920, *New York Times* reported that a German actress named Pola Negri had reported the theft of one million marks worth of jewelry from her Berlin hotel room. Police were said to believe that the culprit had some expertise in jewelry as her imitation jewels, mixed in with her real jewels, had been scattered all over the floor. Apparently he knew exactly what to look for.
25. *Variety*, December 3, 1920, 34.
26. Rothafel edited the picture for length and "taste," most significantly omitting the final shot of DuBarry's severed head being tossed out to the crowd. The American version ends with the guillotine blade falling.
27. *Photoplay*, March 1921.
28. *Variety*, May 13, 1921, 2.
29. *Variety*, May 4, 1921, 45.
30. *Memoirs of a Star*, 184.
31. *Variety*, June 3, 1921, 4.
32. *Ibid.*
33. Taken from *Variety*, October 14, 1921, 43.
34. *Reel Journal*, March 31, 1922.
35. Hake, Sabine, *Passions and Deceptions: The Early Films of Ernst Lubitsch* (Princeton University Press, 1992), 42.
36. Quoted in Eyeman, Scott, *Laughter In Paradise: The Films of Ernst Lubitsch* (New York: Simon & Schuster, 1993), 56.
37. Eyeman, 84.
38. *Reel Journal*, March 12, 1922.
39. *Reel Journal*, July 1, 1922.
40. *Photoplay*, The Autobiography of Pola Negri, Part 2, March 1924.
41. *Picture Play*, January 1922.

Chapter 4

1. *Deseret News*, August 5, 1922.
2. Chaplin, Charles, *My Trip Abroad* (New York: Harper & Bros., 1922).
3. *Powell Tribune*, July 15, 1921, 8.
4. *New York Times*, December 13, 1920.
5. *Salt Lake Telegram*, April 19, 1921, 17.
6. *Picture Play*, May 1921, 52.
7. *Motion Picture*, February 1921.
8. *Wyoming State Tribune*, May 3, 1921, 5.
9. *Salt Lake Telegram*, April 13, 1921, 14.
10. *Salt Lake Telegram*, April 3, 1921, 4.
11. *Exhibitor's Trade Review*, September 10, 1921, 1026.
12. *Ibid.*
13. *Motion Picture*, October 1921.
14. Quoted in *New York Morning Telegraph*, December 22, 1922, 4.
15. *The Exhibitor's Herald*, July 9, 1921, p. 73.
16. *The Exhibitor's Herald*, July 30, 1921, 57.
17. *The Exhibitor's Herald*, August 27, 1921, 65.
18. *The Exhibitor's Herald*, February 25, 1922, 72.
19. *Motion Picture*, March 1922.
20. *Motion Picture*, February 1921.
21. *Variety*, May 13, 1921, 47.
22. Petrie, Graham, *Hollywood Destinies: European Directors in America, 1922–1931* (London: Routledge & Kegan-Paul, 1985), 7.
23. Petrie, 19.
24. *Picture Play*, October 1921, 45.
25. Petrie, 7.
26. *Variety*, May 13, 1921, 42.
27. *The Exhibitor's Herald*, May 7, 1921, 47.
28. *The Exhibitor's Herald*, May 28, 1921, 28.
29. *Billboard*, May 21, 1921, 106.
30. *The Photodramatist*, December 1921, 10.

31. *Photoplay*, "Famous Carmen's," October 1921.
32. *The Exhibitor's Herald*, September 10, 1921, 74.
33. *The Exhibitor's Herald*, October 8, 1921, 27.
34. *The Exhibitor's Herald*, October 1, 1921, 81.
35. *Variety*, April 18, 1921, 8.
36. Quoted in Petrie, 16.
37. *Variety*, May 13, 1921, 19.
38. *Variety*, May 13, 1921, 42.
39. *Motion Picture*, September 1921, 48.
40. *Motion Picture*, September 1921, 105.
41. *Variety*, October 7, 1921, 42.
42. *The Exhibitor's Trade Review*, September 24, 1921, 1180.
43. *The Exhibitor's Trade Review*, November 5, 1921.
44. *The Educational Screen*, January 1922, 29.
45. *Screenland*, December 1921.
46. *Picture Play*, May 1922.
47. *The Davis County Clipper*, April 21, 1922, 6.
48. *The Daily Star*, December 19, 1921.
49. *Billboard*, December 31, 1921, 98.
50. *The Exhibitor's Trade Review*, June 1, 1922, 295.
51. *Variety*, April 7, 1922, 42.
52. *The Exhibitor's Trade Review*, October 29, 1921, 1518.
53. *Motion Picture*, February 1922.
54. *Variety*, January 20, 1922, 35.
55. *Picture Play*, April 1922.
56. *New York Morning Telegraph*, January 27, 1922, 6.
57. *The Exhibitor's Trade Review*, April 15, 1922, 1451.
58. Ibid.
59. Ibid.
60. *Motion Picture*, June 1922, 54.
61. Quoted in *The Exhibitor's Trade Review*, June 24, 1922, 245.
62. *Motion Picture*, September 1922, 116.
63. *The Exhibitor's Trade Review*, August 26, 1922, 876.
64. *Reel Journal*, May 5, 1922.
65. *The Saratogian* (NY), March 17, 1921, 5.
66. *Variety*, May 13, 1921, 45.
67. *Brooklyn Daily Eagle*, May 31, 1921, 6.
68. Hall, Carolyn, *The Twenties in Vogue* (New York: Harmony, 1983, 86).
69. *Picture Play*, April 1922.
70. Vinder, Maximillian, "She Delivers the Goods," *Photoplay*, May 1922, 50.
71. Ibid.
72. Allvine, Glendon, "How Polish is Pola Negri?" *Filmplay*, June 1922.
73. Ibid.
74. Klumph, Helen, "What About Pola Negri?" *Picture Play*, July 1922, 18.
75. Lachenbruch, Jerome, "The Real Pola Negri—A Creature of Fire," *Movie Weekly*, July 7, 1922, 8.
76. "Schwarz" is "black" in German, just as "Negri" is a variation of "black" in Italian.
77. *Billboard*, August 27, 1921, 57.
78. "What About Pola Negri?"
79. *Brooklyn Daily Eagle*, August 21, 1921, 8.
80. "What About Pola Negri?"
81. Ibid.
82. Quoted in *Film Daily*, January 18, 1922, 2.
83. Peterson, Anne Helen, *Scandals of Classic Hollywood: The Most Kissable Hands of Pola Negri*. http://thehairpin.com/2013/11/scandals-of-classic-hollywood-the-most-kissable-hands-of-pola-negri/.
84. *Bella Donna* is the title of a novel by Robert Hitchens and was first made into a movie in 1915, starring actress Pauline Frederick.
85. According to legend, when asked in Customs whether he had anything to declare, Ben Blumenthal, Negri's chaperone on her voyage to America, reputedly stated: "Yes! Pola Negri!"
86. Zierold, Norman, *Sex Goddesses of the Silent Screen* (Chicago: Regnery Press, 1973. 81). From the photos, this is clearly not accurate.
87. Klumph, Helen, "Now We Know About Pola," *Picture Play*, December 1922, 20.
88. *New York Morning Telegraph*, September 17, 1922.
89. *Ogden Daily Examiner*, September 13, 1922, 2.
90. Negri, Pola, *Memoirs of a Star* (New York: Doubleday, 1970), 201.
91. "Now We Know About Pola."
92. *Memoirs of a Star*, 204.

Chapter 5

1. Negri, Pola, *Memoirs of a Star* (New York: Doubleday, 1970), 197.
2. *Motion Picture*, November 1922.
3. *Motion Picture*, February 1923.
4. "Do Women of the Screen Lack Beauty?" *Motion Picture*, May 1925, 32.
5. *Horsham Times*, April 13, 1923.
6. *Brooklyn Eagle*, August 21, 1921, p 8.
7. Harpman, Julia, "Love and War Color Pola Negri's Career," *Schenectady Gazette*, July 10, 1924, 14.
8. *New York Morning Telegraph*, September 12, 1922, 5.
9. *Casper Herald*, October 17, 1922, 10.
10. Underhill, Harriette, "Europe's Most Beautiful Star Here at Last," *New York Morning Telegraph*, September 17, 1922, 2.
11. Faulker, H.H., "Readings of the Noses of Ten Famous Stars," *Motion Picture*, February 1923, 66.
12. *Screenland*, February 1924, 92.
13. *Motion Picture*, "Handwriting of the Stars," April 1927.
14. *Motion Picture*, June 1923, 47.
15. Negri's eyes are recorded in many sources as being "black," "green," "smoky," "velvet," and "gypsy." They were, in fact, gray.
16. Howe, Herbert, "The Real Pola Negri," *Photoplay*, November 1922, 59.
17. *Screenland*, July 1924, 10.
18. Ibid.
19. Negra, Diane, "Immigrant Stardom in Imperial America: Pola Negri and the Problem of Typology," from *A Feminist Reader in Early Cinema*, edited by Jennifer M. Bean and Diane Negra (Duke University Press, 2002), 396.
20. *Motion Picture*, June 1924.
21. Stanlaws, Penrhyn, "What's Wrong With Our Women?" *Screenland*, January 1923.
22. Stanlaws, Penrhyn, "The Most Beautiful Star in the World," *Screenland*, February 1923, 16.
23. http://www.enjoy-your-style.com/pola-negri.html.
24. *Motion Picture*, November 1922.
25. An item in the January 1923 issue of *Screenland* described Negri's appearance at the Grauman's Egyptian Theatre premiere of Douglas Fairbanks' *Robin Hood*: "Pola Negri is new to Hollywood, so her wrap was only mink. Her gorgeous black eyes and olive skin were set off by her favorite headdress—a broad band of gold cloth."
26. The turban, as it turned out, was an accidental

creation. Negri was running late for a party and with no time to set her wet hair, she simply wrapped it up in a scarf and inadvertently created a fashion statement.

27. *Tasmanian Advocate*, March 6, 1926.
28. *Motion Picture*, May 1925.
29. *Lauceton Examiner*, June 20, 1925.
30. *Horsham Times*, November 24, 1925.
31. Howe, Herbert, "The Real Pola Negri," *Photoplay*, November 1922, 59.
32. *Picture Play*, March 1923.
33. *Picture Play*, April 1923.
34. *Adelaide Register*, December 16, 1922.
35. Hall, Gladys and Adele Whitley-Fletcher, "We Interview Pola Negri," *Motion Picture*, January 1923, 22.
36. Carr, Harry, "Behind The Scenes with Pola Negri," *Motion Picture*, June 1923.
37. Negra, 386.
38. *Ibid*.
39. Negra, 397.
40. *Ibid*.
41. *Ogden Daily Examiner*, October 13, 1922, 2.
42. Goldwyn, Samuel, *Behind the Screen* (New York: George H. Doran Co., 1923).
43. *Picture Play*, September 1922.
44. *Photoplay*, September 1922.
45. Howe, Herbert, "The Real Pola Negri," *Photoplay*, November 1922.
46. Leeds, Stanton, "Who is the Sarah Bernhardt of the Screen?" *Picture Play*, December 1922, 16.
47. *Picture Play*, March 1923.
48. *Film Daily*, February 23, 1923.
49. Quoted in *The Exhibitor's Trade Review*, March 17, 1923, 818.
50. Quoted in *Film Daily*, March 26, 1923.
51. *Ibid*.
52. *The Educational Screen*, April 1923, 186.
53. *Variety*, March 8, 1923, 28.
54. *Evening Independent*, March 31, 1923.
55. Carr, Harry, "Behind the Scenes with Pola Negri," *Photoplay*, July 1923, 33.
56. Schallert, Edwin, "The Elegy of Pola Negri," *Picture Play*, March 1923.
57. "Behind the Scenes With Pola Negri."
58. Actor Adolphe Menjou in his 1948 autobiography, *It Took Nine Tailors*, states that the closed set privilege was only extended to top stars, but Pola did not care. When author Ring Lardner stopped by to visit production of *Bella Donna*, she, not knowing who he was, reputedly wanted him removed from the set immediately or she would not going on with her next scene. According to Menjou, when told that Lardner was a famous writer, she said, "Introdooce me, plizz. I weel eenspire heem to write a beautiful sonnet."
59. Zierold, 89–94.
60. *Perth Sunday-Times*, December 9, 1923.
61. *New York Times*, April 15, 1923, Amusement Section, 3.
62. *Picture Play*, August 1923, 23.
63. *Casper Herald*, October 17, 1922, 10.
64. *Perth Mirror*, September 15, 1923, 8.
65. *The Barrier Miner*, August 13, 1938.
66. *Perth Mirror*, October 27, 1923, 8.
67. *The Barrier Miner*, August 13, 1938.
68. *The Syracuse American*, August 7, 1927.
69. *New York Morning Telegraph*, January 28, 1923, 4.
70. "Love and War Color Pola Negri's Career."
71. *Photoplay*, "The Autobiography of Pola Negri, Part 3," April 1924.
72. Howe, Herbert, "The Little People of the Screen," *Photoplay*, September 1924, 30.
73. *Motion Picture*, January 1923.
74. *Variety*, October 27, 1922, 43.
75. "The Autobiography of Pola Negri, Part 3."
76. *Ibid*.
77. *Ibid*.
78. *Ibid*.
79. *New York Morning Telegraph*, April 15, 1923, 6.
80. "The Autobiography of Pola Negri, Part 3."
81. *Screenland*, October 1923.
82. "The Autobiography of Pola Negri, Part 3."
83. *Picture Play*, August 1923, 98.
84. Swanson, Gloria, *Swanson on Swanson* (New York: Random House, 1980), 185.
85. *Rockhampton Morning Bulletin*, March 31, 1923.
86. *Albury Banner and Wonduga Express*, November 28, 1930.
87. Shearer, Michael, *Gloria Swanson: The Ultimate Star* (New York: St. Martin's Press, 2013).
88. *New York Times*, July 26, 1925.
89. Shearer, 42.
90. Quoted in Shearer, 93.
91. Carr, Harry, "The Fight for the Crown," *Motion Picture*, September 1925.
92. *Memoirs of a Star*, 228–229.

Chapter 6

1. Negra, Diane, "Immigrant Stardom in Imperial America: Pola Negri and the Problem of Typology," from *A Feminist Reader in Early Cinema*, edited by Jennifer M. Bean and Diane Negra (Duke University Press, 2002), 400.
2. "Block-Booking" required exhibitors who wanted to book the latest production from a major box-office "name" or attraction to contract to take a number of less desirable pictures as well, otherwise known as "program pictures." The benefit for the studio was to guarantee distribution of all of their product. For the exhibitor it was far less sweet deal. They had to accept pictures that they didn't necessarily want and commit to screening them instead of another picture that might prove more profitable to them.
3. *The Exhibitor's Trade Review*, April 28, 1923, 1107.
4. *Variety*, April 19, 1923.
5. *New York Times*, April 26, 1923.
6. Quoted in *Film Daily*, April 17, 1923.
7. *Ibid*.
8. *The Exhibitor's Herald*, February 2, 1924.
9. *The Exhibitor's Herald*, March 1, 1924.
10. *Photoplay*, June 1923.
11. *Pictures and the Picture-Goer*, June 1924.
12. Carr, Harry, "They Still Twinkle," *Motion Picture*, October 1923, 36.
13. *Motion Picture Classic*, December 1923.
14. *Screenland*, September 1923, 56.
15. *Picture Play*, July 1923, 60.
16. Carr, Harry, "A Ride With Pola Negri," *Motion Picture*, 1924 (Month unknown), 28.
17. *Ibid*.
18. *Photoplay*, August 1923, 44.
19. *Screenland*, August 1923, 49.
20. *The Wyalong Advocate and Mining, Agricultural and Pastoral Gazette*, August 31, 1923.
21. Rice, T., "Protecting Protestantism: The Ku Klux

Klan vs. the Motion Picture Industry," *Film History*, Vol. 20, No. 3, 2008, 367–380.
22. Allen, Bert, "Last of the Temperaments," *Silver Screen*, April 1934, 32.
23. *Variety*, August 30, 1923, 26.
24. *New York Times*, August 27, 1923.
25. Quoted in *Film Daily*, August 29, 1923.
26. *The Exhibitor Trade Review*, September 8, 1923, 660.
27. *New York Morning Telegraph*, September 18, 1923, 5.
28. *Motion Picture*, November 1923.
29. *Variety*, December 8, 1923, 38.
30. *Photoplay*, "The Autobiography of Pola Negri," April 1924.
31. Ibid.
32. *Photoplay*, June 1923.
33. *Photoplay*, December 1923.
34. *Memoirs of a Star*, 221.
35. *Variety*, May 10, 1923, 17.
36. *Variety*, May 10, 1923, 22.
37. Negri, Pola, *Memoirs of a Star* (New York: Doubleday, 1970), 225.
38. Press sheet for *The Cheat*, Paramount Pictures, 1923.
39. *Motion Picture*, October 1923.
40. *Pictures and the Picture-Goer*, June 1924.
41. *Motion Picture*, June 1924.
42. *Motion Picture*, October 1923.
43. *Shadowland*, October 1923.
44. *Motion Picture Classic*, December 1923.
45. In an article for the May 1931 issue of *New Movie Magazine*, Herbert Howe recounted a visit with Negri in 1924 in which he asked her feelings for Chaplin. She replied, "I love him. The trouble is I love him more than he loves me. But don't print that. It would make him more conceited."
46. *Memoirs of a Star*, 205.
47. Cotes, Peter and Thelma Niklaus, *The Little Fellow: The Life and Work of Charles Spencer Chaplin* (New York: Philosophical Library, 1965), 53–54.
48. *Movie Weekly*, April 8, 1922. In the original version of the story, as previously noted, Negri's reply in her broken English is "jazz boy Charlie."
49. *Photoplay*, The Autobiography of Pola Negri, Part 2, March 1924.
50. *Motion Picture*, December 1922.
51. Howe, *The Real Pola Negri*.
52. Hall, Gladys and Adele Whitley-Fletcher, "We Interview Pola Negri," *Motion Picture*, August 1922.
53. Robinson, David, *Chaplin* (New York: McGraw Hill, 1985), 324.
54. *Memoirs of a Star*, 207.
55. Robinson, 325.
56. Ibid.
57. *Variety*, December 21, 1922, 29.
58. *New York Evening Telegram*, January, 16, 1924.
59. According to *Memoirs*, Charlie gave her the diamond as either a birthday present or as her engagement ring. She was miffed at the fact that he gave it to her as a loose gem in a box, telling her that he hadn't had the time to get it set in a ring. She supposedly tossed the box—unopened-into a drawer, telling him she would open it when she had the time.
60. *Salt Lake Telegram*, January, 18, 1923, 1.
61. *Salt Lake Telegram*, January 19, 1923, 1.
62. *Kansas City Times*, January 29, 1923.
63. *New York Evening Telegraph*, January 31, 1923, 4.
64. Menjou, Adolphe and M.M. Musselman, *It Took Nine Tailors* (New York: Whittlesey House, 1948, 103–104).
65. *Photoplay*, March 1923.
66. *Motion Picture*, April 1923.
67. Kelly, T. Howard, "Can Pola and Charlie Be Happy?" *Movie Weekly*, December 30, 1922.
68. *Picture Play*, April 1923.
69. *Motion Picture*, May,1923.
70. *Variety*, April 19, 1923, 32.
71. *Kansas City Times*, March 2, 1923.
72. *New York Times*, March 3, 1923.
73. Robinson, 327.
74. *Variety*, April 3, 1923, 26.
75. *Perth Mirror*, April 8, 1923.
76. Ibid.
77. Ibid.
78. *Salt Lake Telegram*, April 14, 1923.
79. *The Ogden Standard*, April 2, 1923.
80. *The Post Pirie Recorder*, November 19, 1923.
81. Ibid.
82. "William Tilden II Named As Pola Negri's Lover," *Gloversville Morning Herald*, July 31, 1923, 1.
83. *Perth Mirror*, August 4, 1923.
84. Howe, Herbert, "The Loves of Pola Negri," *Photoplay*, July 1923.
85. Ibid.
86. *Photoplay*, December 1923.
87. *New York Times*, December 8, 1923.
88. Quoted in *The Exhibitor's Herald*, December 17, 1923.
89. *Screenland*, January 1924, 51.
90. Quoted in *Film Daily*, October 10, 1923.
91. *The Exhibitor's Herald*, March 15, 1924.
92. *The Exhibitor's Herald*, March 1, 1924.
93. *Niagara Falls Gazette*, September 12, 1933, 8.
94. *Photoplay*, September 1923.
95. *Buffalo Sunday Courier*, 1924, 10.
96. *Screenland*, February 1924, 10.
97. Ibid.
98. *New York Times*, February 8, 1924.
99. *The Exhibitor's Trade Review*, March 1, 1924, 27.
100. *Film Daily*, February 24, 1924.
101. *Film Daily*, March 9, 1924.
102. *Salt Lake Telegram*, February 2, 1924, 10.
103. *Motion Picture Classic*, February 1924.
104. Carr, Harry, "A Ride With Pola Negri," *Motion Picture*, 1924.
105. *Film Daily*, April 14, 1924.
106. *The Exhibitor's Trade Review*, May 3, 1924, 33.
107. "What Kind of Women Attract Men Most?" *Photoplay*, February 1924.
108. *Pictures and the Picture-Goer* Magazine, March 1924.
109. *The Ogden Standard*, April 26, 1924.
110. From *The Exhibitor's Trade Review*, May 17, 1924, 32.
111. Ibid.
112. *Variety*, May 7, 1924, 20.
113. *New York Times*, May 5, 1924.
114. *The Montreal Gazette*, July 15, 1924.
115. *Photoplay*, February 1925.
116. *The Northern Territory Times and Gazette*, May 23, 1924.
117. Carr, Harry, "The Mystery of Pola Negri," *Motion Picture*, February 1925.
118. Marshall, Eunice, "The New Pola," *Motion Picture*, June 1924, 34.

119. *Salt Lake Telegram*, July 13, 1924, 4.
120. *Photoplay*, "Favorite Sweethearts of the Screen," July 1924, 31.
121. *Ibid.*
122. *Photoplay*, June 1924.
123. *Motion Picture*, May 1924.
124. *Variety*, August 27, 1924, 21.
125. *Ibid.*
126. *Variety*, May 7, 1924, 20.
127. *Ibid.* She was probably only teasing, but even so it was a bit mean-spirited to call him "Rudy," particularly in light of what would eventually happen, and more so because La Rocque hated being compared to Valentino. He was often referred to as a "junior Valentino."
128. *Variety*, June 25, 1924, 19.
129. *Variety*, August 27, 1924.
130. *New York Times*, August 25, 1924.
131. *The Exhibitor's Trade Review*, September 6, 1924, 21.
132. Quoted in *Film Daily*, September 27, 1924.
133. Quoted in *Film Daily*, November 6, 1924.
134. Quoted in *Film Daily*, September 27, 1924.
135. Quoted in *Film Daily*, November 6, 1924.
136. Gebhardt, Myrtle, "A Turn in Pola's Career," *Picture Play*, August 1924, 23.
137. *Ibid.*
138. *The Exhibitor's Trade Review*, December 6, 1924, 51.
139. Quoted in *Film Daily*, November 23, 1924.
140. *Photoplay*, January 1925.
141. Harpman, Julia, "Love and War Color Pola Negri's Career," *Schenectady Gazette*, July 10, 1924, 14.
142. *Photoplay*, June 1924.
143. *Motion Picture*, January 1925.
144. *Motion Picture*, March 1925.
145. *Variety*, January 7, 1925.
146. *New York Times*, January 26, 1925.
147. *The Exhibitor's Trade Review*, January 17, 1925, 48.
148. *Brooklyn Daily Eagle*, January 11, 1925, 4.
149. *Perth Mirror*, April 4, 1925.
150. *New York Times*, April 6, 1925.
151. *Variety*, April 8, 1925, 36.
152. *The Exhibitor's Trade Review*, April 18, 1925, 60.
153. *Photoplay*, May 1925.
154. *New York Times*, March 2, 1925, 5.
155. *Brooklyn Daily Eagle*, March 15, 1925.
156. *The Buffalo Evening News*, March 17, 1925, 20.
157. *New York Times*, March 22, 1925, Sec. 2, E.
158. *Variety*, March 25, 1925, 35.
159. *Variety*, April 8, 1925, 16.
160. *The New York Evening Post*, May 5, 1925, 1.
161. *Variety*, May 6, 1925, 19.
162. *New York Times*, July 7, 1925.
163. *The Educational Screen*, June 1925, 364.
164. *Variety*, August 21, 1925.
165. *New York Times*, October 20, 1925.
166. Quoted in *Film Daily*, November 18, 1925.
167. *Film Daily*, July 7, 1926.
168. *Photoplay*, June 1926.
169. *Pictures and the Picture-Goer*, October 1925.
170. *Variety*, June 10, 1925, 32.
171. *Film Daily*, January 7, 1926.
172. *Variety*, August 19, 1925, 31.
173. *Salt Lake Telegram*, September 6, 1925, 4.
174. Mann, William, J., *Wisecracker: The Life and Times of William Haines* (New York: Viking Press, 1998), 109–110.
175. *Ibid.*
176. *Variety*, October 14, 1925, 12.
177. *Variety*, October 20, 1925, 37.
178. *Variety*, December 16, 1925.
179. Quoted in *Film Daily*, December 22, 1925.
180. *Motion Picture*, March 1926.
181. *Photoplay*, February 1926.
182. *Photoplay*, January 1926.
183. *Photoplay*, May 1926.
184. *Photoplay*, March 1926.
185. Quoted in *Film Daily*, April 9, 1926.
186. *Screenland*, June 1926, 49.
187. *Photoplay*, June 1926.
188. *Ibid.*
189. *Photoplay*, June 1927.
190. *Variety*, June 18, 1926.
191. *New York Times*, June 13, 1926.
192. Quoted in *Film Daily*, June 26, 1926.
193. Quoted in *Film Daily*, July 14, 1926.
194. *Photoplay*, March 1926.
195. *Salt Lake Telegram*, October 3, 1926, 18.
196. *New York Times*, January 3, 1927.
197. *Photoplay*, January 1927.
198. *The Exhibitor's Herald*, February, 18, 1928, 63.
199. *Utica Observer Dispatch*, August 10, 1924, 1.
200. *Ibid.*
201. Botham, Noel and Peter Donnelly, *Valentino: The Love God* (London: Ace Books, 1976), 185.
202. *Ibid.*
203. *Motion Picture Classic*, October 1924.
204. *Photoplay*, April 1925.
205. Cooper, Miriam, *Dark Lady of the Silents* (Indianapolis: Bobb-Merrill Co., 1973), 212.
206. Quoted in Ellenberger, Allen R., *The Valentino Mystique* (Jefferson, NC: McFarland, 2005), 25.
207. *Memoirs of a Star*, 258.
208. Ellenberger, 25.
209. *Ibid.*
210. *Ibid.*
211. Quoted in Ellenberger, 26.
212. Botham and Donnelly, 185.
213. *Memoirs of a Star*, 262.
214. *Memoirs of a Star*, 265.
215. Leider, Emily W., *Dark Lover* (New York: Farrar, Straus & Giroux, 2003), 361.
216. Shulman, Irving, *Valentino* (New York: Trident Press, 1967), 315.
217. Ullman, S. George, *Valentino as I Knew Him* (New York: A.L. Burt Company, 1926), 154.
218. *Motion Picture Classic*, August 1926.
219. Leider, 363.
220. Quoted in Ellenberger, 26.
221. *Ibid.*
222. *Motion Picture Classic*, September 1926.
223. Ellenberger, 26.
224. York, Cal, "He Who Got Slapped and Why," *Photoplay*, July 1926, 5.
225. *Motion Picture*, August 1926.
226. In Michael Ankerich's 2012 biography of Mae Murray, *The Girl With the Bee-Stung Lips*, he makes the claim that the time of Murray's wedding to "Prince" David Mdivani, she was still sexually involved with Valentino, unbeknownst to Negri. He writes that George Ullman, seeing the picture of Rudy standing between Pola and Mae at Mae's wedding, and knowing what he knew, thought that the film star looked painfully awkward.
227. Cooper, 212.
228. *Variety*, February 10, 1926, 12.
229. *Salt Lake Telegram*, February 3, 1926.

230. *The Syracuse Journal*, February 4, 1926, 24.
231. *Salt Lake Telegram*, February 2, 1926, 1.
232. *The Buffalo Sunday Express*, February 18, 1926, Sec. 5, 4.
233. *The Ogden Standard*, February 18, 1926, 1.
234. *The Northern Star*, March 8, 1926.
235. *The Buffalo Sunday Express*, February 18, 1926, Sec. 5, 4.
236. Rogers St. John, "Adela, Love and Laughter in Hollywood," *The American Weekly*, October 20, 1950.
237. *New York Times*, March 23, 1926.
238. *Motion Picture*, July 1926.
239. *The Buffalo Courier*, April 20, 1926, 10.
240. *New York Times*, June 30, 1926.
241. Ardmore, Jane, *The Self-Enchanted: Mae Murray, Image of an Era* (New York: McGraw Hill, 1959), 187.
242. *Syracuse Journal*, August 24, 1926, 8.
243. Ellenbarger, 56.
244. Ellenbarger, 71.
245. Shulman, 52.
246. Shulman, 115–116.
247. *Brooklyn Daily Eagle*, August 24, 1926, 2.
248. *The Port Pirie Recorder*, August 30, 1926.
249. *The Daily Star*, August 26, 1926.
250. *Evening Independent*, August 26, 1926.
251. Ibid.
252. Shulman, 71.
253. Ullman, George, "The Real Valentino," *Photoplay*, January 1927.
254. Ellenbarger, 86.
255. *The Daily Argus* (Mt. Vernon, NY), September 3, 1926, 3.
256. *The Syracuse Gazette*, September 20, 1926, 20.
257. In her 1952 biography, *From Under My Hat* (p. 157), gossip columnist Hedda Hopper writes: "Joseph Hergensheimer had a bungalow opposite Pola at Ambassador Hotel.... Joe watched Pola emerge in deep mourning, with the veil thrown back so newsreel cameras could record how she faced going on living with bravery and fortitude. Shots were taken. One cameraman yelled: "Pola—the light's not good on your face—will you do it again?" And, Joe reported to me with awe. "Darned if she didn't! It's the only time I ever saw a retake on mourning!"
258. *Motion Picture*, December 1926.
259. *The Adelaide Mail*, August 6, 1932.
260. *Screenland*, November 1927.
261. *Motion Picture*, November 1927.
262. *Variety*, August 10, 1927.
263. *The Exhibitor's Herald*, January 21, 1928, p. 75.
264. *Photoplay*, May 1927.
265. *Salt Lake Telegram*, April 14, 1927, 1.
266. *Motion Picture*, January 1927, 40.
267. Leone-Moats, Alice, *The Million-Dollar Studs* (New York: Delacorte Press), 1977.
268. *Motion Picture*, July 1927.
269. *Photoplay*, May 1927.
270. *New York Times*, March 23, 1927.
271. *Memoirs of a Star*, 196.
272. *Memoirs of a Star*, 299.
273. *Photoplay*, December 1926, 16.
274. *Memoirs of a Star*, 300.
275. *New York Times*, March 3, 1927.
276. *Photoplay*, May 1927.
277. *Photoplay*, July 1927, 74.
278. Mdivani, David, "Prince Serge Mdivani was Perfect Lover," *Australian Woman's Weekly*, August 15, 1936.
279. *The Buffalo Courier Express*, April 27, 1927, 2.
280. Mdivani.
281. *The Syracuse American*, April 24, 1927, 3.
282. *The Buffalo Courier Express*, April 27, 1927, 2.
283. *Perth Daily News*, April 27, 1927.
284. *The Ogden Standard*, May 15, 1927, 1.
285. Ankerich, 193: "Mae Murray was livid over the prospect of two 'Princess Mdivani's' in Hollywood. When Louella Parsons was told by Pola that she would be marrying Serge and that she had known the Mdivani since childhood, Mae went to great lengths to deny it and accused Louella of lying."
286. *The Ogden Standard*, May 15, 1927, 1.
287. *Memoirs of a Star*, 314.
288. *The Ogden* (UT) *Standard-Examiner*, May 29, 1927, 4.
289. *Memoirs of a Star*, 315.
290. *Picture Play*, September 1927, 10.
291. Letter from E.G., Cape May, NJ, printed in *Picture Play*, January 1928, 10.
292. *Photoplay*, September 1927.
293. *Photoplay*, June 1927, 74.
294. *Variety*, September 28, 1927.
295. *New York Times*, September 26, 1927.
296. *Film Daily*, October 2, 1927.
297. *Variety*, January 25, 1928, 6.
298. *The Exhibitor's Herald*, March 10, 1928, 62.
299. *Salt Lake Telegram*, November, 8, 1927, 5.
300. *Memoirs of a Star*, 317.
301. *Variety*, June 1, 1927, 1.
302. *Variety*, March 14, 1928.
303. *New York Times*, March 12, 1928.
304. *Photoplay*, December 1927.
305. *The Exhibitor's Herald*, March 31, 1928, 54.
306. *Variety*, March 21, 1928, 7.
307. *Film Spectator*, March 3, 1928, 57.
308. Oettinger, Malcom H., "The Queen Receives," *Picture Play*, January 1928, 74.
309. *Variety*, January 4, 1928, 8.
310. *Picture Play*, May 1928, 112.
311. *Variety*, April 25, 1928.
312. *Film Daily*, April 29, 1928.
313. *Photoplay*, June 1928.
314. *Film Spectator*, April 28, 1928, 12.
315. *Variety*, May 2, 1928, 7.
316. *Picture Play*, March 1928, 9.
317. *New York Times*, July 26, 1928.
318. *Variety*, August 1, 1928.
319. Quoted in *Film Daily*, August 5, 1928.
320. *Moving Picture Herald*, May 24, 1929, 63.
321. *Variety*, August 22, 1928, 28.
322. *Moving Picture Herald*, May 11, 1929, 61.
323. *Picture Play*, August 1927, 30.
324. *The Exhibitor's Trade Review*, July 9, 1928.
325. *Variety*, November 7, 1928.
326. *Photoplay*, September 1928.
327. *The Motion Picture News Daily*, November 11, 1928.
328. *The Exhibitor's Trade Review*, November 7, 1928.
329. *Variety*, December 12, 1928, 3.
330. *The Daily Star*, May 19, 1928, 6.

Chapter 7

1. http://lavidak.org/Biografias/index.php?b=Pola-Negri.
2. Hall, Leonard, "The Passing of Pola," *Photoplay*, December 1928, 29.

3. Chamberlin, Willard, "Too Continental or What?" *Picture Play*, November 1930, 88.
4. Letter to *Picture Play* from Lillian Dusky, Gisborne, New Zealand, April 1929.
5. Letter to *Picture Play* from Rosa Sheptner, Krementchug, Russia, October 1929.
6. *Perth Daily News*, October 24, 1928.

Chapter 8

1. Howe, Herbert, "Pola Speaks," *The New Movie Magazine*, November 1930, 59.
2. Kotowski, Mariusz, *Pola Negri: Hollywood's First Film Fatale* (Lexington: University of Kentucky Press, 2014), 159.
3. *Exhibitor's Daily Review*. October 10, 1928.
4. *Photoplay*, September 1928.
5. *Exhibitor's Daily Review*, July 14, 1928.
6. *New York Times*, August 17, 1928.
7. *Film Daily*, September 11, 1928.
8. *New York Times*, September 9, 1928.
9. *Ibid*.
10. *The Barrier Miner*, September 12, 1928.
11. *The Brisbane Sunday Mail*, December 2, 1928, 1.
12. *Film Daily*, December 12, 1928.
13. *Variety*, December 26, 1928, 35.
14. Motion Picture Daily News, March 23, 1929.
15. *New York Times*, June 1, 1933.
16. *Ibid*.
17. *Variety*, January 16, 1929, 1.
18. *The Yonkers Statesman*, April 12, 1929, 11.
19. *The Northern Miner*, April 13, 1929.
20. *Ibid*.
21. *Variety*, March 12, 1929.
22. *The Geraldton Guardian and Express*, July 2, 1929.
23. *Variety*, May 4, 1930, 43.
24. *Motion Picture* in its August 1931 issue described it as "a tug of war" between the two women for Mdivani's affections.
25. *The Milwaukee Sentinel*, November 30, 1929.
26. *New York Times*, December 18, 1929.
27. *The Milwaukee Sentinel*, December 15, 1929.
28. *The Pittsburgh Press*, December 21, 1929.
29. *Variety*, June 6, 1930, 65.
30. *Mt. Vernon Daily Argus*, November 13, 1930, 1.
31. *Variety*, October 29, 1930.
32. *Sydney World News*, March, 18, 1931, 26.
33. *The Standard Union*, March 20,1931.
34. *Central Queensland* (Australia) *Herald*, April 9, 1931.
35. Alexis, the youngest of the "Marrying Mdvani's," had divorced Van Arlen to marry Woolworth heir Barbara Hutton. He died in an automobile crash in 1935.
36. Sharon, Mary, "Lovelorn," *Silver Screen*, September 1931, 18.
37. *Ibid*. One wonders is her mention of "being denied" children an admission of her miscarriage?
38. The *Ogdensburg Republican Journal*, May 5, 1931, 1.
39. Negri, Pola, *Memoirs of a Star* (New York: Doubleday, 1970), 353.

Chapter 9

1. *Photoplay*, May 1931.
2. *Motion Picture*, February 1929.
3. *Picture Play*, October 1930.
4. *Picture Play*, April 1931.
5. *Picture Play*, April 1930.
6. *Ibid*.
7. *Picture Play*, December 1930.
8. *New Movie Magazine*, May 1930, 43.
9. *The Milwaukee Sentinel*, May 8, 1931.
10. *Photoplay*, June 1931.
11. *The Milwaukee Sentinel*, May 8, 1931.
12. *Photoplay*, June 1931.
13. *New York Times*, July 19, 1931.
14. *Modern Screen*, August 1931, 10.
15. *New Movie Magazine*, September 1931, 12.
16. Sharon, Mary, "Lovelorn," *Silver Screen*, September 1931, 18.
17. *Photoplay*, October 1931.
18. Pryor, Nancy, "Pola Comes Back to Hollywood," *Motion Picture*, August 1931, 14.
19. *Film Daily*, August 8, 1931.
20. *The Brisbane Courier*, October 28, 1931, 8.
21. *The Niagara Falls Gazette*, December 12, 1931, 8.
22. *The Perth Western Mail*, February, 18, 1932.
23. *Photoplay*, March 1932.
24. Hall, Mordaunt, Pola Negri Heard, *New York Times*, January 29, 1932.
25. *Film Daily*, January 31, 1932.
26. *Photoplay*, February 1932.
27. *Motion Picture*, May 1932.
28. *Motion Picture*, April 1932.
29. *Motion Picture*, January 1932.
30. *The Hollywood Reporter*, January 24, 1933.
31. *The Perth News*, June 1, 1932.
32. *Ibid*.
33. Berle, Milton, *Milton Berle: An Autobiography* (New York: Applause Theatre and Cinema Books, 1974), 139.
34. *The Salt Lake Times*, August 12, 1932, 4.
35. *Variety*, March 15, 1932, 36.
36. *Pittsburgh Post-Gazette*, August 6, 1932.
37. *Perth Mirror*, January 27, 1933.
38. *Variety*, October 11, 1932, 34.
39. *Moving Picture Herald*, January 21, 1933, 25.
40. *Variety*, February 29, 1933, 3.
41. Hall, Gladys, "Valentino Still Lives—For Pola Negri," *Motion Picture*, January 1935, 46.
42. *The Hollywood Reporter*, June 25, 1934, 1.
43. Negri, Pola, *Memoirs of a Star* (New York: Doubleday, 1970), 365.
44. *The Palm Beach Post*, July 20, 1933.

Chapter 10

1. Golden, Eve, "The Opportunist: Pola Negri On Her (More or Less) Centenary," *Classic Images*, December 1997.
2. Negri, Pola, *Memoirs of a Star* (New York: Doubleday, 1970), 368.
3. *Memoirs of a Star*, 372.
4. *Schenectady Gazette*, February 2, 1935, 10.
5. *Ibid*.
6. *The Australasian*, February 9, 1935, 3.
7. *Memoirs of a Star*, 373.
8. *Ibid*.
9. Ott, Frederick W., *Great German Films* (Secaucus, NJ: Citadel Press, 1986), 156.
10. *The Adelaide Advertiser*, March 6, 1937.

11. *Memoirs of a Star*, 375.
12. *The Niagara Falls Gazette*, November 25, 1935, 8.
13. *Ibid.*
14. *New York Times*, May 6, 1935.
15. *Perth Mirror*, January 25, 1936. The article states that she had also let her hair go "back to its natural color—a Titian red." True? Previously, her natural hair color had been deemed to be brown.
16. *Variety*, April 4, 1936, 3.
17. *Variety*, October 28, 1936, 15.
18. *Variety*, August 13, 1936, 3.
19. *The New York Post*, April 17, 1937, 6.
20. *The Sunday Perth Times*, June 16, 1937.
21. *The Gloversville Morning Herald*, June 31, 1937, 6.
22. *The Milwaukee Sentinel*, September 10, 1938.
23. *The New York Post*, October 30, 1937.
24. *Variety*, June 2, 1937, 23.
25. *Ibid.*
26. *New York Times*, October 30, 1937.
27. *Memoirs of a Star*, 381.
28. *Memoirs of a Star*, 384.
29. Kotowski, Mariusz, *Pola Negri: Hollywood's First Film Fatale* (Lexington: University of Kentucky Press, 2014), 181.
30. *The Townsville (Australia) Daily Bulletin*, January 12, 1939.
31. *The Perth Sunday Times*, July 2, 1939.
32. *Memoirs of a Star*, 391.
33. *The Townsville Daily Bulletin*, April 7, 1941, 5.

Chapter 11

1. Even though Milton Berle had denied being her lover in his autobiography, he later told the tabloids that Pola had been his girlfriend until she had been "stolen" by Adolph Hitler. Perhaps he intended it as a joke.
2. Negri, Pola, *Memoirs of a Star* (New York: Doubleday, 1970), 399.
3. *The Milwaukee Sentinel*, February 2, 1942.
4. *The Perth Western Mail*, October 23, 1941, 14.
5. *The Buffalo Courier Express*, March 22, 1943, 20.
6. *The Buffalo Courier Express*, September 8, 1943, 22.
7. *New York Times*, October 1, 1942.
8. *New York Times*, July 28, 1942.
9. *Ibid.* "Paula Schwartz" was a name that had been ascribed to her back in the days before anyone in America knew anything about her. Seeing that name again this late in her career makes one stop and consider whether there was actually something to it.
10. *Ibid.*
11. *The Pittsburgh Press*, December 6, 1942.
12. *Memoirs of a Star*, 401.
13. *New York Times*, September 24, 1943. If the critic was referring to her silent film acting, then the comparison wasn't apt since, as already discussed, it's a different kind of acting altogether.
14. *Deseret News*, June 1, 1943.
15. *Schenectady Gazette*, August 8, 1946, 14.
16. *Memoirs of a Star*, 403.
17. *Memoirs of a Star*, 406.
18. *The Buffalo Courier Express*, November 16, 1949, 9-C.
19. *Memoirs of a Star*, 408.
20. *Memoirs of a Star*, 409.
21. *Memoirs of a Star*, 412–413.
22. *The St. Petersburg Times*, November 10, 1948.
23. *The Chicago Tribune*, March 15, 1950.
24. *The Buffalo Courier Express*, December 3, 1950, 33A.
25. *The Sydney Morning Herald*, November 4, 1954.
26. *Memoirs of a Star*, 412–413.
27. Slide, Anthony, *Silent Players: A Biographical and Autobiographical Study of 100 Silent Film Actors and Actresses* (Lexington: University of Kentucky Press, 2002), 382.
28. Leider, Emily W., *Dark Lover* (New York: Farrar, Straus & Giroux, 2003), 271.
29. Slide, Anthony, *Silent Topics: Essays on Undocumented Areas of Silent Film* (Lanham, MD: Scarecrow Press, 2005 [e-book]).
30. Grey-Chaplin, Lita, and Vance, Jeffrey. *The Wife of the Life of the Party* (Lanham, MD: Scarecrow Press, 1998), 63.
31. Watters, James, *Return Engagement: Faces to Remember—Then and Now* (New York: Crown Publishers, 1984), 107.
32. Quoted in obituary, *Los Angeles Times*, August 3, 1987.

Bibliography

Books

Anger, Kenneth. *Hollywood Babylon*. New York: Simon & Schuster, 1975.
Ankerich, Michael G. *Mae Murray: The Girl with the Bee-Stung Lips*. Lexington: University of Kentucky Press, 2012.
Ardmore, Jane. *The Self-Enchanted*. New York: McGraw-Hill, 1959.
Basinger, Jeanine. *Silent Stars*. New York: Knopf, 1999.
Berle, Milton. *Milton Berle*. New York: Applause Theatre and Cinema Books, 1974.
Botham, Noel, and Peter Donnelly. *Valentino: The Love God*. New York: Ace Books, London, 1976.
Bruno, Michael. *Venus in Hollywood*. New York: Lyle Stuart, 1970.
Chaplin, Charles. *My Autobiography*. New York: Simon & Schuster, 1964.
_____. *My Trip Abroad*. New York: Harper & Bros., 1921.
Cooper, Miriam. *Dark Lady of the Silents*. Indianapolis: Bobb-Merrill, 1973.
Cotes, Peter, and Thelma Niklaus. *The Little Fellow*. New York: Philosophical Library, 1951.
Eisner, Lotte. *The Haunted Screen: Expressionism in the German Cinema and the Influence of Max Reinhardt*. Berkeley: University of California, reprint, 1977.
Ellenbarger, Allan R. *The Valentino Mystique*. Jefferson, NC: McFarland, 2005.
Eyeman, Scott. *Laughter In Paradise: The Films of Ernst Lubitsch*. New York: Simon & Schuster, 1993.
Franklin, Joe. *Classics of the Silver Screen*. New York: Cadillac Publishing, 1959.
Goldwyn, Samuel. *Behind the Screen*. New York: George H. Doran, 1923.
Grey-Chaplin, Lita, and Jeffrey Vance. *The Wife of the Life of the Party*. Lanham, MD: Scarecrow Press, 1998.
Griffith, Richard, and Arthur Meyer. *The Movies*. New York: Simon & Schuster, 1957.
Griffith, Richard. *The Movie Stars*. New York: Doubleday, 1970.
Hake, Sabine. *Passions and Deceptions: The Early Films of Ernst Lubitsch*. Princeton University Press, 1992.
Hall, Carolyn. *The Twenties in Vogue*. New York: Harmony, 1983.
Hopper, Hedda. *From Under My Hat*. New York: Doubleday, 1952.
Huff, Theodore. *Charlie Chaplin*. New York: Henry Schuman, 1951.
Kear, Lynn, and James King. *Evelyn Brent*. Jefferson, NC: McFarland, 2009.
Kobarski, Richard. *An Evening's Entertainment: The Age of the Silent Feature Picture, 1915–1928*. Berkeley: University of California Press, 1990.
Kobel, Peter. *Silent Movies*. New York: Little, Brown & Co., 2007.
Krafsur, Richard, P., Ed. *The American Film Institute Catalog of Motion Pictures Produced in the United States, Part 1*. New York: R.R. Bowker, 1976; Berkeley: University of California Edition, 1997.
Leider, Emily W. *Dark Lover: The Life and Death of Rudolph Valentino*. New York: Farrar, Straus & Giroux, 2003.
Mann, William, J. *Wisecracker: The Life and Times of William Haines*. New York: Viking Press, 1998.
Menjou, Adolphe, and M.M. Musselman. *It Took Nine Tailors*. New York: Whittlesey House, 1948.
Muller, Jurgen, ed., *Movies of the 20s*. Munich: Taschen Books, 2007.
Negra, Diane. "Immigrant Stardom in Imperial America: Pola Negri and the Problem of Typology." *A Feminist Reader in Early Cinema*. Jennifer M. Bean and Diane Negra, eds. Durham, NC: Duke University Press, 2002.
Negri, Pola. *Memoirs of a Star*. New York: Doubleday, 1970.
Ott, Frederick. *The Great German Films*. Secaucus, NJ: Citadel Press, 1986.
Petrine, Graham. *Hollywood Destinies: European Directors in America, 1922–1931*. London: Routledge & Keagan-Paul, 1985.

Quinlan David. *Wicked Women of the Screen.* New York: St. Martin's Press, 1987.

Robinson, David. *Chaplin.* New York: McGraw-Hill, 1985.

Schickel, Richard, *The Stars.* New York: Bonanza Books, 1962.

Shearer, Michael. *Gloria Swanson: The Ultimate Star.* St. Martin's Press, 2013.

Shipman, David. *The Great Movie Stars: The Golden Years.* New York: Da Capo Press, 1979.

Shulman, Irving. *Valentino.* New York: Trident Press, 1967.

Slide, Anthony. *Silent Players: A Biographical and Autobiographical Study of 100 Silent Film Actors and Actresses.* Lexington: University of Kentucky Press, 2002.

_____. *Silent Topics: Essays on Undocumented Areas of Silent Film.* Lanham, MD: Scarecrow Press, 2005 (e-book).

Swanson, Gloria. *Swanson on Swanson.* New York: Random House, 1980.

Ullman, S. George. *Valentino as I Knew Him.* New York: A.L. Burt, 1926.

Watters, James. *Return Engagement.* New York: Crown Publishers, 1984.

Zierold, Norman. *Sex Goddesses of the Silent Screen.* Chicago: Regnery Press, 1973.

Movie Magazines and Trade Journals

Billboard
Cinelandia
The Educational Screen
The Exhibitor's Herald
The Exhibitor's Trade Review
The Film Daily
Film Play
The Hollywood Reporter
The Hollywood Vagabond
Modern Screen Magazine
Motion Picture Classic
Motion Picture Daily
Motion Picture Magazine
Movie Classic
Movie Weekly
The Moving Picture Herald
New Movie Magazine
Pantomime
The Photodramatist
Photoplay
Picture Play
Picture-Play
Pictures and The Picture-Goer (UK)
The Reel Journal
Screenland
Shadowland
Silver Screen Magazine
Variety

Magazine Articles

Allvine, Glendon. "How Polish Is Pola Negri?" *Filmplay Magazine,* June 1922.

Allvine, Glendon. "Meet Miss Chalupez … and Learn the Real Truth About Pola Negri." *Filmplay Magazine,* September 1922, 21.

Biery, Ruth. "Inside the Politics of the Studio." *Photoplay Magazine,* July 1931, 48.

Carlisle, Helen. "The Negri Legend." *Motion Picture Magazine,* May 1927.

Carr, Harry. "Behind the Scenes with Pola Negri." *Photoplay Magazine,* July 1923.

_____. "The Fight for the Crown." *Motion Picture Magazine,* September 1925.

_____. "The Mystery of Pola Negri." *Motion Picture Magazine,* February 1925.

_____. "A Ride With Pola Negri." *Motion Picture Magazine,* 1924 (month unknown).

_____. "They Still Twinkle." *Motion Picture Magazine,* October 1923, 36.

Chamberlin, Willard. "Too Continental or What?" *Picture Play Magazine,* February 1930, 88.

Denbo, Doris. "What Do Women Seek in Marriage." *Motion Picture Magazine,* January 1927, 40.

Faulker, H.H. "Readings of the Noses of Ten Famous Stars." *Motion Picture Magazine,* February 1923, 66.

Gaitsei, Eduardo. "Pola Negri Se Pone Tragica y Sentimental." *Cinelandia,* 1922.

Gebhardt, Myrtle. "A Turn in Pola's Career." *Picture-Play Magazine,* August 1924, 23.

Hall, Gladys. "Valentino Still Lives—For Pola Negri." *Motion Picture Magazine,* January 1935, 46.

Hall, Gladys and Adele Whitley-Fletcher. "We Interview Pola Negri." *Motion Picture Magazine,* January 1923, 22.

Hall, Leonard. "The Passing of Pola." *Photoplay Magazine,* December 1928, 29.

Hamilton, Sara. "*Ach,* that Pola!" *Photoplay Magazine,* January 1932, 40.

Howe, Herbert. "The Little People of the Screen." *Photoplay Magazine,* September 1924, 30.

_____. "The Loves of Pola Negri." *Photoplay Magazine,* July 1923.

_____. "Pola Speaks." *The New Movie Magazine,* November 1930, 59.

_____. "The Real Pola Negri." *Photoplay Magazine,* November 1922, 59.

_____. A Trip Though Europe's Filmland." *Picture-Play Magazine,* March 1921, 17.

Kelly, T. Howard. "Can Pola and Charlie Be Happy." *Movie Weekly,* December 30, 1922.

Kingsley, Grace. "A New Vogue for Flappers." *Photoplay Magazine,* February 1923, 30.

Klumph, Helen. "Now We Know About Pola." *Picture-Play Magazine,* December 1922, 20.

Lachenbruch, Jerome. "The Real Pola Negri—A Creature of Fire." *Movie Weekly,* July 7, 1922, 8.

Leeds, Stanton. "Who Is the Sarah Bernhardt of the Screen?" *Picture Play Magazine,* December 1922, 16.

Lyon, Ben. "Vampires I Have Known." *Photoplay Magazine*, February 1925.
Mad Love Pressbook, Goldwyn Pictures, 1922.
Malinson, Russell. "Wielding Woman's Weapons." *Pictures and the Picturegoer Magazine*, May 1923, 15.
Marshall, Eunice. "The New Pola." *Motion Picture Magazine*, June 1924, 34.
McClegg, William. "Is Acting Madness?" *Photoplay Magazine*, December 1930.
Mdivani, David. "Prince Serge Mdivani Was Perfect Lover." *Australian Woman's Weekly*, August 15, 1936.
Negri, Pola. "The Autobiography of Pola Negri, Pt. 1." *Photoplay Magazine*, February 1924.
_____. "The Autobiography of Pola Negri, Pt. 2." *Photoplay Magazine*, March 1924.
_____. "The Autobiography of Pola Negri, Pt. 3." *Photoplay Magazine*, April 1924.
Oettinger, Malcolm H. "The Queen Receives." *Picture Play Magazine*, January 1928.
"Press Sheet for *The Cheat*." Paramount Pictures, 1923.
Pryor, Nancy. "Pola Comes Back to Hollywood." *Motion Picture Magazine*, August 1931, 14.
"Review of *Barbed Wire*." *Motion Picture Magazine*, November 1927.
Rice, T. 2008. "Protecting Protestantism: The Ku Klux Klan vs. the Motion Picture Industry." *Film History*, Vol. 20, No. 3, 367–380.
Rogers-St. John, Adela. "Love and Laughter in Hollywood." *The American Weekly*, October 20, 1950.
Schallert, Edwin. "The Elegy of Pola Negri." *Picture Play Magazine*, March 1923.
Sharon, Mary. "Lovelorn." *Silver Screen Magazine*, September 1931, 18.
Stanlaws, Penrhyn. "The Most Beautiful Star in the World." *Screenland Magazine*, February 1923.
_____. "What's Wrong with Our Women?" *Screenland Magazine*, January1923.
Ullman, George. "The Real Valentino." *Photoplay Magazine*, January 1927.
Vinder, Maximilian. "She Delivers the Goods." *Photoplay Magazine*, May 1922, 50.
"We Interview Pola Negri." *Motion Picture Magazine*, 1923, 22 (Actual date of publication unknown).
York, Cal. "He Who Got Slapped and Why." *Photoplay Magazine*, July 1926, 5.

Newspaper Articles

"Chaplin's Secret Is Out." *Kansas City Times*, January 29, 1923.
Hall, Mordaunt. "Pola Negri Heard." *New York Times*, January 29, 1932.
Harpman, Julia. "Love and War Color Pola Negri's Career." *The Schenectady Gazette*, July 10, 1924.
Negri, Pola. "Secrets in Pola Negri's Life." *Sydney Times*, April 22, 1923.
"Pola Negri Jilts Chaplin," *Kansas City Times*, March 2, 1923.
"Pola Negri, 'Vamp' of Silent Films, Dies." *Los Angeles Times*, August 3, 1987.
Underhill, Harriette, "Europe's Most Beautiful Star Here at Last," *New York Morning Telegraph*, September 22, 1922.
"William Tilden II Named as Pola Negri's Lover." *Gloversville* (Australia) *Morning Herald*, July 31, 1923.

Newspapers

Adelaide (Australia) Advertiser
Adelaide (Australia) Mail
Adelaide (Australia) Register
Albury Banner and Wondunga Express (Australia)
Australasian
Barrier (Australia) Miner
Brisbane Courier
Brisbane Sunday Mail
Brooklyn Daily-Eagle
Brooklyn Standard-Union
Buffalo Courier
Buffalo Courier-Express
Buffalo Evening News
Buffalo Sunday-Courier Magazine
Casper (WY) Herald
Central Queensville (Australia) Herald
Charleville Times (Australia)
Chicago Tribune
Daily Argus
Daily Star
Davis County Clipper
Deseret (UT) News
Evening Independent (Australia)
Geraldton (Australia) Guardian and Express
Gloversville (Australia) Morning Herald
Hobart (Australia) Mercury
Horsham (Australia) Times
Kansas City Times
Lauceston (Australia) Examiner
Milwaukee Sentinel
Montreal Gazette
Mt. Vernon Daily Argus
New York Call
New York Evening Post
New York Evening Telegram
New York Morning Herald
New York Morning Telegraph
New York Post
New York Times
New York Tribune
Niagara Falls Gazette
Norrn (Australia) Miner
Norrn (Australia) Star
Norrn Territory (Australia) Times and Gazette
Ogden (UT) Standard
Ogden (UT) Standard-Examiner
Ogden Daily Examiner
Ogdensburg Republican Journal
Palm Beach Coast
Perth (Australia) Daily News

Perth (Australia) Mirror
Perth (Australia) Western Mail
Perth (Australia). Times
Pittsburgh Post-Gazette
Pittsburgh Press
Post Pirie (Australia) Recorder
Powell Tribune
Rochester Democrat Chronicle
Rockhampton (Australia) Morning Bulletin
Salt Lake Telegram
Saratogian (NY)
Schenectady Gazette
Sheridan (WY) Enterprise
St. Petersburg Times
Sunday Perth Times
Sydney (Australia) Morning Herald
Sydney Times
Syracuse American
Syracuse Gazette
Syracuse Journal
Tasmanian Advocate (Australia)
Townsville Daily Bulletin
Utica Observer-Dispatch
Whaling Advocate and Mining, Agricultural and Pastoral Gazette (Australia)
Wyoming State Tribune
Yonkers Statesman
Youngstown Vindicator

Internet Articles

Golden, Eve. "The Opportunist: Pola Negri On Her (More or Less) Centenary." *Classic Images Magazine.*
Long, Christopher, "Barbara Apolonia Chalupec," *Handbook of Texas Online,* http://www.tshaonline.org/handbook/online/articles/fchtm.
Peterson, Anne Helen. "Scandals of Classic Hollywood: The Most Kissable Hands of Pola Negri." http://thehairpin.com/2013/11/scandals-of-classic-hollywood-the-most-kissable-hands-of-pola-negri/.

Websites

http://archive.org/details/mediahistory
http://archive.org/search.php?query=subject%3A%22movie%20fan%20magazine%22&page=1
http://www.boxoffice.com/the_vault
http://www.enjoy-your-style.com/pola-negri.html
http://lavidak.org/Biografias/index.php?b=Pola-Negri
http://www.polanegri.com/home_pola.html
http://www.silentsaregolden.com/
http://www.stanford.edu/~gdegroat/negri.htm

Index

Numbers in **_bold italics_** refer to pages with photographs.

Anger, Kenneth 5, 130
Ardmore, Jane 106
Arlen, Michael 75, 90
Arme Violetta 18, 38, 143; *see also The Red Peacock*
Aryanism 152, 153, 158
Die Augen der Momie Ma 17, 19; see also *Eyes of the Mummy*

Barbed Wire 101; story 109–110; reviews 110, ***111***, 117
Basinger, Jeanne **5**
Bella Donna 41, 48, 50; reviews 59, 61, 66, 67, 68, 74, 75, 130; story 57, ***58***; studio censoring 52, 56
Die Bergkatze 18, 26; review of in *Variety* 27
Berle, Milton 147
Berlin, Germany 16; departure from 29; difficulties in wartime 16; return to 150
Botham Peter 102
Bow, Clara 45, 99, 129
Brenon, Herbert 72
Bret, David 103, 167
Buchowetzki, Dimitri 27, 77, 80, 81, 96, 97

cancer 169
Cap Ferrat, France 90, 154, 160, 164
Carmen 17, 19–20, ***21***, 29, 56; see also *Gypsy Blood*
The Carousel of Love 37
Carr, Harry 2, 49, 52, 55, 60, 104
cats 54, 168
Chalupec, Apolonia 8, 9; *see also* Chalupec, Barbara Antonia
Chalupec, Barbara Apolonia 8, 9; *see also* Chalupec, Apolonia
Chalupec, Jerzy Mathias (father) 9; arrest and trial 10, 12; death 12; exile to Siberia 12

Chaplin, Charles 3; meeting Negri 31, 32, 52, 56, 64; romance with 65–71, 88, 90, 101, 103, 105, 106, 117, 162, 167
The Charmer: reviews 88; story ***87***–88
Chateau Seraincourt, France 90, 113, 117, 133
The Cheat 56; reviews 62–63, 65, 68, 70, 74, 75, 131; story 61–62
Colombo, Russ 147
Cooper, Miriam 102, 105
The Crown of Lies 56; story and reviews 96, ***97***
Cruze, James 61

Davies, Marion 42, 102
De Acosta, Meredith 143
The Devil's Pawn: reviews 38, 47
Dietrich, Marlene 3, 142
Dombski, Count Eugene 23; marriage and breakup 24, 30; reaction to Negri and Chaplin's engagement 69, 135
Donnelly, Peter 102

East of Suez: reviews 85–***86***, 93; story 85
Eisner, Lotte 7
End of Hollywood contract 125
Eyes of the Mummy 29; review 38; see also *Die Augen der Momie Ma*

Falcon's Lair 104, 106, 109
Famous Players–Lasky Company 1, 2, 26, 29, 37, 38, 41, 43, 48, 65, 68, 93, 96, 99, 100, 106, 115, 120, 121, 125, 129, 130, 131, 157, 162; *see also* Paramount Pictures
Fanatisme 148, ***150***
First National Picture 31, 36
"Fits of Temperament" 6, 50–51, 53, 61, 63, 76, 78, 146, 148, 156, 165, 168
Fitzmaurice, George 52, 60, 64
Die Flamme 19, 28, 29, 76; *see also Montmartre*
Flower of Night: story and reviews 91, ***92***
Forbidden Paradise 29; reviews 84; story 82, ***83***
Die fromme Lüge 159

Garbo, Greta 3, 45, 130, 141, 142, 143
Der Gelbe Schein 17; *see also The Devil's Pawn*; *The Yellow Ticket*
"German invasion" of movies 33, 34, 35.38
Die geschlossene Kette 18
Goebbels, Joseph 152, 153, 159
Golden, Eve 151
The Goldwyn Company 48
Good and Naughty: story and reviews ***98***–99
Griffith, Robert 7
Gypsy Blood 1; reviews 34–35, 125, 141; *see also Carmen*

Haines, William: reported engagement 93–94, 101
Harris, Mildred 69
Hertz, Alexander 14, 15, 23
Hi Diddle Diddle 162, ***163***
Hitler, Adolf 149, 152, 153, 154; rumored relationship with 157, 158, 159, 161
Hollywood 61
Hollywood Babylon 5, 130
Hotel Imperial: story and reviews 100
Howe, Herbert 8, 22, 45, 46, 51, 65
Huff, Theodore 22
Hulewicsz, Casimir de 12, 13, 14, 90, 115, 154

Imperial Academy of Dramatic Arts 12
Intrigue: review 37, 38; see also Das Martyrium

Jannings, Emil 19, 20, 22, 150
jewelry smuggling 90, 124

Das Karussell des Lebens 18; see also The Carousel of Love; The Last Payment
Kaufman, Al 63
Kidston, Glen 137, 138; death 139, 167
Kielczeska, Eleonora de (mother) 9, 11, 12, 93, 148, 116, 160, 164, 165, 166, 167
Klumph, Helen 39, 40
Komtesse Doddy 18
Kotowski, Mariusz 8, 11, 159
Kozarski, Richard 5
Kreuziegt Sie! 18

Laemmele, Carl 149, 152
La Rocque, Rod 78, 82, 94, 101
The Last Payment: reviews 37
Leider, Emily 102, 104, 167
Liedtke, Harry 19, 20
Lily of the Dust: story and review 80, **81**, 93
Lipino, Poland 9
loss of personal fortune 137
love 47, 71, 108, 139
Love and Passion 14, 16
Loves of an Actress: story and reviews 126, **127**, 130
Lubitsch, Ernst 8, 17, 19, 24, 26, 27; Negri's "sadistic" relationship with 28–29, 36, 39, 52, 55, 60, 63, 82, 84, 97, 141, 149
Lyon, Ben **81**, 82

Mad Love: reviews 48; see also Sappho
Madame Bovary: story and reviews 157
Madame DuBarry 18, 20–21, **22**, 26, 29, 30, 56, 112; see also Passion
Mallinson, Russell P. 6
Mania **17**
Die Marchesa d'Armiani **18**
Das Martyrium 18; see Intrigue
Mazurka 149, 150, **151**; story and reviews 154
Mdivani, David 104, 113, 115, 116, 117
Mdivani, Serge 106, 112; courtship and engagement 114–115, 128, 131, 133, 134; divorce 139; introduction to 113; legal separation 135; reconciliation 137; re-start divorce from 138
Memoirs of a Star 8, 10, 11, 19, 23, 42, 65, 105, 113, 116, 117, 132, 133, 140, 153, 159, 162, 168
Men: story and reviews 77, **79**
Menjou, Adolphe 67, 82, 84, 162

Montmartre: reviews 76; see also Die Flamme
The Moonspinners 166, 168
Moscow Shanghai: story and review 156
My Confession 138

Die Nacht der Entscheidung 159
Negra, Diane 45, 56
Negri, Ada 12
Negri, Pola: acting 47, 82; American citizenship 166; anti-German sentiment 35; arrival in America 41, **44**; cancer 169; and cats 54, 168; end of Hollywood contract 125; failure of American career 130–132; as fashion trendsetter 46, 87; fatalist in love 23, 102, 103, 117, 137, 139; health problems 144, 147, 149, 155, 157; ignoring lawsuits 90, 112, 138, 151, 162; jewelry smuggling 90, 124; loss of personal fortune 137; money problems 138, 161–162; negative perceptions of acting 60, 63, 72, 76, 91, 95; negative reactions to Mdivani wedding 117–118, 130; pregnancy and miscarriage 132–133; publicity 31, 39–41, 43, 45, 46–50, 142; Red Cross volunteer 160; relations with the press 6, 52; return to America 141; rumored engagements 70, 89–90, 139, 146, 147, 154, 155; sexuality 166–167; unhappiness with Hollywood 63, 76, 82, 132; variations on birthdate 8; variations on eye color and height 44; variations on nationality 39; variations on surname of "Chalupec" 8; vaudeville appearances 138, 139, 147–148, 149, 155; xenophobia 33–34, 68
Niewolnica zymslów 14; see also Slave of Sin

One Arabian Night: reviews 36, 61; see also Sumurun (film version)

Paramount Pictures 5, 31, 46, 56, 59, 61, 63, 64, 71, 74, 77, 80, 84, 85, 87, 91, 96, 98, 100, 109, 118, 121, 124, 126, 129, 130, 131, 136, 141, 142, 143, 146, 156, 161; see also Famous Players–Lasky Company
Parsons, Louella O. 102, 106, 113, 161
Passion 1, 26, 31; reviews of 31–32, 39, 56, 63, 72, 75, 125, 131, 141; see also Madame DuBarry
Pickford, Mary 7, 52, 61, 72, 86, 108, 143
The Polish Dancer 37
Pour Vous libel trial 158–159

The Queen's Necklace 134–135

Rambova, Natacha 103, 106
The Red Peacock 37; reviews 38; see also Arme Violetta
Reinhardt, Max 15, 16, 88
R.K.O.-Pathé 140, 142, 143
Rogers, Adela St. John 95, 103, 104, 150
Rozmaitości (Polish national theater) 13
Russian Imperial Ballet School 11–12

St. Clair, Malcom 94, 98, 99
San Antonio, Texas 166
Sappho 19, **27**; see also Mad Love
Saturn Films 17
Schleber, Wolfgang George (Polonius) 25–26; breakup with 29–30
Schoenbrunn, George 167
The Secret Hour: story and reviews 121
Shadows of Paris: reviews 74–**75**; story 74
Shaw, George Bernard 134
Silent Film Stars (book) 5
Slave of Sin 14, 23, 37; see also Niewolnica zymslów; The Polish Dancer
Slide, Anthony 166, 167
The Spanish Dancer 64; reviews 72, 73; story 71–72
Sphinx Films 14; films done for Sphinx 15; release from contract 15
Styka, Tadeusz 30, 68, 168
Sumurun (film version) 18, **24**–25, 56; see also One Arabian Night
Sumurun (stage play) 15, 16–17, 40
Sunset Blvd. 165
Swanson, Gloria 5, 52; feud with 53–55, 64, 74, 76, 85, 91, 126, 164, 165

Tango Notturno 158, **159**
Three Sinners 124
Tilden, Bill **70**, **101**
Trinity College 168, 169
A Trip to Pressburg 149, 155

Ufa 17, 19, 23, 24, 26, 27, 28, 38, 97, 125, 128, 135, 138, 143; refusal to return to 160; return to 152, 153, 154, 156, 158, 159
Ullman, George 103, 107, 108

Valentino, Rudolph 2, 3, 5, 26, 72, 101; death 106; doubts about engagement 106; experimental engagement with 105; first meeting with 102–103; publication reaction to Negri's claims 107–109, 112, 116, 133, 135, 164, 167; re-assertion of engagement

with 107; relationship with 103–105
vampire 20, 28, 37, 47, 52, 54, 82, 131
Vega, Marina 70
Vendetta 18; review 37, 38

Warsaw Imperial Ballet 12
West, Margaret 164; death 166; relationship with 165
Wilder, Billy 156
A Woman Commands 130, 131, 143, 144; reviews 146, 147; story 144–*145*
The Woman from Moscow 57; stories and reviews 128–*129*, 130
The Woman He Scorned 136
A Woman of the World: reviews 95, 99, 168; story 94
The Woman on Trial 118; story and review *119*–120
World War I 13–14

xenophobia 33–34, 68

The Yellow Ticket 17–18, 38; *see also Der gelbe Schein*

Zierold, Harold 50

www.ingramcontent.com/pod-product-compliance
Ingram Content Group UK Ltd.
Pitfield, Milton Keynes, MK11 3LW, UK
UKHW050524150426
5217IPUK00026B/1779